THE HANGMAN'S KNOT

LYNCHING, LEGAL EXECUTION, AND AMERICA'S STRUGGLE WITH THE DEATH PENALTY

Eliza Steelwater

A Member of the Perseus Books Group

Copyright © 2003 by Eliza Steelwater

Westview Press books are available at special discounts for bulk purchases in the United States by corporations, institutions, and other organizations. For more information, please contact the Special Markets Department at the Perseus Books Group, 11 Cambridge Center, Cambridge MA 02142, or call (617) 252–5298 or (800) 255–1514 or email j.mccrary@perseusbooks.com.

Published in the United States of America by Westview Press, 5500 Central Avenue, Boulder, Colorado 80301–2877 and in the United Kingdom by Westview Press, 12 Hid's Copse Road, Cumnor Hill, Oxford OX2 9JJ.

Find us on the World Wide Web at www.westviewpress.com

A Cataloging-in-Publication data record for this book is available from the Library of Congress.
ISBN 0–8133–4042-X

The paper used in this publication meets the requirements of the American National Standard for Permanence of Paper for Printed Library Materials Z39.48–1984.

10 9 8 7 6 5 4 3 2 1

TABLE OF CONTENTS

DEDICATION

This book is dedicated to the memory of two strong women who cared about me: Biki and Miss Rose Saitta.

ACKNOWLEDGMENTS

Thanks to:

- the Alumni Federation of Louisiana State University, which provided an extraordinary four years of full financial support to me as a student long ago;
- Elizabeth Hines, Ph.D., geographer and college professor, for moral support above and beyond;
- my agent, Jeff Kleinman, and Westview senior editor Jill Rothenberg, for seeing me through;
- Westview's Wendy Halitzer, Art Director, Carmel Huestis, Director of Editorial Production, Greg Houle, Senior Publicist, and Trish Goodrich, Promotions Administrator, and Andrew Brown, Manager of Editorial Services at Scribe, for all their help; and
- my husband, John Odland, for happiness and love every day.

A legal execution in the Arizona Territory.

The Hanging of George Woods

I sit at a long oak table in a quiet, high-ceilinged room. Outside on the street the sun is blinding, but I've been at the table for hours and I'm almost cold. I wear white cotton gloves in order not to damage the photograph I'm about to pick up. I take it by a corner and pull it from its envelope.

I find myself looking down a sloping pasture on the edge of a raw mountain town. It looks like a Western mining town of the late 1800s, with its half-built, false-fronted Main Street running along a railroad track at the back of the picture. The pasture is full of people; the photographer must have stood at the top of the hill to get them all in. Some seated, some standing or perched on wagon beds, they face away from me. A child whose head comes only to her father's waist holds his hand.

Only slowly, because the photograph is grainy and the object of attention far away, I realize I am witnessing a hanging. There at the center of the photograph is the gallows, densely surrounded by people. Rising from a platform at about shoulder height are wooden posts and a crossbar. These are heavy, square timbers, well braced. Between the posts a taut rope hangs straight down. The dark object at the end of the rope is a man. His head is covered by a short hood and below it I think I can even distinguish the stretched narrow column of his neck—four inches in diameter once the hanging is completed, I read somewhere. I turn over the photograph. It is labeled only with the place of execution and the name of the condemned: "Arizona Territory, the hanging of George Woods."

The public hanging of George Woods probably took place between 1870 and 1890, some 275 years after the first known executions in

America. These took place in Jamestown, Virginia, in 1608 and 1622, when one man was hanged for spying and one for theft. By the late 1800s, executions in many states had been made non-public because they had become rowdy spectacles, exercises in crowd control. Yet the 150 or so people on the hillside in this unknown town don't appear to be gawkers come for a chance to get drunk or fight or pick someone's pocket. Instead, they have an air of quiet attentiveness. They seem to have gathered to watch a story unfold, a story whose ending is known by heart yet awaited with a certain tension.

This is the community at work, the photograph seems to say. The community passed judgment on one of its own and it came—man, woman, and child—intending to see that judgment carried out. And now it is over. In a moment, perhaps, those who are sitting on the hillside will rise and check their clothes for dust and bits of grass, giving themselves time to arrange their faces and cross the little chasm back to life. They will straggle away to their everyday world, calling out to one another about commonplace things. Except for the man at the end of the rope.

Thinking of the father and daughter in the photograph, I try to imagine the family's dinner table that night. *What did they say to the child?* In reality I know that school-aged children like the one in the photograph aren't particularly compassionate. The adult idea of "shielding" them doesn't belong to the time and place of George Woods's death. When a parent or teacher did not take them to an execution as a moral lesson, children were only too apt to attend on their own.

The child in the photograph probably just had a few of those inconvenient questions that children ask: *Was the man really dead? Can I touch him? Why did he die?* And very likely she was given a few of those highly unsatisfactory adult answers: *Yes. No. Because he was a bad man.*

He was a bad man. It sounds like the end of a story. Good met evil and they struggled. Finally, good won out, and here's the proof—evil has just been hanged by the neck until dead.

That's it exactly—I've seen the end of a story. It's one we've been telling ourselves for so many years. Soon after I saw the photograph of George Woods meeting his death, I learned that over 15,000 convicted criminals have been executed since the United States became a nation. In the name of vigilante justice, we've also extralegally executed—lynched—thousands more. Each hanging, electrocution, gassing, shooting, or lethal injection has added something to our story of execution as justice until, now, our story of good versus evil carries a heavy cargo of messages:

- We must be responsible for our own individual behavior.
- As a democratic nation, we the people can judge each other.
- At the same time, we must practice fair play.
- Because justice must be done.
- We must keep ourselves safe from evildoers.
- We must make an example of those whom we catch.
- There must be payback to society, retribution for evils done.
- Because it's wrong to kill.

Some of these ideas may be shared by citizens of countries all over the world. But the *combination* of democracy, individual freedom, and stern morality goes to the root of who we Americans are as a people. Our European heritage was government explicitly tied to religion, and the Puritans carried this concept about as far as it could go.

At the same time, our heritage has also been to battle and dispute about who's in charge. Issues of authority in the U. S. go back at least to the tug of war between British colonial government and its American colonists. Ever since, we as Americans have argued the supremacy of national versus state governments, states versus their counties, "the state" as a whole versus the rights of its citizens. Later, the rise of big business led to contention over the rights of workers versus those of employers. Capital punishment has figured in these debates since the beginning. The framers of our Constitution avoided giving federal government the power of life and death over its citizens except for federal crimes, such as treason. Instead, the Constitution distributed most of the power to condemn and execute to each state individually. Most states have considered whether to execute. At their formation, some states argued that Americans should reject execution as the barbaric practice of our former overlords, the British—that taking our own citizens' lives would make us as brutal as the British were. Others argued that a state simply didn't have the right to take its citizens' lives—that "consent of the governed" did not go that far.

But we didn't go on to abolition, not even in the late twentieth century as other leading democracies did so. Of 195 countries listed by Amnesty International, 112 don't use the death penalty. Of these 112 nations, nineteen haven't held an execution in ten to fifty years—for example, the Congo, Papua New Guinea, and Sri Lanka. Sixteen permit execution only by the military or for wartime crimes, for example, Greece, Israel, and Turkey. Seventy-six nations have outlawed the penalty completely, including the United Kingdom, France, Germany, Spain, Italy, and *all* other western European nations. Venezuela has outlawed executions since 1863. Six of fifteen other Latin American countries ban the death penalty absolutely, five more allow it only in military circumstances. Support and opposition for the death penalty are mixed together in every world region except for a band of pro-execution nations extending across north Africa, the Middle East, and Asia. Examples are Libya, Egypt, Nigeria, Afghanistan, India, China, Vietnam, and Japan.

True, for Americans to outlaw the death penalty nationwide, a decision to abolish would have to be made in each of 50 states. But nations with decentralized decision-making powers like ours—Australia and Mexico—have abolished the death penalty. Our pro-death-penalty policy places us in the company of such human-rights dropouts as China, Saudi Arabia, and Iran. These are the governments that carry out most of the executions in the world—along with the United States.

I wrote this book because I couldn't understand how we as Americans could come so close to abolishing the death penalty, then return to it—not once, but three times. I wanted to know how the story of execution as part of justice became such a compelling one for us— so compelling that even men and women who are sentenced to death sometimes admit they supported capital punishment until they found themselves on death row.

The more I learned about U. S. capital punishment, the more I came to believe it's about our past—mostly about our many battles over who's in charge. The death penalty as part of our past, our national identity, is the hook for me both as a scholar and as a person.

I was born into what I think of as the Southern white guilt generation. I must harbor a little more than the average amount of that guilt, or I wouldn't be writing about a subject that has so much to do with American mistreatment of persons of color. I didn't know until long after I was grown how fully capital punishment is part of the history between white and black, white and yellow, white and red. But I don't think I ever had to learn the idea of systematic abuse. Or the lesson that some people were, and are, more vulnerable to abuse than others. Long before my first day of consciousness, these were facts of life around me. I think I was supposed to understand that my light skin and straight blond hair made me safe; I wasn't one of the vulnerable ones. But that lesson didn't take. When I write about people who suffer disproportionate punishment or are punished for no crime at all, I write from my own childhood nightmare of vulnerability: *If it can happen to anyone, it can happen to me.* This is my inheritance from the past.

The idea of studying capital punishment came to me when Miles Richardson, anthropologist and geographer at Louisiana State University, challenged his students, including me, to write about some one place where the most powerful moments of life were passed. I don't doubt that it's my feeling of being unsafe in some basic way that drew me toward the execution chamber.

At LSU, I was only fifty-five miles from the electric chair at the infamous Louisiana state penitentiary and prison farm called Angola. When I visited Angola, I found out that I'd need to come back another time with permission from the prisoner's lawyer before I could talk to a prisoner on death row. That day, I toured the prison grounds, viewed death row from the guards' office, spent an hour with the warden, and ate lunch with the captain of guards. I took note of the isolation, the razor wire, the economic activity of farming, the offices full of secure employees, and the way the warden and the officers spoke of just doing their job—as if they were Greek classical actors raised above the human on platform shoes, talking through masks that made all their voices sound deep and reassuringly masterful. By the end of my visit, I realized I had nothing to offer a condemned prisoner, neither spiritual or emotional comfort nor legal advice. Calling someone out to be brought shuffling in chains to a visiting booth to answer my naive questions would be asking that person to exhibit himself to me like a zoo animal, and to about as much purpose.

I was pretty sure I could find a willing prisoner, because any distraction from the tedium of a cell and the thought of one's impending death has some value. I could be a zoo animal for the prisoner, too— "the scholar," if I wanted to flatter myself. Instead, I went home to really become a scholar. Eighteen years later, I see that what I learned about the death penalty hasn't had much to do with how I've earned a living— mostly in the field of historic preservation. But I couldn't let go of the question that formed as I studied for a Ph.D. I had to find out why so little of the story of capital punishment was about the individual who is convicted and put to death.

I call it "the story" because I know, as a person and a scholar, that human beings operate on stories. All human beings share the kind of mind that looks for the story, the meaning, the conclusion, the lesson, in every event. Most of the time, closure is way more important to us than facts. Our stories are built up over individual lifetimes and over generations as we talk and listen to others at home, at school, at work, in legislatures and law courts, in conversation, in books, on television and in the movies. Stories depend on where we stand in life and when we stand there, and so we come to have a "Southern story," a "white story," a "story of privilege," and their opposites. All of these and more are included in the American story and make it different from that of other countries. Our distinctive story has been forming for some 400 years, and I've come to believe that telling it, as it concerns the death penalty, is the best way of understanding why we are where we are now, today, with the death penalty. That is the purpose and method of this book.

Next to the story of love and the story of success, the story of good and evil is one of the most powerful we know. The story has characters in white hats and characters in black hats and, ideally, an ending that distributes ultimate punishment to whomever wears the black hat. The ones who take that punishment in our story, the American story, are those men who occupy the cubicles on death row until they are shuffled in chains to the gurney and strapped down to die.

But those men aren't really chosen from all the people who commit whatever we decide is the ultimate crime. That's what I learned from studying American capital punishment. How we decide whom to kill is a matter of history—the history of particular groups of peoples in states and nations. As we talk and listen to others, and participate in getting and spending through generations, we form and reform the ideas we use to govern ourselves and be governed, to distribute wealth and power. In this process we exclude certain people from vulnerability and target others to endure it.

Since that day in the library with the photograph of George Woods, I've seen many more photographs of hangings, legal and illegal. Arizona was one of the later states to make executions non-public. This step was taken because many legal executions—not just lynchings—*were* mass spectator events, attended by the disengaged and the up-to-no-good. On these occasions, the authorities had a hard time preserving order. As the public came to be excluded, newspapers began reporting every detail. They described the demeanor and dress of the condemned, the springing of the trap, the official doctor's count of rising and falling pulse rate per minute as the heart struggled in the dangling body—119, 104, 31, 42, 22, 19, 32—finally stopping as long as 50

minutes later. Cameras were by no means forbidden. Any unusual feature was prized, and no wonder, since the photographs were often sold.
They were even made into postcards: "Dear Em: Have been here a
week. Weather hot. George and Sally well." No mention of the picture
on the reverse—a suit-coated young man jauntily waving his hat to the
crowd as he enters the execution shed, like a salesman boarding a train.

I have seen a man standing on the gallows beneath an enormous
metal weight that was about to pull him into the air. The weight
smashed his head into the gallows crossbeam instead of hanging
him—a miscalculation by the local authorities.

I have seen the photographic series: before, during, after. It is surprising how much of who we are is in our body language. Very little
that is individual survives a strict application of the law of gravity over
an hour or more.

I have even seen a photograph of an electrocution—the famous
bootlegged photograph of Ruth Snyder taken by a witness to her death
in 1928 in Sing Sing. Sitting in the wooden armchair strapped, masked,
and attached to electrodes, she wears a dress and pumps with heels.
Ruth Snyder's photograph is blurry. I am haunted by the question of
whether it was the photographer or the chair that shook as the current
changed her from a person into a thing.

Most, I am haunted by a photograph I've never seen—death by
injection. It's the photograph that can't be taken. How can a photograph capture the experience of a lethal chemical traveling along the
veins, overtaking the lungs, the heart, and the brain? The condemned
lie on a gurney in a clean, well-lighted cubicle. Except for being
strapped down from chest to ankles, they look as if they are giving
blood or receiving chemotherapy.

I have also seen photographs of homicides. The archive of a city
police department is enough to sicken anyone for life. The word *butchery* comes to mind and there are photographs that exude a stench of
agony. If there is a calculus of suffering, many a victim of murder
endures more than all but a few victims of legal execution.

The difference is that homicide victims were killed by individuals. Execution is killing at the hands of all of us—man, woman, and child. Serving as executioners is just as much part of who we grow up to be now, as American citizens, as it was for the community members who watched George Woods die.

Of course, it's easier now because there's no mess. And it all takes place so far away. We have learned to say, *He was a bad man,* or *We don't talk about those things at the dinner table.* But we are all former children. Somewhere inside each of us is still the question: How did we become George Woods's executioners?

A prisoner's view of the electric chair, Louisiana State Penitentiary.

1

"The Right Type of Case"
Capital Punishment, Prisoners without Capital, and Public Support for Executions

History, tradition, and the promise of power up for grabs is what links George Woods in the 1880s to events that happened only three years ago: John Lamb was executed, Sammy Gravano was not. Guess which of them murdered one person, and which murdered nineteen people.

John Lamb was a destitute drifter who had been arrested more than once. He shot and killed a man who offered him a ride and then made a sexual overture. Lamb stole the man's credit cards and his automobile and escaped to Florida, where he was arrested after trying to rob a convenience store. "I think he's exactly the type of case for which the death penalty is designed," said Hunt County District Attorney Duncan Thomas. "He's someone who kills someone, steals all their belongings, and then tries to kill someone else." Lamb was put to death by lethal injection in Texas on November 17, 1999.

Sammy "The Bull" Gravano is apparently not the kind of case for which the death penalty is designed. The man who killed nineteen people is a former mob enforcer for the Gotti family. Gravano was later convicted of running a drug distributing ring, and may even spend some time in prison. But he will never be prosecuted for the premeditated murders he committed, because he testified against a rival crime family, the Gambinos. Gravano's theoretically punishable killings are on record in seventy-six pages of FBI testimony, and his biography is selling well. When interviewed by one reporter, Gravano was eating filet mignon at Ruth's Chris Steak House in Phoenix, Arizona. It was not his last meal.

Good conquers evil—unless evil happens to have a team of skilled attorneys and/or something to trade with the prosecutor. If you had enough money to buy this book, or the wits to borrow it from a library, you can probably commit murder without worrying about ending up on death row.

It can't be that the American story of good and evil draws its power from the effectiveness of the death penalty, which is applied to so few murderers that some defense lawyers have argued it has become cruel and unusual punishment. Even in theory, a murderer has only a *one-third of one percent* chance of being executed. An average of 22,000 homicides are committed each year, but only 300 persons are sentenced to death. It took death rows a while to fill up—the population on January 1, 2003, was 3,692—and the average time to execution is some ten years. The number executed each year from 1976 to 2003 has varied even over the last decade—from a low of 31 in 1993 and 1995 to a high of 98 in 1999. Currently, of the 300 murderers per year sentenced to death, more than two-thirds of those who have their sentences reviewed are given a new trial, have their sentence commuted, or are pardoned. Capital punishment today is tokenism. Some even say it's a lottery. But that would mean the penalty is handed out at random. It isn't. It's given out to those whom a jury are most frightened by—such as African-American men convicted of murdering someone who is not black—and especially to those who can't defend themselves financially.

All but about one percent are men. One-third of the 850 persons executed from 1976 to 2003 were African-American although African-Americans make up only about twelve percent of the general population. John Lamb wasn't African-American; still, his chances of being executed for murder "improved" drastically because he was poor. It's hard to discover how many on U. S. death rows are in poverty, but estimates range upward from ninety percent just for those who get as far as being charged with capital murder. If their case comes to trial, many of them are represented by court-appointed attorneys, often inexperienced in fighting capital charges. Even the few highly knowledgeable attorneys who volunteer for charity cases can be overwhelmed by the intense work and high caseloads involved, and they are losing money every hour the case lasts.

When Lamb was arrested for the murder he committed, he was unwise enough to thank the authorities for capturing him before he killed someone else. Later he was offered a forty-year prison term if he pled guilty. He refused because he thought he could get a better deal by exercising his right to a trial. Sammy "The Bull" Gravano had access to a whole staff of attorneys through his employment with the Gotti family. Gravano's attorneys negotiated so successfully on his behalf that he may never have made a single unprotected admission of guilt.

John Lamb's chances of being executed also got "better" when he committed murder in Texas. Out of the thirty-eight states that inflict the death penalty, Texas has racked up the most executions by far— over one third of executions since the death penalty was reinstated in 1976, and more than the next-ranked four states of Virginia, Missouri, Oklahoma, and Florida when their totals are combined. Even with all its executions, Texas's homicide rate isn't lower than that of other states. The murder rate in the South overall, including Texas, is substantially higher than that of the West, Midwest, and Northeast.

Supposedly, this high murder rate is the reason for high Southern rates of execution. But no study has ever shown that murder is cause and execution rate is effect. Rather, the study of history suggests that both illegal and legal killing comes from relying on violence to resolve both personal matters and political matters, or from institutionalizing this strategy as laws, law enforcement, and the lack of either one. The higher-executing states today are probably those in which lawmakers, politicians, and bureaucrats have gone the farthest in exploiting historical public support for violence. Texas, for instance, differs from even other southern states in its criminal trial laws. The law in Texas is so punitive toward the defendant that at least one person was executed *after* he was found to be innocent. New evidence can only be filed in a Texas death-penalty case within thirty days of the original verdict. This man died because the time limit had expired.

At a 1984 trial in Texas, the court-appointed attorney slept through the prosecution's presentation of its case. Calvin Burdine was found guilty of murdering his homosexual lover and sentenced to death. The trial judge, the Texas Court of Criminal Appeals, and the U. S. Court of Appeals for the Fifth Circuit all agreed that defense by a sleeping lawyer is "not ineffective." "Not ineffective" was the standard; actual effectiveness need not be demonstrated. One lower court ruled that the attorney hadn't slept through the important parts of the trial. And anyway, as a judge pointed out, the U. S. Constitution doesn't require that the attorney be awake. Only on the third round of appeals, in 2001, did Burdine win the right to a new trial at the state's discretion.

Yet another Texas defendant, James Colburn, was so heavily drugged to subdue his schizophrenia that he fell asleep again and again during his *own* trial and may not have heard the death sentence.

John Lamb was not among those on the nation's death rows who was cleared of guilt or thought to be insane. But we have begun to discover how many of the condemned *are* wrongfully convicted. Since 1976, 107 condemned persons (and counting) have been released from death row. As many as twenty-three of the unjustly condemned are known to have been executed. The most common cause of wrongful conviction is simple lying on the part of a prosecution witness. In about 35 percent of cases, the innocent who manage to avoid execution are saved when the real murderer confesses.

Most other unjust convictions occur as a result of one of the following: low-quality police investigation under pressure from superiors, eyewitness error, false confessions obtained through police coercion, guilty pleas by innocent defendants trying to escape the death penalty, and prosecutors' refusal to dismiss cases where evidence is weak.

Former governor George Ryan of Illinois declared a moratorium on executions after discovering that thirteen men were wrongly condemned to death in the state during the previous thirteen years. After hearing a report from the investigative commission he empaneled, Ryan, just before stepping down as governor in January, 2003, commuted the sentences of all those on death row.

Previously, Nebraska legislators also voted to declare a moratorium, but were overridden by the governor's veto. The governor of Maryland declared a moratorium on that state's executions also, but the next elected governor ended the moratorium.

U. S. Supreme Court Justice Harry A. Blackmun, death penalty supporter for twenty years, concluded shortly before his retirement in 1994: "The death penalty experiment has failed." He delivered this statement as part of a dissenting opinion when the court refused to review a death sentence in the case of Callins versus Collins. Blackmun was one of the justices who voted against discontinuing the death penalty in 1972, when the Supreme Court declared only 5-4 that the death penalty as then administered was unconstitutional. After hearing death-penalty cases over the years since then, Blackmun finally came to call the goal of a Constitutionally administered death penalty a "delusion."

———

When people support capital punishment, they usually believe one of three things: First, that executions deter potential murderers from killing. Second, that executions are less expensive for the public than keeping those convicted in prison for life. Third, that for justice to be done, both the public and the survivors of someone who was murdered need to know the killer will be executed. All three of these arguments in favor of capital punishment have been around for a long time, and have been amply debated.

The first argument is deterrence. Most specialists in the field say: Forget about it. Some forty years of statistical research have led to no conclusion, just a dead end of technical argument. Experts have tried, but no one has been able to show that the death penalty deters capital crime. It was not a deterrent in England in the 18th century, when the rate of execution was truly staggering, and it is not a deterrent here and now. No wonder polls show that only about half of the general public take the idea of deterrence seriously.

The second argument is cost. Many people believe that execution is less costly than keeping the condemned in prison for life. In reality, the average cost of a capital trial has been estimated at $2 to $3 million, versus $1 million for a fifty-year prison sentence. Execution would be less expensive than prison only if our legal system completely abolished the right to appeal a conviction. We would also need to cast aside mistrial, resentencing, and other items of the "due process of law" guaranteed by Article V of our Bill of Rights. No wonder that a judge in Vinton County, Ohio, wanted to refuse a capital murder charge in 2002 because of crippling expense to the county. The judge also feared that financial considerations would affect the quality of the defendant's trial and appeals. Prosecutors pressured him to reconsider, and now the county and state may pay defense costs as high as $350,000 on behalf of the defendant, who is indigent. The county's share of this sum would be six percent of its annual budget.

The third argument in favor of capital punishment is a little different because it isn't an argument from facts. It's an argument about what's right—what is "just desserts" for human behavior. This argument, or question, has been around the longest. Revenge, retaliation, retribution—they are often described as "justice" and are central themes of the Old Testament and certain holy writings of other world religions. The reason most often given for death-penalty support, as the Gallup pollsters summarize it: "an eye for an eye," "they took a life," "it fits the crime." In spite of the Old Testament phrasing, most persons who give this response don't seem to base it on explicit religious beliefs. Rather, "death for murderers" appeals to us intuitively—almost fair, almost practical, if you don't look too closely.

I keep going back to that little girl who watched George Woods die at the end of a rope. The scene of judicial death has so much dramatic appeal that children have gone home from witnessing an execution and hanged themselves—perhaps not understanding that the operation they had just witnessed was permanent. Other children, trying to learn the lesson, begin testing it out by applying it to everything.

> *Daddy killed someone in the war; is someone going to kill Daddy?*
> *No, because that was war.*
> *Is the man who killed the bad man today going to be killed?*
> *No.*
> *Why not?*

This is the point at which the parents of a really persistent child might have said, *We don't talk about those things at the dinner table.*

Not everyone agrees. Phil Donahue, host of an evening talk show, thinks executions should be able to be televised as part of Americans' right to free speech. "If you think the death penalty is a deterrent," Donahue added, "what better way to enhance its deterrent value than to let the kids see what happens if you're a bad person."

Sometimes now we use the word "bad" ironically, admiringly. But "bad," or some word like it, is still a serious word in the world of a child. It's a scare word, a stop word, the trump card in a parent's hand. As in: *You've been bad, and I'm going to tell your father.* We all think we know what "bad" means. It's a word we use when we can't bring ourselves to go into detail, or when we want to condemn.

The word "bad" is the end of the discussion, and that is the way we teach it to our children. It has an effect like that of an unpleasant smell. Over time, it convinces our children, as it convinced us, that nothing good can come of looking more closely. It isn't any use questioning society's decisions—that's the real lesson. By the time the child is grown, she has learned to answer hard questions with a story and, when the story itself is hard to tell, end her stories with a scare word. She reserves her real energy for private life and has prepared a respectful face of indifference for the rest.

Much of America wears this face of indifference. In a 1998 poll, over half of those responding said they favor capital punishment even if innocent people are sentenced to death. Over half said the poor are more likely to receive a death sentence. Over half said they favor capital punishment even if it doesn't deter crime.

Over half even admitted they couldn't afford a lawyer themselves if charged with murder.

———•———

It sounds crazy. Why would people who couldn't afford a lawyer support a penalty that, above all others, calls for a good lawyer? But people's positions become a lot easier to understand when you realize that the people most in favor of capital punishment are those least likely—in fact, not at all likely—to be condemned to death.

In another poll, respondents were asked, "What do you think should be the penalty for murder—the death penalty, or life imprisonment with absolutely no possibility of parole?" Poll takers broke down the answers according to income, age, gender, race or ethnicity, and other specifics.

People who are over sixty-five years old and those whose income is less than $20,000 per year supported the death penalty—if no other choice was offered. But when the choice of life imprisonment was offered, most of the elderly and those with low incomes preferred not to execute. The only other group in which a majority preferred not to execute was persons of color, especially African-Americans.

Obviously, for these respondents punishment was a safety issue. They didn't want a particular punishment. They wanted protection from violent crime.

But motives of respondents with the highest incomes are harder to understand. Given a choice of penalties, their opinion changed very little. For those with an income of $75,000 or more, support for the death penalty was only two per cent less when they could choose to sentence murderers to life in prison instead of execution.

Only two percent decrease, compared to thirty-four percent among the poor—yet it is the well-to-do who have least to fear from murderers.

The Bureau of Justice Statistics has demonstrated that persons with household incomes under $15,000 per year are "significantly" more likely to be victims of violent crime. Victims are also more likely to be black. In 2001, the most recent year for which numbers are available, some 47 percent of homicide victims were African-Americans, 51 percent whites, and two percent other race. By contrast, only 12 percent of the U. S. population were African-American, and 73.1 percent white.

To make a long story short, those who most persistently favor the death penalty are Republicans, men who haven't attended college, Westerners, and Southerners. Many of these poll respondents are people with higher incomes who are self-described conservatives. Many come from the two regions where the death penalty was used most heavily in historical times.

In fact, the death penalty—not always administered under law— played a formative role in politics in the South and West. In virtually all parts of the nation, both legal execution and lynching, or vigilante execution, were used by established financial and political interests against the newcomers, the upstarts, and especially the immigrants and former slaves. In nearly every part of the country, support for capital punishment was a badge of conservatism, just as it is today. Support for capital punishment was used and sustained by those who held power or wanted to be identified with the powerful.

Taking both opinion polls and history into account, it's possible to say that Americans have used the death penalty for exactly the same reason that totalitarian regimes like China or Iran do: the ability to execute is the supreme political power.

Yet I don't think that intimidation explains America's continued use of capital punishment today. Rather, the fact that we used capital punishment as intimidation in the past has made it a potent, if empty, symbol of authority now. Above all, it is a club for one politician to use against the other, and a way to reassure voters who really have little or nothing at stake. And the inhabitants on death row really don't have much political clout, do they?

Puritan magistrates believed that a witch's body had physical signs.

2

The Worst of the Worst
Punishment, Puritans, and Political Power

Now I'm part of the audience. It's a cool autumn night in Indiana, and three people are on stage in this college auditorium under the lights. They, and we, are here to debate the death penalty. The second speaker waits at the table with the moderator, sipping water to occupy her hands and mouth, while the first speaker stands at the podium and lays out his case. He has been sent by the state attorney general's office—a youngish man in a pearl gray suit and a red power tie. We'll call him Mr. Prosecutor. His theme is "the worst of the worst." That's who the state executes now, he says, and our state's legal process is the best in the nation. After the indictment and trial, we have an appeal, we take it to the state, we take it to federal court, we take it to the U. S. Supreme Court. We hire experienced attorneys for the defendants at each stage. We give them money to carry out their own investigation of the crime in order to find any gaps in the police inquiry. Our state law calls for a death-penalty jury, when setting the sentence, to consider a whole list of facts about the crime and the defendant. These facts are divided into "the aggravators" and "the mitigators."

I can't remember whether Mr. Prosecutor said that the defendant's attorneys are given money to hire experts, but he probably did. The night of the debate, he's certainly hitting all the points. He mentions that the governor appointed a commission to investigate our use of the death penalty. The commission spent nineteen months in study and found out that, with only one procedural change, our death penalty will have sufficient safeguards. In the course of his talk, our speaker also mentions the pardons board and possibility that every con-demned person has of being pardoned by the governor.

The taxpayers' money is clearly at work here, and I'm impressed. Maybe we've been bending over too far backward on behalf of these people who are, after all, the worst of the worst. It's only when Mr. Prosecutor starts on the anecdotes, the little stories, that I begin to notice something. He argues like an attorney in court. By this I mean that he presents one side of the case only. Our second speaker, although an opponent of the death penalty, isn't an attorney but an activist. She'll treat our debate more like an inquiry into an issue that concerns us, stating certain points for the other side as she makes the case for her own. The prosecutor will talk about the anguish of mur-der victims' families, and so will the activist. But only she will point out how few of the bereaved get to experience the "joy" of ultimate revenge against their loved one's murderer.

Mr. Prosecutor, like any good attorney, sticks to saying what makes his client—the state—look good, just as he would do if his audience were a jury trying a death penalty case. He selectively leaves out facts that damage his case, and he implies, insinuates, and suggests what damages our opinion of the defendant but isn't really evidence.

Realizing I'm being treated as a juror gets me wondering about those points Mr. Prosecutor has been making. Just how much does the state spend prosecuting each of its cases, and how much was each defendant given for his defense? What is the comparative batting average of the prosecutor in previous death penalty cases versus the record of each defending attorney drawn, we are told, from a pool?

Mr. Prosecutor told us about the favorable findings of the gover-nor's Criminal Law Study Commission. But Mr. Prosecutor didn't tell us that ninety percent of those on the commission were law enforce-ment officials. In Illinois, where a similar commission had a more diverse membership, commissioners made eighty-five recommenda-tions for change. Illinois's justice system may be in worse shape than

Indiana's, but I doubt that the difference is great enough to account for only one recommended change versus eighty-five.

The Indiana Supreme Court's commission on race and gender fairness has spent the last four years studying race and gender bias in the courts. I know this—but not because Mr. Prosecutor mentioned it. He didn't.

Soon after his talk, the Supreme Court's commission admitted they hadn't gotten to the bottom of bias and would recommend a panel for further study. In spite of Mr. Prosecutor's you're-in-good-hands presentation, the end is not in sight.

I am also struck by the storytelling techniques that Mr. Prosecutor uses as he makes his case to us, the audience. During a description of one crime, Mr. Prosecutor alleges that the now-convicted defendant "dressed in camouflage clothes" before picking up a rifle and driving to his ex-wife's home.

A jury found that this man killed his ex-wife and two other persons. But, I wonder, what's the relevance of the "camouflage clothes"? It isn't evidence of intent—the defendant could have dressed that way to go duck hunting or attend a costume party—but I'll bet Mr. Prosecutor described those clothes in court. In one crisp detail, his words paint a color image of the criminal for me as I sit in the audience tonight. And I'll bet it made the jury see the defendant about to commit murder more clearly than they saw him sitting in front of them in court, wearing a suit.

How would we react, I can't help wondering, if Mr. Prosecutor had told us that the defendant dressed in a pearl gray suit and a red power tie and put a weapon in his briefcase before driving to his ex-wife's house?

Might we have thought, *Poor man, he must have gone insane?*

Might he never have been charged with capital murder at all?

When the prosecutor has finished speaking, the activist rises to speak. In her talk, she really makes only one point:

In spite of all the changes we as Americans have made to the death penalty, almost everyone who's executed today is poor.

There's nothing new about this fact of life and nothing new about pointing it out. Thomas Paine said the same thing in almost the same words in *The Rights of Man*, written in 1791. Paine, former soldier in George Washington's army and renowned defender of revolution, called the poor "the exposed sacrifice of vice and legal barbarity." He said, "When, in countries that are called civilized, we see age going to the workhouse and youth to the gallows, something must be wrong in the system of government."

Mr. Prosecutor's tactics and techniques go back at least a hundred years before Thomas Paine—back to a case we've all heard of. In this case too, most of the condemned, as abundant testimony showed, were not very well liked or very important to anyone. They were too poor and unconnected to influence the court, and they were defenseless when the prosecutor introduced details that weren't relevant to the case but made the defendants look bad.

The first to be accused were a slave and two old women, one bad-tempered, one simply homeless and probably not sane. The three were Tituba, who had no last name because legally she was property, Sara Osborn, and Sarah Good. But the first to be tried was a little different, not young but evidently a still sexually attractive woman who wore the female equivalent of combat fatigues—a tight red dress and lots of lace.

The elements of the case were so much like those Mr. Prosecutor described—a heinous crime, an ample number of eyewitnesses, the outrage of the community, a formal indictment, the advice of experts, and a panel of distinguished judges led by a future governor of the state of Massachusetts. Members of the jury were seated and the accused brought forward.

Her name was Bridget Bishop. She was in her late fifties, married for the third time, and ran not one but two successful local taverns. She dressed flamboyantly, not as an honest married woman should. Rumor had it that she led an irregular lifestyle. Everyone knew she had been hauled into court on previous occasions—more than once for creating a disturbance by quarreling publicly with her husband.

This time the charge was more serious: witchcraft. This capital offense had been on the books in England and its colonies since 1641 and now, in 1692 in Salem, Massachusetts Bay Colony, it was taking victims as seldom before. On April 19, Bishop had been indicted on four separate counts of witchcraft, that is, being assisted by Satan or using supernatural powers to harm others. Bishop was accused of bewitching five young women in the township so that their bodies were "hurt, afflicted, pined, consumed, wasted, and tormented." These powerful young accusers sat in court and, whenever Bishop looked at them, contorted their faces and bodies as if in pain. The youngest of them, Ann Putnam, was about twelve years old, and the oldest was in her late teens. Ann, the daughter of local landowners and leading citizens, ended by accusing sixty-two people of witchcraft. In all, nineteen citizens of Salem went to the gallows and one was tortured to death.

From the perspective of our own time, it's easy to point to the limitations in understanding of the Puritan judges and townspeople who condemned these thirteen women and seven men. Above all, the accusers understood their own motives very poorly. Some motives were innocent—boredom, nosiness, and a desire to explain natural phenomena in an age of little scientific knowledge. Other motives were the kind you can see in hindsight were going to bring devastation to anyone who stood in the way—resentment, greed, desire for revenge, unbridled personal and political ambition.

What made the ill-wishing and profit-taking deadly is that they were so completely rationalized. After studying Mr. Prosecutor's technique, I've wondered how much may *not* have changed since Puritan times. It's worth studying how the Puritan authorities accomplished what they did—the unjustified killing of 20 members of their own community.

The witch trials were a textbook example of picking the victims first and tailoring the accusations to target them alone. Only later would women become a protected class when capital punishment is applied. In Puritan society, women were the core group of the punishable for religious and moral offenses because they bore the brunt of scrutiny. If someone wished to attack a woman, or to attack others through her, there was often a misstep she had made that could be brought to the attention of the authorities and prosecuted. Puritan authorities concealed their damaging strategy of social control under a blizzard of Bible quotations, legalistic arguments, and verbal intimidation. No matter how we refine the definition of a capital offense, the authority of office, the very use of language in the act of argument make it easy to let ambition slip through—to invoke animosity and prejudice in the guise of presenting evidence. The means can be as simple as focusing attention on the defendant's clothing.

Records of Bridget Bishop's indictment and trial show that more than two dozen members of the community testified against her at her indictment before a grand jury, not counting those who accused her at trial. Bishop said again and again that she was innocent and, in fact, didn't know what was meant by witchcraft.

Most readers of these depositions today would agree with Bishop that witchcraft was pretty hard to define, let alone demonstrate. Men (never women) claimed Bishop came in ghostly form and provocative clothing to sit on their chests in bed at night. Mothers blamed Bishop for insanity, retardation, ill health, and death among their young children. Some simply repeated what others had said—especially "Doctors and foreigners" who had solemnly given their opinion that such-and-such a child was bewitched. A dyer said that Bishop had brought him pieces of lace that were too small to be worn *in a normal way*. More to the point, perhaps, the money she paid for having the lace dyed then disappeared—and the dyer's apprentice *swore* he didn't know what happened to it!

In one case, a neighbor said he was visited by Bishop's evil spirit after he and she disputed over her chickens coming into his orchard. The pastor of her church said that a number of the congregation complained to him that Bishop's late hours and rowdy company were corrupting the youth of the village. In addition, she was blamed for the psychotic depression and eventual suicide of another congregant, Christian Trask. The pastor, who was not a medical expert, testified that Trask could not have cut her own throat with the short pair of scissors found near her body.

The evidence was all guesswork, hearsay, and retelling of the dreams, fantasies, and petty day-to-day disputes within a small community—yet the end result was the deaths of twenty people. It's true that the rules of evidence were different then: hearsay was admitted, and simply making an accusation automatically put the accused on the defensive. Bridget Bishop, who evidently had common- and business-sense in abundance but didn't understand much about religion—or politics—must have felt she was caught in a nightmare. She wasn't even accused of murder or assault, simply of ill-wishing Mrs. Trask and the children by a kind of remote control until, with Satan's assistance, they sickened and died. The death penalty was sought for the witchcraft itself. On June 2, 1692, Bridget Bishop was sentenced to be hanged by the neck until dead.

Bishop's sentence was carried out eight days later. This "lengthy" reprieve was granted under a law that stipulated the condemned must have at least four days to prepare themselves for death. Bishop was the first of nineteen convicted witches to be hanged in Salem in less than four months. A twentieth, Giles Corey, was killed for refusing to be tried at all. He was pressed to death under a pile of heavy stones, a form of torture that took two days to result in death. Corey's act was probably a desperate attempt to keep his farm, which he had willed to his daughters' husbands, from being confiscated by the state upon his conviction. Both Giles Corey and his wife Martha, who was hanged the day after he died, had been accused of witchcraft after they publicly criticized the accusers. Three of those hanged were sisters whose family, the Townes, had a long-standing quarrel with the Putnam family. At least five others among the accused died in irons while imprisoned, awaiting a trial that didn't come. As for the homeless and probably crazy Sara Good, her four-year-old daughter Dorcas, incredibly, was arrested as a witch and jailed with her mother. They remained in prison together until the mother was taken away to be hanged. In later years, the orphan's father reported that Dorcas had lost her reason and was, in effect, mentally incompetent for life.

Early residents of the Massachusetts and Plymouth colonies lived in a harsh world ruled by, as they understood it, the God of Moses. When a seventeenth-century American Puritan fell short of God's expectations, catastrophe was the outcome. Indians attacked; wolves devoured the livestock; spouses, children, and animals alike fell ill and died. Crops failed or were destroyed by storm, drought, insects, or disease. Milk went sour and grain spoiled. Money that was hard earned and sorely needed disappeared. Holes even appeared in the ground— another occurrence that one witness blamed on Bridget Bishop, and we can now speculate was an aftereffect of one of the region's several earthquakes. So acutely did the Puritans feel their dependence on God that, although holidays such as Christmas were not celebrated, and people married and were buried without services, the colonies held days of either public humiliation or public thanksgiving following events considered significant manifestations of God's favor or disfavor.

Witchcraft charges in this troubled society became epidemic when two of the future accusers, children living in the household of Samuel Parris, preacher to Salem village, became caught up in the idea of witchcraft—a titillating subject that had been in the air of the colony for several years after a popular book, *Memorable Providences*, was published in 1688. The author was none other than Cotton Mather, third-generation Puritan elite and pastor of Boston's Old North Church.

The two girls began playing fortune-telling games with Parris's slave Tituba, an Arawak Indian brought from Barbados. Perhaps it was only a way to pass the winter, but matters soon got out of hand. Betty Parris—a preacher's daughter who could well have felt guilty and afraid after indulging in the forbidden—began complaining of being pricked with pins, pinched, and choked without apparent cause. Tituba panicked, making a charm against Betty's bewitchment. When Betty's father found out, the girls turned on Tituba. Then Samuel Parris beat his slave until she "confessed" to an extraordinarily active ring of witches infesting Salem township. Pastor Parris used his pulpit as a forum to declare a conspiracy of evil. Satan, he said, was aiming an attack against the Parris household and the village at large. Girls outside the Parris household began showing symptoms like Betty's as well as speaking gibberish and hiding under chairs and tables. The father of ringleader Ann Putnam was the patron who had brought Samuel Parris into the village as pastor.

Looking back, we can see that Ann Putnam and the others were probably acting the way preadolescent and adolescent girls still act sometimes—showing off their intellectual curiosity, their social and sexual discomfort, and their budding social skills by mocking and imitating those around them. With typical lack of perspective, once the examinations and trials began, the young women might have found it harder to confess that their stories were lies than to see a few community members die. After all, the condemned were old, by adolescent standards, and of low status by anyone's reckoning. By now it was summer and the young accusers, joined by Ann Putnam's mother and Tituba, were acting out the witchcraft story to large audiences who came from all over the region. It's impossible to know whether they were pretending or, like the best salespeople, had become sincere believers in their own story.

Because each step was understandable in its own way, a need for attention and a fit of group hysteria are sometimes offered as the explanation for what happened next. But there is more to know about developments in Salem village so terrifying that they could turn a momentary loss of perspective into the deaths of twenty.

Not only did Tituba, the children, individual townspeople, and magistrates and other officials act on inappropriate personal motives, but also the township was split by an economic dispute. In the course of telling the history of the death penalty, I'll come back again and again to a financial and political contest in the background of capital trials where justice doesn't seem to have been served. Even today, the location of some trials is moved away from the county where the crime was committed. Change of venue is sought not only because of pretrial publicity, but also because undisclosed factionalism may play a part in the selection of jurors and the conduct of attorneys and the judge. Tension between two sets of interests, played out within the community, makes quarrels escalate and sometimes causes the parties involved to seek a way to disable their opponents permanently.

The town of Salem was a thriving port that depended on sea trade; Salem village traded with inland agricultural regions. But the two settlements, as part of one township, were under one government. Like a modern county's officials, the township authorities oversaw a number of villages and towns. Township government could determine the fortunes of most local business, from prosecution of criminals to who got public jobs and the way tax money was apportioned among the county's various settlements—for example, whether the town's resources went into sea trade versus farm trade. Meanwhile, residents of Salem village themselves could not agree over how closely the village should be tied to the port. One village faction was led by the Putnams and Parrises, the other by a clan called the Porters. Their quarrel entered the day-to-day relations of neighbor and neighbor, and influenced what delegates the township as a whole sent to meetings of the colonial government.

Samuel Parris, like any town preacher of the time, was in the thick of the power struggle. Today, his role is more likely to be taken by a newspaper editor or the management of a radio or television station, but Parris's involvement in the witch trials typifies both the personal financial stake of such opinion-makers and the way they can serve as a conduit for the political views of those who hire them. In larger Puritan settlements, several churches could appoint and individually support their own pastors. However, under Puritan law, the town also had a preacher. The Puritans, who had managed to finesse the British in order to govern themselves in New England, combined church and state and based much of their law on the contents of the Bible, taken verse by verse. Therefore, the township and the church parish were one governing unit, and pastors strongly influenced policy and administration.

Massachusetts towns appointed a pastor and supported him with a salary, a house to live in, and supplies. But the Parrises were in trouble. Before John Putnam brought Samuel Parris in as pastor to Salem village, Parris had been a planter in Barbados. He had no theological training and, apparently, no fortune to fall back on. After only two years as the village pastor, in October, 1691, Parris had alienated his contentious congregation to the point where they quit paying his wages or supplying his firewood. Interestingly, it was only three months later, in January 1692, that Parris's daughter began to act as if possessed.

Within a month after that, Parris coerced Tituba into confessing witchcraft and implicating two others. The preacher's prompt action, whatever motivated it, had the effect of turning the spotlight away from his congregation's dissatisfaction with him. When other ministers hastened to join the witch hunt, Parris's leadership was assured. As for the community, the discovery of an enemy within did not unite them. Rather, it caused them to take sides, many along the lines of their existing Putnam or Porter allegiances.

Soon after the accusations began in late February, county magistrates John Hathorne and Jonathan Corwin issued arrest warrants for the accused and conducted an initial examination. Hathorne was a merchant and local politician, active in church affairs, whose examining style was like that of a prosecutor rather than a judge.

> Hathorne: How do you know that you are not a witch?
> Bishop: I do not know what you say ... I know nothing of it.
> Hathorne: Why look you, you are taken now in a flat lie.

In other words, Bishop could be a witch without knowing she was a witch. But she was still held responsible for knowing this thing that she didn't know, so that not knowing that she was a witch made her a liar. And if she was a liar, she was not in a position to demonstrate that she was not a witch.

Nowadays, most of us—I hope—would consider Hathorne's logic suitable only for dysfunctional families, Stalinist Russia, or other totalitarian regimes. But Hathorne and other Puritan leaders upheld their position by an even stronger piece of circular reasoning: The Almighty gave me authority, therefore I am right. And since I am right, the Almighty must have given me authority. This reasoning process hid an enormous presumption and, with it, a great capacity to ignore contradictory evidence. It took a great deal of time for someone who thought this way to doubt a stand he or she had taken. Some of the inquisitors, like Hathorne, never did.

The spectacle of witches on trial before awesomely well-spoken, well-dressed, self-assured Puritan ministers sounds very much like celebrity trials of our own time that are interminably broadcast on television and, as a topic, play an important part in our social lives. Another layer of drama was added by the great amount of arbitrary power that Puritan officials could wield, compressing into minutes or hours cliffhanging decisions that we now consider worthy of months of deliberation. People came to Salem village from miles around to escape the smallness of their worlds and peek into the lives of those more adventuresome—exotically tormented young women possessed by Satan, mind-bogglingly evil old women who consorted with the Prince of Darkness. It was a live drama of thrilling, vicarious wickedness, and it offered the satisfaction of watching from a position of safety while payback was administered to others.

By the middle of May, so many had been accused of witchcraft that the courts were clogged. Just at this time, the new governor of the Massachusetts Bay Colony, Sir William Phips, returned to the colony from receiving his royal appointment. Phips was a protege of the incalculably influential Mather family. Increase Mather was president of

Harvard College—and father of Cotton, who had recently written the book on witchcraft that helped start the scare.

Perhaps anxious to show decisive leadership, new governor Phips ordered those imprisoned on witchcraft charges to be placed in chains. This action probably contributed to the deaths in prison even though Phips also convened a special court to try the cases more quickly. For this court, Phips appointed his new lieutenant governor, William Stoughton, to head the prestigious panel of judges. Several of the judges, like Phips himself, enjoyed friendship or patronage from the Mathers.

William Stoughton was a pastor in Dorchester before entering Massachusetts politics during the colony's power struggle with England in the 1670s, and he went on to take charge of the colony's courts of justice in the 1680s. Like many other judges, who were chosen from the ministry, Stoughton had no legal training and permitted court procedures that violated even the slender rights of defendants in that time. Most fateful was Stoughton's admitting "spectral evidence." This was the clause that made most of the witchcraft convictions possible. Accusers could testify, and be taken seriously, that the specter or spirit of an alleged witch had separated from the witch's body to visit them with malicious intent.

It appears from a letter written by Cotton Mather to one of the judges that at first Mather urged that spectral evidence be admitted. Mather was considered the leading expert on witches, and his recommendation did its work. Accusations continued to pour in, and began to come not only from Salem but from neighboring settlements such as Andover. One child, Martha Jacobs, accused her own grandfather. Five more convicted witches were hanged on July 19. Another five, including Martha Jacobs's grandfather, were hanged on August 19. On September 19 through 21, Giles Corey was pressed to death. On September 22 eight more of the convicted, including Martha Corey, were hanged.

Cracks in the prosecution's case appeared early on. One of the accusers admitted she was lying, then took back her confession. Later, the accused Rebecca Nurse, aged 71, was actually found not guilty. But when the jury's verdict was read, spectators and accusers raised such an outcry that more testimony was taken and the jury told to reconsider. Aided by Nurse's deafness and confusion that produced ambiguous answers to Justice Stoughton's questioning, the jurors this time found her guilty. A petition from the community did not save her from being hanged in July.

A celebrity defendant was added when former Salem minister George Burroughs found himself among the accused. Burroughs had left Salem over a salary dispute. He had also had arguments over money with John Putnam. Under arrest, Burroughs was brought back from Maine to Salem, jailed, and quickly convicted. Burroughs's standing in the community cut two ways. Thirty-two respected residents of the village petitioned for his release. One of his accusers admitted that she had invented her testimony. But, because Burroughs had been a leading figure in community life, he was a great catch for accusers and judges—much more so than an old woman, even a respectable one. Burroughs was portrayed as a sorcerer and ringleader of the witches. At his hanging, Burroughs did something thought impossible for a witch—he recited the Lord's prayer correctly. Bystanders cried out for the hanging to be stopped. But Cotton Mather, who was on hand as a witness, pressed the sheriff's men to carry out the hanging.

The momentum of the witch hunt was so great that the convictions and hangings didn't stop for over five months after the first uncertainties appeared.

Increase Mather finally began to have doubts when some of the "witches" he conscientiously visited in prison took back their confessions in spite of the fact that confessing would have saved them from execution. It may have mattered as much, or more, that the growing numbers of accusers overreached themselves. How could it happen, one local pastor asked, that so many respectable people all in one location, at one time, became allies of the devil? It is said that rumor even began to accuse members of the Puritan elite, such as the wives of Governor Phips and Increase Mather, of witchcraft. Mather had already called for the discontinuance of spectral evidence, and he would soon publish a 39-page tract, *Cases of Conscience*, that explored the question further.

On October 8, 1692, Governor Phips forbade the use of spectral evidence in witchcraft trials. Three weeks later, Phips released many of the accused and dissolved the special court. Another court was convened to take up prosecution of the witches, and in January, 1693, Justice William Stoughton attempted to have those convicted witches executed who had been reprieved for pregnancy. Phips overrode Stoughton's order, releasing most of those arrested on the basis of spectral evidence. A few months later, Phips pardoned the last three still in prison.

Ann Putnam's mother and father both died soon after the trials, leaving their daughter to raise their other children and never marry. In 1706, Ann Putnam apologized in church for her false accusations, stating that she had been tricked by the Devil.

Preacher Parris, who had by now expressed remorse for his accusations but continued to blame others more than himself, clung on to his ministerial post in Salem Village. He even brought his case to court, but was eventually forced out of the job.

Tituba, who had been in jail all through the trials except when brought into court to testify, was sold to a new master.

Sir William Phips was called to London to explain charges of improper financial conduct in his administration. He died in 1695, blaming William Stoughton for the witchcraft trials.

Stoughton became the next governor of the Massachusetts colony. He never admitted to any wrongdoing.

Cotton Mather was given the official records of the Salem witchcraft trials for the purpose of writing a book about them that would reflect well on the conduct of the judges. The book, *Wonders of the Invisible World*, came out in 1693. For Stoughton and Mather, who never admitted improper conduct, the trials had been an unbeatable career builder.

———•———

How different the world is now—or is it? As I began to write this book, I argued with myself about including the Puritans in a book about U. S. capital punishment today. But the more I read about Puritan trial procedure and compared it with the motives of the witches' accusers and prosecutors, the more I saw how lack of self-awareness, and the rules themselves, could smuggle injustice into the courtroom. True, in our own time we stretch out the process of condemnation over months and years. But how much arbitrary power courts should exert remains an open question today.

As I write, the Supreme Court has voted 8-1 that federal appeals courts must hear a condemned prisoner's appeal on constitutional grounds, even if the prisoner's case for error isn't airtight. Courts had been applying the higher standard as well as compressing two appeals steps into one.

Also being debated is how long evidence of innocence can continue to be heard. During an appeal in February, a judge on the Missouri Supreme Court found herself wondering if she had heard correctly. "Are you suggesting," she asked the prosecutor, that "even if we find Mr. Amrine is actually innocent, he should be executed?" Many prosecutors have no trouble answering yes to this question. But for me it points up the absurdity of applying the irreversible act of execution when we know so well—dating all the way back to the Puritans—that the discovery of *actual innocence* doesn't take place on the prosecutor's time table.

———•———

People sometimes say that Americans inherited attitudes from the New England Puritans—for example, a habit of judging severely, excessive personal modesty, or extreme disapproval of sex. These traits actually belonged more to Cotton Mather as an individual, a man who was incredibly gifted and extremely rigid, than to the Puritan leadership as a whole.

But nineteenth and twentieth century Americans carried on the Puritan concern with right and wrong conduct. The importance of examining one's conscience in light of a moral code can be traced historically from Puritan Massachusetts to Maine and south to Georgia as the Great Awakening, a Christian revival movement of the 1730s and 1740s begun by renegade Puritan minister Jonathan Edwards. Edwards called for a return to the original Calvinist faith accompanied by a purification of behavior. He urged Gospel standards of charity toward others, encouraged the expression of religious ecstasy, and inveighed against "reveling, frolicking, profane and unclean conversation, lewd songs, fornication, and tavern haunting," among a very long list of forbidden behaviors. Edwards's movement spread morally conservative Protestantism to all parts of the American colonies, making his views a social force that remains potent in our day. For us more than some other nations, the debating of moral issues has combined a personal quest, a communal value, and a binding social glue.

A

SERMON

Preached on the Occasion
Of the EXECUTION
OF

Katherine Garret,
an Indian-Servant,
(Who was Condemned for the

Murder

of her Spurious Child,)
On *May* 3*d.* 1 7 3 8.

To which is Added some short Account of
her Behaviour after her Condemnation.

Together with her Dying WARNING
and EXHORTATION.
Left under her own Hand.

By ELIPHALET ADAMS, M. A.
And Pastor of the Church of CHRIST *in* N. London.

N. LONDON,
Printed and Sold by T. GREEN, 1738.

Katherine Garret heard this sermon, later printed, before she was hanged.

3

"A Vast Circle of People"
Authority, Public Execution, and Crowd Control

Whoever Cotton Mather was as an individual, he was also the last of a breed—the Puritan divines who could govern New England from a pulpit, marshaling the fears and beliefs of entire communities at occasions such as a hanging.

Cotton Mather secured his place in the Puritan power structure through his expertise in moral judgment. In early Puritan days, ministers were the masters of law, of innocence and guilt.

When the state took a human life, the presence of ministers lent legitimacy to an act that was otherwise too nakedly appalling to contemplate. In return, ministers who succeeded were accorded as high a status as anyone in the land. Mather in particular was the learned authority on heaven and hell. There could be no more climactic moment than when the condemned was about to be sent for all eternity to one realm or the other. Mather took a special interest in the crime of fornication or "uncleanness" and, during his career, saw two young women to the hangman for murdering their illegitimate infants. Many ministers in Mather's place might have felt real compassion, but all saw themselves as comforters whose primary responsibility was to the soul, not the body or the emotions of those who were to be hanged. Mather feared that the condemned women could not be spiritually saved. He performed all parts of his duty scrupulously, but his diary entry makes clear that contact with the prisoners was tedious. They weren't on his social or intellectual level and were probably awed to silence when he visited them in prison. "Many and many a weary Hour, did I spend in the Prison, to serve the Souls of those miserable Creatures," he wrote in a diary entry after the execution on June 8, 1693.

Ministers who upheld state religion and the executions it sponsored don't seem to have acknowledged, probably not even to themselves, the professional benefit they received. But Mather's diary reveals a real root of his zeal for attending the condemned. After his sermon for the execution of the two condemned women on the same day, he told his diary with pride that "one of the greatest Assemblies, ever known in these parts of the World, was come together" to hear him preach. He also recorded the later satisfaction of seeing his sermon "immediately printed, greedily bought up, and afterwards reprinted at London."

But, you'll say, all this has changed. No one in our society derives the kind of authority or status from the death penalty that Cotton Mather attained. A secular bureaucracy has taken the place of ministers both in law courts and at the place of execution. To see the connection between support for capital punishment and the aggrandizement of authority figures today—you'll protest—we have to go to Islamic nations where religious texts are still the law of the land.

All right—I'll indulge you in this argument before we return to the end of Cotton Mather's time and the beginning of ours. Let's take the case of Nigerian felon Amina Lawal.

In March, 2002, a Nigerian religious court convicted Lawal of adultery. The man she named as the father of her child swore on the Qur'an that he was not the father, therefore the court found him innocent. He was released. Amina Lawal, the mother, was reprieved until the religious authorities judge that her infant is old enough to be weaned. Then she will meet a death perhaps more cruel than that of Giles Corey, who had stones piled on top of him until he suffocated. In Lawal's case, the stones will be thrown at her head until she is broken, blind, and faceless, then more stones will be piled over her. In the darkness she'll be left to die of shock, blood loss, or brain swelling while still buried in the ground up to her shoulders.

Even if Amina Lawal weren't unlettered, poor, and without influence, she is similar to early Puritan defendants in having few rights under the law. Lawal's conviction was supported by the chapter and verse of Islamic religious law, the Sharia. The sanctity of the Qur'an is so central to northern Nigerian society that Lawal's lover was declared innocent simply for swearing on the holy book. Any other verdict would place the authenticity of the Qur'an in question. So judges turned a blind eye to the lover's obvious self-interest—avoiding being executed. Lawal's stoning, it's clear, will also serve to stress the authority of Nigeria's religious leadership in their power struggle with secular politicians. To carry out an execution is to assert that one holds the highest authority in the land.

But, you'll protest, authoritarian government in the United States ended with the American Revolution.

Oh, did it? If power struggles using the death penalty as a symbol have ended in the American nation, how did they end, and what came afterward?

In the 1700s, colonists' growing diversity of income and origin all over the British colonies of America fostered moral and religious diversity. It became difficult to prosecute unorthodox beliefs and moral offenses under law. Early Puritans had several times punished Quakerism with death during the 1600s. Later, in a live-and-let-live atmosphere, accepted Protestant sects ranged from Anglicanism and Quakerism to a kind of early Unitarianism and to the conservative, evangelical Christian belief that Jonathan Edwards preached. By 1750 when Edwards, as Puritan pastor of Northampton, chastised his congregation for drifting away from original Puritan beliefs, church members simply removed him from his job.

With the move away from morals prosecutions, the focus on women as capital offenders disappeared. Adultery was last punished with legal execution in the 1640s, and no one was executed for witchcraft after 1692. After the 1730s, the law seldom singled out murdering a newborn as morally distinct from other kinds of killing. Thirty-six of the 135 recorded executions in the Plymouth, Maine, and Massachusetts Bay colonies during the 1600s—about one-quarter of all executions—were of women. Twenty-five of these women were executed as witches in

Connecticut and Massachusetts. During the 1700s, the total fell to only fifteen of 179, fewer than ten percent of the female population. Ultimately, women (except for the poorest) would be sequestered at home as the keepers of lost human innocence—those whom prosecutors and juries professed to believe were almost incapable of a crime deserving the death penalty. We are now fewer than two percent of all those on death row in the United States.

Slaves, both men and women, were executed historically at a higher rate compared to their total population than unenslaved persons. But after about 1800, unenslaved men, especially young immigrant men, became a preferred target of punishment along with slaves. African-American men were to become the most targeted group of all. This change began around 1800 when the newly prosperous American society grew more concerned about keeping order and protecting property than inquiring into their neighbors' beliefs and conduct. Most executions since we became a nation have been for murder, robbery, theft, or arson.

Today, to shed light on the fate of Amina Lawal, we have to read about executions of women in the 1700s. The American holy men who walked these two women to the gallows told almost nothing about the women who died, but left a full record of what they were thinking. During the 1730s, their insecurities about their own authority began to show.

Rebekah Chamblit was convicted of murdering her illegitimate infant shortly after his birth. To escape hanging, Chamblit would have had to prove that the child was born dead. However, Chamblit gave birth alone and buried the child without telling anyone. Chamblit's burying her baby could have been reported by anyone whom she inconvenienced—a spiteful neighbor, a member of her family, or the baby's father. In a "confession" dated the day before her execution in Boston, on September 27, 1733, Chamblit maintained that when the child was born she wasn't sure whether it was alive or not.

Chamblit may have made this halfway admission in hopes she would be spared. But she became an example of the fate that awaited the morally tainted—what one of Cotton Mather's execution sermons called a warning from the dead. The horror of Chamblit's death was supposed to deter other young women from fornication, the crime of unwed sex. Whether or not this effect was achieved, the death sentence, the execution sermon, and the appearance of ministers on the scaffold underscored the worldly power of Puritan divines in a very pertinent way: they were able to cause lives to be taken. But the lesson, whatever it really was, had to be public. Terror was part of the punishment, and so was dying for the edification of a crowd. In his professional capacity, the attending minister at an execution was bound to hope the crowd was a large one.

What really happened to the baby and what Chamblit felt as she wrote her confession—whether she even wrote it without help amounting to dictation—will never be known. Almost everything that remains of Chamblit's twenty-seven years of life is contained in an execution sermon of the kind that Puritan ministers commonly made up into pamphlets or books. The sermon as published typically included the lecture given the Sunday before the execution, the confession of the doomed prisoner, and a description of the last hours of life. But the writing of these documents is so tightly scripted, so stuffed with piety and hellfire, that it's hard to imagine the real scene.

Chamblit, her prison fetters having been struck off and the hanging rope placed around her neck, walked to the gallows behind her own coffin. The Reverend Mr. Byles went with her. Even if she hadn't been terrified, I wonder if she could have heard his words over the noises made by the crowd. Chamblit couldn't expect much sympathy. Many bystanders were doubtless active supporters of her punishment; others were just looking for entertainment, or feeling the delicious pleasure of not being in Chamblit's shoes. Many would have been used to witnessing and experiencing suffering in their own lives.

As Byles walked with Chamblit in procession to the gallows, he carried out his moral duty by describing her evil nature in much the same terms that proponents of the death penalty make use of today. About one man condemned by a Houston jury in 1992, a sheriff said in a typical comment, "he is absolutely the most vicious and savage individual I know." In theory, Pastor Byles, unlike this modern-day sheriff, was speaking directly to Chamblit, but both Byles and the sheriff knew their comments would be recorded and widely read.

"You are now walking to a dismal execution!" Byles tells us he began.

Perhaps most of what's in his record is for the benefit of us, the readers. And maybe young women like Chamblit were so used to hearing this kind of talk from their pastors that it seemed normal. On their way to the place of execution, Byles tells us he found time to touch on Chamblit's "raging corruptions," "vicious habits," and "the obstinacy of her wicked heart."

Byles's comments were lengthy; as for Chamblit, "Her answers indeed were but short." As they reached the place of execution, which was a tree growing on Boston Common, Chamblit "grew disordered and faint, and not capable of attending further to continu'd discourse." It may be that Chamblit, like most of the condemned, was able to keep herself from believing what was going to happen. But dignity came to an end at the hanging tree. Byles's flat summary probably meant that, when Chamblit saw the executioner and the sheriff's men, the burst of body heat and the cold sweat and piss and shit of mortal fear took her over. The human system is made to retain consciousness as long as resources of body and mind remain, but Chamblit may have had to be physically supported in her appointed position, standing on a wagon. She had to be rendered helpless and immobile before she could be killed, and so her hands were tied, and perhaps ropes tied around her arms and her legs. A handkerchief or cloth bag was placed over her head and the rope, already around her neck, was thrown over a tree limb and secured while Byles continued to pray aloud.

Then the sheriff's men whipped up the horse and drove the wagon away.

Hanging always worked, unless the rope wasn't prepared correctly or just broke and the whole operation had to be repeated, but it could kill in different ways. Chamblit probably swung off the wagon and dangled from the rope, instead of being dropped so that her neck was caught abruptly and fractured by the noose. Modern medical evidence suggests that hanging victims like Chamblit didn't usually die either from spinal cord injury or from having their air cut off but because the noose compressed major veins, arteries, or nerves in the neck. The condemned might die in five minutes to an hour following the destruction of brain cells or disruption of the heart's rhythm. We don't know how long it took to become unconscious.

Chamblit's execution was an ordinary one—like several hundred others we can learn about through execution sermons. Nothing the commentators said suggested that they, or the crowd, objected to the proceedings. But an execution sermon five years after Rebekah Chamblit's came to terms, possibly for the first time, with both opponents of execution and the darker motives of bystanders.

Katherine Garret was an American Indian and, like Rebekah Chamblit, was a servant convicted of the death of her illegitimate infant. Before Garret was hanged in New London, Connecticut, on May 3, 1738, Eliphalet Adams, pastor of the Puritan or Congregational church, chose somewhat strangely to preach on the text from Proverbs 27:17, "A man that doth Violence to the blood of any person, shall flee to the Pit, Let no man stay him." In his sermon, Adams inveighed against lesser punishments than death and applied some of the same reasoning death penalty supporters use today.

Adams said that the "Pit" he referred to was a Bible term for the grave. He spent fully thirty-one pages of his thirty-seven-page sermon outlining the reasons that no one should prevent the formal killing of one who killed. There may have been some feeling in New London against Garret's execution, even some fear of retaliation by the Indian community. Adams spoke the Pequot language and had opened Indian schools in Lyme, Connecticut. He may have been considered an acceptable figure of authority to uphold Puritan law. But his note of defensiveness had rarely been heard on previous occasions.

Adams was even at pains to spell out that a killer's becoming a fugitive and exile like Cain was no longer sufficient punishment. After Cain murdered Abel, said Adams, God expressed His wrath by means of the

Biblical flood, and afterward He said to Noah (Genesis 9:6): "Whoso sheddeth man's blood, by man shall his blood be shed: for in the image of God made he man." Adams also recognized that pity was natural, and some in his audience would want to help a condemned individual escape execution. The sermon spelled out forbidden stages of resistance to the law—forcibly preventing arrest, suppressing testimony at the trial, aiding a prison escape.

Adams went on to give some of the same reasons that death penalty supporters still use to avoid granting mercy to the condemned. Commutation of sentence, Adams said, made the merciful one an accessory to the guilty one's crime. It invited God's judgment on the whole community. It allowed the freed felon (if he or she was ever freed) to commit another crime. As if even these reasons were not enough, Adams then justified the penalty of death for murder on grounds that (1) it was God's law and (2) it was practiced by, as he claimed, the whole world.

Adams couldn't help boasting about the size of the crowd— "more Numerous, perhaps, than Ever was gathered together before, On any Occasion, in this Colony"—but he admonished spectators who attended for the wrong reasons. If many in the crowd jeered, got drunk, and picked each others' pockets, it was nothing new. But Adams, because of his official capacity and his religious belief, was adamant for the execution as a religious occasion and a moral lesson. Spectators were there to witness God's will being done and should behave accordingly.

To make matters difficult for the Reverend Mr. Adams, however, a greater population and better communications within the colonies were making execution crowds larger. At the same time, ideas were changing fast, throwing the authority of both church and state into doubt.

During the second half of the 1700s, both evangelical Protestantism and Enlightenment philosophy affected debate. The cult of reason prompted each citizen to think independently; democratic evangelical fervor called for direct communication with a God who cherished each individual. Unexpectedly, reason and religion worked together to undermine the severity of colonial law. A milestone of public discussion was Cesare Beccaria's anti-execution *Essay on Crimes and Punishments*, first published in 1764. Beccaria's work was reprinted and discussed by reformers almost as quickly in the United States as in France or England. By the end of the century, some new American states were at pains to distinguish their application of justice from the bloodthirsty behavior of the British, as when Quaker reformers William Bradford and Benjamin Rush, a physician and member of the Continental Congress, used Beccaria's arguments to rewrite the colonial-era Pennsylvania criminal code. The Pennsylvania laws of the 1790s established two degrees of murder and instituted imprisonment, rather than corporal punishment, as the norm for offenses less than first-degree murder. Other newly formed states followed more or less slowly in revising their legal codes.

But the crowd roared louder and louder. Executions after Independence, held at county seats, took on the atmosphere of a combined market day and festival. The crowd at a 1784 execution in Reading, Pennsylvania, was estimated at 15,000 to 20,000. As late as 1806, the minister at an execution in Haverhill, New Hampshire, it is said, preached a two-hour sermon and led the crowd of 10,000 in singing and prayers. But, if it even happened that way, the pastor was there by invitation of the community, not as a representative of state religion. As crowds grew more raucous, ministers may have been invited less often to address them. Or the ministers may have withdrawn voluntarily, unable to insist on the edifying example of a hanging, eventually attending only when the condemned individual asked them to. By 1820, accounts of many executions state that the pastor's participation was limited to a brief prayer.

After attending the execution of a man named Bennet as part of an enormous crowd at the hanging in July of 1820, the Quaker and prominent Philadelphia merchant Thomas Cope asked himself, "Can this be the best mode of managing such cases?" Cope wrote in his diary, "Is this the way to reform him, or even to deter others from the commission of crime?"

The way that Cope spoke of the condemned man was new: as an individual rather than a stick figure manipulated to make a point. The young Bennet, Cope wrote sadly, was "in the prime & vigour of manhood." Convicted of murder, however, Bennet seemed "a most hardened, abandoned culprit, evincing nothing like contrition or repentance even under the jibbet. Till the hour of his execution he has been visited by any person who chose it & his time since condemnation appears to have been spent in obscene conversation, in drinking & abuse of courts, juries &c." A criminal like Bennet could now feature in popular imagination, and spur the cottage industry of tradespeople and printers as the published broadside detailing the culprit's crime replaced the execution sermon. In this new format, every detail of the crime, then of the culprit's manner and bearing in prison and on the scaffold, was detailed. As the preacher's role faded into obscurity, the condemned criminal became a celebrity.

"If society will persist in the infliction of death for crime, why thus suffer the criminal to be exposed to idle, vicious company? Why not, rather, by seclusion from the world, afford him the opportunity of reflection & repentance?" Thomas Cope continued. People like Cope believed in the importance of individual atonement. But they also saw to it that public executions ceased in state after state because they believed that the disadvantage of public disorder had won out. Public execution had become the opposite of a demonstration of governmental authority.

Does the fact that we no longer execute publicly mean that executions are no longer a power play on the part of government? A recent headline says it all: "Under Ashcroft, Judicial Power Flows Back to Washington." U. S. attorney general John Ashcroft, morally self-assured supporter of capital punishment, recently overruled twenty-eight recommendations from local federal prosecutors who had decided *not* to seek the death penalty. Ashcroft's actions aggrandized the power of federal government by exerting the ultimate governmental decision of death over life. Ashcroft is less able to impose his position directly on state governments, but he has already attempted to do so by trying to overrule Oregon's law allowing physician-assisted suicide.

Ashcroft's aggressive positioning of the federal government, as it takes a new ideological tack, opposes the historical American fight for states' rights over those of the central government. Legal execution has been one of the tokens in this chess game since the death-penalty debates of the 1790s. The American federal system has always made use of the death penalty for a maximum number of offenses—more than most states have authorized. But, traditionally, as a sign of autonomy from centrally determined policies, some American states held tightly to their right to execute while others vigorously rejected the death penalty.

I doubt that John Ashcroft is an especially cruel individual—no more than Cotton Mather, John Byles, Nigerian religious leaders, or the men of Amina Lawal's community who'll throw the stones. The father of Lawal's child may be among the stone-throwers just as Chamblit's and Garret's lovers were likely to be in the crowd when their child's mother was hanged. You could say decision-makers like these are callous, indifferent. But that attitude is the one they need. I think they've weighed the value of a condemned prisoner's life to them against the value to them of their public standing and their careers. Is it surprising if, however unconsciously, they've decided in favor of self-interest? Lawal and others waiting on death row are like rabbits who wandered into the hunter's gunsights just when the hunter needed a rabbit. Those who judge are those least likely ever to have to play the role of rabbit. And those who witness execution or help inflict it may feel they're buying themselves insurance against meeting such an end themselves. The Nigerian local courts and the U. S. Justice Department are playing to different audiences, perhaps. American power mongers, unlike Nigerian ones, have learned that they can act effectively without risking the fully informed debate, much less the riot potential, of a live-audience public execution.

Cell block seven, Eastern State Penitentiary, Philadelphia (1829).

4

"Darkness, Threatening, Ruins, Terror"
The Penitentiary and Capital Punishment

E xecutions today are the tip of America's punishment iceberg. Capital punishment in the United States was once considered the opposite of imprisonment—each execution seen by reform-spirited citizens like Thomas Cope as society's failure.

At the end of October 2002, 3,697 prisoners were on death row in 37 states and 2 federal jurisdictions, civil and military. Sound like a lot? These condemned men and women were about *three-tenths of one percent* of the total 1,406,031 prisoners in state and federal prisons nationwide. Another 702,044 were awaiting trial or serving sentences in county and city jails, or on probation or parole. According to a World Prison Population List maintained by the British government, more than half the world's prisoners are in the United States.

Trying to compare the rate of punishment to the crime rate is tricky, I find. For instance, the number of persons in American prisons rose dramatically each year for twenty years—from 1980 to 2000. Crime rates have risen, fallen, risen, and fallen again in those years and are now comparable to 1970s rates. A University of Texas study group estimated that only twenty-five percent of our drop in crime can be accounted for by putting more people in prison for longer sentences. These researchers credited most of the decrease to our recently strong economy, improved policing, and a drop in sales of crack cocaine. When crime and imprisonment rates are compared state by state, there's even less relationship between crime and punishment than the national rates suggest.

The history of crime legislation is more telling than the history of crime rates. In 1968, during an era of anti-war protests and urban riots, Richard Nixon was elected on a platform that emphasized crime as a problem. In the same year, Congress approved major funding for local law enforcement and mandated that federal government become more involved in local enforcement. In an uneasy nation, Nixon's "war on drugs" was every bit as popular as Cotton Mather's wars on witchcraft and adultery. Popular response hasn't diminished under presidents since Nixon. His initiative was taken up by the states when Nelson Rockefeller as governor of New York encouraged mandatory prison sentences of benchmark severity for drug-related crimes. Rockefeller's move was imitated nationwide.

But both liberal and conservative experts—for example, criminologist Franklin Zimring of the University of California, Berkeley, and U.S. Supreme Court Justice William Rehnquist—have described mandatory sentencing as punishment by political decision.

If political candidates are making hay out of our fear of crime, it's nothing new. The creation of penitentiaries was an important step in politicizing punishment, and the United States was a leader in developing the penitentiary—*a place of repentance in captivity*. Stimulated by reformers, lawmakers intended this type of prison to replace corporal punishment and most capital punishment. The first American penitentiary was the Walnut Street Jail in Philadelphia, built in 1773 and made into a penitentiary in 1790. Today, at last estimate, the United States has 1,196 "confinement facilities," or twenty-four per state if they were distributed evenly. Add to this total at least one county jail in each of our more than 3,000 counties.

It's hard to believe that our only places of imprisonment in colonial times were town jails—few, small, and insecure. A typical example was built in a Maryland town in 1693, an iron cage fifteen feet square placed on the courthouse grounds. In some frontier locales, prisoners were boarded in a locked room in the jailer's house, or held in caves or mines. These jails didn't have cells, just a common space, and mostly held arrestees waiting for trial. If the prisoners survived the cold, heat, bad water, scanty food, and vermin-borne illnesses of confinement and were convicted, the wealthier and more influential citizens might be allowed to pay a fine and perhaps make public confession or monetary restitution. Some who were convicted of murder were pardoned with only a brand on the thumb—for one murder only—if they could show they were able to read. For the rest found guilty of an offense, the luckier ones would only be placed in the stocks or pillory so that the public could mock them and throw refuse, animal and human excrement, and sometimes rocks. The less lucky men and women were whipped until their backs and breasts were scarred for life, branded on the face, had their ears cropped or their noses slit. All of these punishments served as public entertainment. Afterward, some convicted felons may have remained in the community. But many left voluntarily or were driven away.

When Pennsylvania's new legislators first mandated the penitentiary, they were rebelling against the harsh, Puritan-style criminal code that the British crown had imposed on them. American Quakers of the 1700s, led by the social thought of William Penn, believed unshakably in both reform and the deterrent value of public example. They felt penitentiaries would supply these two goods. They were also responding to a fact of postcolonial life that Pennsylvania felt with special intensity—the growth of population. At some point, the beatings, the pillorying, the branding and cropping, and the hangings would be continuous. As with execution crowds, spectators at other public punishments created a consuming exercise in keeping order. From the point of view of an elected state government, it wasn't feasible anymore to put every offender out of town. Sooner and sooner, the next town would be complaining of their arrival.

—◆—

"To reclaim rather than to destroy"—Pennsylvania's legislators started at the top when they stated their goal for criminal justice in 1786. These words are dusty now, vague and hard to grasp, an epitaph for a theory of a system. Reading them in the half-dark stacks of a university law library in the twenty-first century, I marvel at the optimism and self-confidence of the reforming lawmakers who wrote them. The same whirlwind of social change and intellectual energy that brought about the American and French revolutions led reformers to the idea of the penitentiary—to the idea of reform itself. It certainly *sounds* as if Pennsylvania's lawmakers intended, or at least hoped, to return their straying citizens to a productive place in the community. Distinguished Europeans such as Tocqueville and Dickens who visited our first penitentiaries couldn't have guessed that over the next half-century these elaborately designed "houses of reclamation" would be remodeled again and again, first to house more prisoners, then to contain a death chamber.

The prison theory that created the penitentiary came partly from sixteenth-century European experiences with workhouses, where the poor were trained to work. Governments later began to detain vagrants, disobedient servants, and even unruly children at labor in houses of correction. These institutions introduced the idea of the prison as residence—of very tightly regulated work as the road to redemption. Workhouses may always have had a profit motive, but reformers tried to adapt them as a humane alternative to corporal punishment and public humiliation. To do so, they needed to overcome the standard conditions of jail detention: enforced idleness, indiscriminate mixing of genders, ages, and kinds of offense, and extortion of prisoners by jailers and other prisoners. Reformers sought, it seems, to model good social relations through an exemplary life under lock and key. Both English and American houses of correction took off from the idea that criminals were created by a disorderly social environment in which they never learned the virtues of industry and a "regular" life.

This idea hasn't been disproved. But in well over 200 years we've made relatively few offenders into productive citizens by any system of imprisonment. The first penitentiary regimes were the Pennsylvania and Auburn systems. Both called for only one prisoner per cell and the inmates' complete silence at all times. Under the Pennsylvania system, prisoners worked alone in their cells, but the Auburn system called for work in groups. The Pennsylvania system was sponsored by the Philadelphia Society for Alleviating the Miseries of Public Prisons, organized in 1787 by Benjamin Franklin, Benjamin Rush, and other leading Philadelphians. Drawing on Quakers' belief in solitary meditation, the Pennsylvania system prescribed isolation. Prisoners weren't even allowed to get a glimpse of one another or of their jailers. Work such as shoemaking or weaving, which was optional, was performed alone in one's cell. The only reading was the Bible. There were no letters, no visits except from official prison visitors.

Officials first introduced Pennsylvania's "unremitting solitude to hard labor" at the Walnut Street Jail in 1790-1792 simply by adding a block of isolation cells in the jail yard. The Pennsylvania government had a very difficult time getting taxpayers to go even this far into spending money on reform. Within a decade, reformers were deploring overcrowding in the Walnut Street Jail. Meanwhile, from about 1797 to 1817, other states from New York to Georgia constructed Pennsylvania-system prisons that provided individual isolation cells.

Then the competing Auburn system made its debut in New York state with a macabre experiment. To prove the Auburn system's superiority to that of Pennsylvania, Auburn's prison officials chose a comparison group of eighty offenders to be placed in solitary confinement, with no work, for two years from Christmas 1821 to Christmas 1823. An unknown number of these prisoners died or went insane. Nonetheless, back in Pennsylvania, legislators persuaded themselves that a new prison especially for solitary confinement should be built near Philadelphia. The $780,000 prison, begun in 1829, was one of the most expensive buildings in the United States.

"Darkness, threatening, ruins, terror," Francesco Milizia wrote in his *Principles of Public Architecture* in 1785. A prison should look like a house of horror. To visit Eastern State Penitentiary, which has stood empty since 1971, is—almost—to understand and be converted by the concept of architectural deterrence. Architect John Haviland designed a fortress-like Gothic Revival exterior in rough stone with battlements, an intimidating, overscaled entry, and nearly a half-mile of high stone wall with guard towers at each of four corners. Inside the walls, cellblocks were arranged like spokes, converging on a central guard station. The purpose of the Boston Prison Discipline Society in hiring Haviland, they wrote, was to create "architecture adapted to morals." This principle made the interiors of prisons much more frightening than the exteriors. Haviland explained in his prospectus that each cell wall, adjacent to the central corridor, would contain "a feeding-drawer and peephole." The wall itself was eighteen inches thick, and the drawer was made so that food and clothing were passed to the prisoner without his or her being able to see the keeper. This arrangement, Haviland went on, was considerably cheaper than a door for the same purpose.

Not mentioned on elegant occasions such as the presentation of architectural plans was another purpose of solitary cells: the sheer need to control a rapidly increasing population of prisoners. Reporting on New Jersey's original, congregate penitentiary (built 1797 with additions in 1820), a legislative investigating committee found in 1830 that the guard room "[commanded] a view of neither the yard, the shops, the wings, or the walls of the prison." The prisoners, the committee reported, "might rise upon the under keepers, in the shops; the prisoners, in the cells of either the north or south wing, might make their escape; the sentinel, on the wall, might sleep at his post, and the principal keeper and his deputy, in the guard room, be so far removed from hearing, and cut off from sight, as to know nothing of it."

"In a prison, thus constructed," the New Jersey committee concluded, "there can be no discipline." In a penitentiary on the Pennsylvania plan, by contrast, where prisoners were "in their places," silent, and constantly under surveillance, "there would be comparatively little need of severe punishment, because rebellion and villainy would be prevented in the very beginning." But, at the Eastern State Penitentiary, it took thirteen years to build the first 250 cells. By then, authorities realized that the prison was too small, and the rest of the building's history was a scramble to fit more and more cellblocks into the radial design. Crowding obliterated design features that were meant to enforce silence, such as the high, vaulted ceilings that magnified sound and the separate exercise space for each prisoner.

Jails as short-term holding areas needed to be convenient to the courthouse and police station or sheriff's office, but long-term confinement after sentencing could be carried out elsewhere. After the economic advantage of prisons in creating community employment became apparent, politicians in many states vied to locate these facilities within their district. Penitentiaries were also sited for large, cheap land parcels and some kind of resource suitable to convict labor. Sing Sing, for example, was built at the village of Ossining near a river and a quarry, and convicts from the Auburn penitentiary mined the construction rock. Sing Sing's first cell house was 482 feet long, containing about 800 cells, seven by three and one-half feet in size, in five tiers. "Solitary" systems proved unsuccessful at reform, a fact that was quickly discovered by impartial observers though only slowly and reluctantly acknowledged by officials. Superintendents and wardens took over from charitable prison boards, and the prison bureaucracy was born. Prison labor, touted as self-sustaining or profitable in response to taxpayer and voter concerns, seldom paid the state (though it was sometimes profitable for individual contractors) but found its importance as a means of occupying the inmates' time and attention. Corporal punishment was not abolished with the construction of cellular prisons. It flourished for another one hundred years and more within penitentiary walls, and one of the most dreaded disciplinary measures was solitary confinement.

As American states developed other kinds of reform institution, penitentiaries became a warehouse for unemployable trouble makers, ranging from career criminals to brawling immigrants. As early as 1850, Massachusetts prison records show that a third of all those incarcerated in the state were foreign born—over twice their percentage in the general population. The Irish formed 11.4 percent of the states' population and 17.6 percent of its prisoners. African-Americans, 0.9 percent of the population, made up 8.6 percent of prisoners.

From what we know of wrongful conviction and unequal punishment in more recent times, it's safe to say that judge and jury prejudices and no money for a good attorney contributed to these statistics. In these years, even right-minded reformers like Samuel Gridley Howe could use the expression "the criminal or dangerous class." If this class of irredeemables existed, they made an unstated argument for the permanent need of capital punishment. The circle of such reasoning was completed by placing the execution within the penitentiary.

Before this ironic conclusion was reached, the spirit of human reclamation that drove prison reform also raised the possibility that capital punishment could be replaced by imprisonment.

Politically conservative thinkers had justified capital and corporal punishment for centuries as retribution, a deterrent, and a tool for maintaining civil order. In the new nation, conditions and opinions were changing. Crowd behavior at executions accorded less and less with the idea of order. Juries were often unwilling to convict if a verdict of guilty automatically meant the death penalty. It's hard to know so long after the fact how broad public support might have been for abolishing capital punishment, but during the 1820s to 1840s nearly every state had an anti-death penalty movement. Leaders relied on several arguments, for example that a government by consent of the governed had no right to take a citizen's life. They also pointed to or drew on the psychological thought of John Locke. Contrary to Calvinist belief in sinful human nature, Locke—and some reform-minded Christians as well—proposed that a human life began as a blank slate and was written on by experience. If this were so, society shared responsibility for the individual's actions. Moreover, the individual could be changed by a different quality of experience.

By 1809, the governor of Pennsylvania began asking the legislature to abolish the death penalty. The anti-capital-punishment movement was in full swing by the 1820s. It drew on, and added to, the high energy of other causes such as prison reform and abolition of slavery.

Liberal thinkers and writers such as Lydia Maria Child and John Greenleaf Whittier, celebrities of their time, supplied a link between legislative arguments and the public. Boston Universalist minister Charles Spear publicized the arguments of jurists such as Edward Livingston and Robert Rantoul, and also united with John Greenleaf Whittier and others to form a Massachusetts society to abolish the death penalty. The abolitionist leadership generated petitions to end capital punishment that were frequently presented to state legislatures in New York and Pennsylvania, among other states, during the 1840s.

Another influential abolition campaigner was Edward Livingston, an attorney, former mayor of New York and later member of Congress and U. S. Secretary of State. After moving to New Orleans, Livingston drafted a liberalized legal code for Louisiana. It was not adopted but was studied by several other state legislatures. Livingston spoke against capital punishment in many venues, citing England's high crime rate to show that the death penalty didn't deter even petty thieves. Unfortunately, he based his case most strongly on one debatable point—that executions brutalized the populace who witnessed them. This argument appealed to individuals like Thomas Cope who were members of a rising middle class and held the liberal religious views of Quakerism or Unitarianism. More and more, prosperous Americans supported public order and the dignity of the individual. They frowned on the raucous street life and street politics that the previous generation had considered appropriate during the Revolutionary War.

Edward Livingston didn't foresee how easily his opponents could adapt his argument to a politically much simpler solution: hold the execution in private. In 1833 Rhode Island became the first state to hold private executions, followed by fourteen other states between 1834 and 1849. But counties, not states, held the execution in their prisons. The central location at a county seat, and the frequent lack of truly secluded indoor gallows, made it possible for the public, with or without official connivance, to outwit most counties' halfhearted privacy measures. When Samuel Mills, a 26-year-old miner, was executed in New Hampshire on May 6, 1868, the hanging was watched by approximately 3,000 persons. Bystanders criticized the sheriff for holding the hanging earlier than the announced hour, an eyewitness later said. The train from Littleton hadn't yet arrived, and "some folks didn't think it fair that the trainload should be cheated out of the sight of the hanging."

The hanging took place in the jail yard and was not officially public. The gallows, "a rough hemlock joist projecting five or six feet from the window of [Mills's] cell on the second floor of the jail," could be seen from the street and surrounding fields of Haverhill. There was no death walk—Mills just stepped over the window sill to an improvised gallows platform built onto the jail yard walls. The sheriff and his assistants, Mills's attorneys, and several newspaper reporters waited on the platform. When the condemned climbed through the window, he bumped his head. As if the occasion were quite an ordinary one, he cried out loudly, "Hel-*lo!*" After he reached the platform and stood himself over the trapdoor, below which the earth had been excavated to a depth of nine feet to provide a drop, "the death warrant was read, and a prayer was offered." Mills, who had robbed and murdered an elderly neighbor in Franconia, wasn't admonished about his sinful nature or his slim chances in the next world. Rather, Mills, like the condemned man Thomas Cope described in his diary, was supported by those around him in keeping up his bravado. "Tell the people that Samuel Mills died like a man," Mills requested. He called out a goodbye to friends he saw in the crowd, and they simply replied, "Goodby, Samuely."

"There was a fence, about as high as my piazza, built around it, so when the body dropped, it couldn't be seen," the eyewitness said. Elmore Whipple was twelve years old at the time and had sneaked away to Haverhill from Franconia with a friend. They heard Mills speak his last words and saw the hood placed over his head. "The man was instantly dangling at the end of the rope," said Whipple. After Mills was cut down, he was placed in a coffin to be viewed. Many in the crowd had already lined up; but "the funny part of it all," as Whipple expressed it, was that some found themselves unable to watch. Whipple and a friend named Harry had urged their other friends to attend, but "when we got to Haverhill and the hanging commenced, Harry had to leave; he was sick as a dog." As for himself, the eyewitness turned his head away. "I couldn't eat any lunch and I wanted to go home."

In spite of the squeamishness of Whipple and his friend, New Hampshire was one of the few states at that time where a majority of voters was known to support capital punishment. They upheld death penalty laws in an 1844 referendum and defeated the attempt at compromise of a "Maine law" five years later. The "Maine law," originating in that state in 1837, was the last kind of reform legislation that abolitionists tried. Condemned criminals were to be incarcerated for one full year between sentencing and execution, then to be executed only on a written warrant issued by the governor at his discretion. The law was written by anti-gallows crusaders, and the then-governor of Maine interpreted the law as a mandate to discontinue capital punishment. But only in Maine and Kansas did this law of delay prevent execution for any length of time. In Vermont (1842), Massachusetts (1852), and New York (1860) as well as New Hampshire, similar laws were either short-lived or didn't have the intended effect.

In these years legislators began to realize that executions held under county authority wouldn't ever really be removed from public view. The Haverhill jail yard where Samuel Mills died was in the heart of town, and like most jails it had no room with a ceiling high enough for an indoor execution. Penitentiary execution was the chosen solution, first put in place by the state of Vermont in 1864. Samuel Mills was the last to be hanged by county authorities in New Hampshire. By revised state legislation, subsequent hangings were held within the walls of the 1812 penitentiary at Concord on a scaffold built by Isaiah Wilson of Portsmouth, having a crossbeam, we are told, 17 feet high. On November 9, 1869, Josiah L. Pike was the first to be hanged from Mr. Wilson's gallows. It was the first of America's "invisible executions"— now, the only kind that we conduct—under the control of a state prison bureaucracy and completely limited to invited witnesses. The "reform" of moving executions to the penitentiary proved much more popular than that of abolishing the death penalty altogether.

The U.S. military executed this Union soldier for attempted rape (1864).

5

The Will of the People
Early Reactions Against Capital Punishment

In Wisconsin, during a public execution in 1851, the crowd had more than enough time to witness the experience of death by hanging. The condemned man, James McCaffry, was quite obviously conscious as he struggled and strangled for five full minutes at the end of the rope. Only then did he become unconscious and slowly suffocate.

Imagine you are one of the spectators and try timing a period of five minutes.

After this hanging was widely reported, a Milwaukee jury refused to convict a defendant generally believed to be guilty, because their finding of guilt was an automatic death sentence.

Abolition of Wisconsin's death penalty took place in 1853 and has never been repealed. How did it happen that activism in Wisconsin and Michigan led to abolishing the death penalty while the efforts of abolitionists in New York, Massachusetts, Ohio, and Pennsylvania came to nothing during these years?

Wisconsin is one of three states, with Michigan (1846) and Rhode Island (1852), to abolish the death penalty in the years before the Civil War. Michiganians, it is said, were made nervous shortly before repealing capital punishment by the execution of someone who was wrongly convicted. When it was too late, the real murderer confessed and the hanged man was revealed to be innocent.

The story of abolition and recall in many states goes the same way: A gruesome or unjust execution is carried out; legislators vote to end the death penalty. Then a gruesome murder occurs; legislators vote to bring the death penalty back. Or else, the death penalty is repealed because too many juries refused to reach a guilty verdict in capital cases. Then the death penalty is reinstated because the number of homicides—sometimes of lynchings—seems to be rising.

At other times citizens and their legislators have remained unmoved. The rope has broken or the electric current has failed even to make the condemned unconscious. But the execution was resumed, and followed by many more, without a change in the law. In such states, even the deaths of persons later shown to be innocent may not bring about abolition.

Back and forth we go with our hopeful "becauses," trying to get to the bottom of differences between one American state and another. Some states have gone full circle, even more than once. At any single point in time, the decision to repeal or restore the death penalty seems almost accidental.

But the cases of Michigan, Rhode Island, and Wisconsin are a little different. These three states haven't authorized an execution in over 150 years—a record in the United States or, for that matter, in the English-speaking world. Something was happening in these states, and a few others at a later date, that goes beyond a legislature's whim, a governor's intervention or non-intervention, or the momentary changes of heart of a state's voters.

Michiganians debated capital punishment from the beginning, when they wrote their state constitution in 1835. But the constitutional convention chose to write in the death penalty. This outcome was the same as in other states during the 1830s, when legislative committees in Massachusetts, New York, Ohio, and even Louisiana presented reports that did not, finally, result in abolition legislation. But in Michigan the debate came back. The state's legal code was due to be revised, so between 1843 and 1846 the legislature conducted a full debate of the code and the proposed changes.

Senator Stanford M. Green presented the revisions. Green favored the compromise of the Maine law, with executions to be carried out after a year's delay on the governor's instructions. As Green rewrote the Michigan code, capital punishment wouldn't be abolished.

Surprisingly, the legislature soon lined up pro and con in two camps of about equal strength. After considerable vote-switching and bargaining, legislators made Michigan the first state to end capital punishment.

The first version of the new law simply substituted "imprisonment in the state prison for life," but the words were immediately re-amended to "solitary confinement at hard labor in the state prison for life." The Senate did not agree to this version, and proposed omitting "at hard labor." However, after a joint committee was convened, both House and Senate passed the version prescribing both solitary confinement and hard labor in place of the death penalty. The death penalty was retained for treason, a crime that has never been prosecuted at the state level.

Michigan eliminated capital punishment only after legislators came up with a substitute penalty terrifying enough to appease execution supporters. In practice, perpetual solitary confinement, which was capable of driving prisoners insane and also made hard labor impracticable, was tried for only four years in Michigan. But abolition of the death penalty endured in Michigan law, and it wasn't until 1929 that reinstatement really came close. When both legislative houses passed a reinstatement bill, it would have become law if not vetoed by Governor Fred W. Green. Two years later, the return of capital punishment seemed even more certain when a bill was passed and, this time, actually signed by Governor Wilber M. Brucker. But Brucker had signed only with the provision that a referendum be held, and Michigan voters defeated reinstatement by 352,000 to 269,000, or 56.7 to 43.3 percent of the vote.

What we know about the public's views on capital punishment in past times is very spotty. But I'm pretty sure that Michigan's result was exceptional. It's also hard to explain.

Liberals didn't dominate Michigan politics around 1930, or both houses of the legislature wouldn't have tried repeatedly to bring back the death penalty. The most liberal legislative segment was a minority coalition based partly on labor leaders. What seems to have happened is that eight Upper Peninsula counties very strongly opposed restoration of the death penalty. Voters' numbers were great enough, and their opposition strong enough at over 80 percent, that these counties swayed the whole state's outcome.

"No law shall be enacted providing for the penalty of death." Michigan's constitutional convention of 1961-1962 made executions unconstitutional. This provision meant that treason was eliminated as a capital offense. Michigan officials enacted the change after they found they couldn't prevent a federal execution for treason that was held in their state. As long as Michigan had the death penalty for any offense, federal authorities were empowered under United States law to execute for federal crimes committed within the state's borders.

The Michigan public has shown less support for the death penalty over the years than voters in most other states. A poll of Detroit voters in a 1986 primary showed that two-thirds of European-Americans, and about half of African-Americans, favored capital punishment. These Michiganians were much less supportive than the public nationwide, who favored the death penalty at the rate of 82 percent of European-Americans and 57 percent of African-Americans.

Of course, that was still a majority of Michiganians who supported the death penalty. On May 19, 2001, as support for capital punishment declined nationwide, a poll by the *Detroit Free Press* found that fifty-three percent of Michigan respondents supported the death penalty. But support dropped to thirty-five percent when respondents were offered the choice between the death penalty and mandatory life imprisonment plus restitution to the victim's family.

As the case of Michigan shows, public support doesn't correspond completely with law. It's hard to compare support among individual states because national poll sizes aren't big enough, and statewide polls vary in how they take a sample and word their questions. Generally, poll respondents in eastern and midwestern states show lower rates of support than do respondents from southern and western states. But the difference between most and least support may be no greater than that between Republicans (more supportive) and Democrats (less supportive).

Looking back over Michigan's years of opposing the death penalty, what's exceptional is that *some* part of the electoral system has always produced enough opposition to keep capital punishment from coming back—now the legislature, now the governor, now the public.

What are the pieces of Michigan's puzzle? How did they come together to create such an unusual picture? When I think of Michigan in the 1840s I think of it as a young state. Its European-American population, recently settled, were mostly small farmers and other homesteaders. Cities weren't very significant yet as an economic or political force. The state had only 59 miles of railroad in 1840, and land speculation, timbering, mining, and manufacturing were just beginning to be sources of great fortune for the few. In contrast to the situation in older states like Massachusetts or New York, in Michigan there hadn't been time or means for any one group of people with like interests to become entrenched as a power elite.

Judging from the record of legislative debate, members of the Michigan state assembly held the spectrum of views on capital punishment that were current in their time. In favor of the death penalty, George E. Hand, James A. Van Dyke, Hiram Stone, and others argued:

- A maximum amount of government authority is needed in order to keep a stable social order.
- Government has the right to take a citizen's life—the same right of self-defense that an individual has.
- The idea of capital punishment deters other criminals best because fear of death is our most compelling fear.

Hiram Stone, as a death-penalty supporter and writer of a minority committee report, was more concerned that a guilty murderer might later be freed from prison than that an innocent one would be hanged. Michigan legislators like Flavius Littlejohn, Charles Bush, and William A. Pratt, who opposed capital punishment, didn't meet this argument head-on, but presented a five-and-a-half page majority report stating their disagreement with Stone. The report written by Pratt made these points:

- Authoritarian government belongs to a barbarous past, not to the enlightened age of American nationhood.
- Government and church should be separate, with government paramount in worldly decisions. For this reason, it's improper to defend capital punishment on the authority of the Bible or any religious text.
- Government is made legitimate only by the consent of the governed. It would be a mockery of justice to force a citizen to "consent" to his own execution.
- Human individuals are redeemable. They can be influenced by environment and atone for their wrongs, but execution is irreversible and cuts off all possibility of reform.

Religion played a part in Michigan's death-penalty debate—maybe the biggest part, when you count the number of words devoted to the subject. Both abolitionists and retentionists cited either the Bible or "divine law" in support of their position. But their issue doesn't seem to have been whether religious teaching favored executions. Legislators were wrangling over *authority*. Where did it come from? How much of it did we need? Who should wield it? Should we keep the penalties "which terrified the people of the middle ages into submission"? Was consent of the governed no more than a "newfangled theory," as one exasperated legislator protested?

Those who favored capital punishment favored strong authority and feared social chaos above all else. "Traitors and pirates, and murderers and robbers," said Hiram Stone in a minority report of 1844, "may be deemed the common and mortal enemies of mankind, against whom society may wage a war of extermination." Those who favored abolition, on the other hand, insisted on limiting the authority of government to less than the power of life and death. Every power the government held, they felt, cut off some portion of the individual citizen's human potential. Moreover, to invoke God as the basis of government was to bring back established religion and, with it, the kind of traditional hierarchy that Americans endured under British rule.

Rebellion against authority runs through the biographies of some legislators who opposed the death penalty and wanted to see its use discontinued. A few abolitionists were known as opponents of evangelical religion. Jonathan Graham described himself as a rebel against the Puritanism of his upbringing in Connecticut. Charles P. Bush opposed the observance of Sunday as a holy day. Austin Blair, legislator during the 1840s, was governor of Michigan 1861-1865. While at school in Cazenovia Seminary, New York, Blair led student opposition to the official annual religious revival. Like fellow abolitionists Michael Patterson and Austin Wing, Blair was later a regent of the University of Michigan. His father had advocated the abolition of slavery, and Blair was one of very few politicians in his time to support the vote for African-Americans. Such a profile was unknown for any legislator who supported capital punishment.

The biographies of representative pro-capital-punishment legislators, by contrast, showed a respect for tradition, social hierarchy, and the privileges and responsibilities of wealth. James Van Dyke was a "prominent Detroit lawyer" and trustee of copper companies who later represented railroad interests. William Fenton came from a banking family in Norwich, New York. His father "was one of the first citizens in wealth and social position, being a prominent banker and an elder in the Presbyterian Church, of which he was one of the main pillars of support." The Presbyterian connection can be traced from the East Coast to Detroit, where the First Presbyterian Church had an elite membership and was pastored by George Duffield, Michigan's best-known supporter of capital punishment. William Fenton married a judge's daughter, emigrated to Michigan, and bought the land that later became Fentonville. Fenton ended as "Colonel Fenton," a distinguished Civil War veteran, a former mayor, and a bank president like his father. William Gray and George E. Hand were also described as prominent Detroit lawyers and representatives of the railroads.

Legislators' party affiliation doesn't really predict where individual representatives would stand on capital punishment, abolition of slavery, temperance, free public education, or other reform issues of their

decade. Both Whig and Democratic parties in Michigan were internal-
ly split and in transition between 1830 and 1860. You can only tell by
looking forward to the 1850s that some of Michigan's state legislators
during the 1840s were already riding the crest of a breaking wave.
Michigan and Wisconsin were the birthplace of the new Republican
Party, soon to elect Abraham Lincoln president of the United States.

One-fourth of all legislators favoring abolition of the death penalty
were future Lincoln Republicans. None of the death-penalty retentionists of known affiliation became Republicans.

Michigan Republicanism at the start was very much a coalition of
interests, but their common position was opposing Southern slave-
owning interests on behalf of small farmers. As judged by the political
offices they gained, these legislators made a successful career of their
reformist, man-of-the-people stance. They held many more offices at
state level, while traditionalist legislators who supported the death
penalty became influential only locally. For example, members of the
Detroit-Wayne-County elite monopolized the offices of mayor and
alderman there. William B. Sprague, a physician and mill owner, was
prominent as the first town clerk of Coldwater, an associate judge of
the county court, and judge of probate. Like three-fourths of his fellow
retentionists, he held no state-level offices other than membership in
the legislature.

In keeping with the emphasis on authority, several of Michigan's
well known death-penalty supporters were leaders in the military.
Augustus C. Baldwin was a brigadier general of the state militia;
Colonel Fenton donated to the establishment of Michigan's first Civil
War regiments and led one of them into battle; Isaac deGraaf Toll was
a career officer in the state militia and captained a company in the
Mexican-American War. The only death-penalty opponent whose military service is mentioned is Marcus Wakeman, who fought in the War
of 1812.

Among abolition supporters, James M. Edmunds was a teacher and
merchant who lived in Detroit, where he served as comptroller. His
main focus was state politics. Besides serving two terms each in the

state House and Senate, he was a delegate to the 1850 constitutional convention and chairman of the state Republican committee for six years. He held several Presidential appointments including the post-mastership of Washington, D.C., for twenty years. Eighteen of thirty-two abolitionists held state-level offices like Edmunds's or leadership positions in the legislature. Austin Blair was governor of Michigan throughout the Civil War (two terms); and Orrin N. Giddings, after moving to New Mexico, became governor there.

The 1820s through 1850s were a crusading era all over the northern states. But Michigan, like Wisconsin, differed from the states of the Northeast in that its social order wasn't yet set in stone. Political power in the upper Midwest was shared between liberals and conservatives, who took different routes to a position of influence.

Prominent Detroit lawyers, husbands of judges' daughters, supporters of the First Presbyterian Church: such persons no doubt attained the kinds of influence most important to them through connections that were half-social, half-business. This elite and their sympathizers could be expected to support capital punishment as a byproduct of their belief in a hierarchical social order.

But Michigan legislators who opposed authoritarian tradition, and weren't themselves members of an elite, were able to be more effective politically than their counterparts in the Northeast. State government wasn't dominated by a long-standing establishment like that of the orthodox Puritans of Massachusetts or the Dutch-English leadership of New York. Michigan legislators' later careers as Lincoln Republicans would show their skill at promoting an ethical position through compromise while advancing their political careers. Wisconsin, with a similar settlement pattern in the years just before statehood, appears to have shared this political culture.

Within New England itself, only Rhode Island succeeded in abolishing capital punishment during the antebellum reform period. Theirs was a tradition of liberal dissent and suspicion of central government, and executions that had taken place under colonial rule in Rhode Island may have had less public support than elsewhere.

By the 1850s, nationwide tensions over slavery eclipsed other topics in public debate and directed political action away from the death penalty. State legislators closed ranks in order to promote their economic and political interests against those of other sections of the country. Most states' opponents of capital punishment, so vigorous in sponsoring speeches, debates, and conferences, seem to have neglected to convince the decision makers. As early as 1841, the New York legislature narrowly defeated death penalty abolition and followed with a powerful pro-execution memorandum. The New Hampshire referendum of 1844 revealed strong public support in that state. The 1850 Ohio constitutional convention, after decades of anti-death-penalty activism, upheld capital punishment.

<hr />

History matters—that's what the case of Michigan demonstrates.

What happened in the past, especially as a state was being organized, is probably more important than public opinion at any given moment. Today, twelve states have laws against the death penalty—Alaska, Hawaii, Iowa, Maine, Massachusetts, Michigan, Minnesota, North Dakota, Rhode Island, Vermont, West Virginia, Wisconsin—and so does the District of Columbia, a federal jurisdiction.

Seven of these states fit the Michigan pattern: younger midwestern and upper-plains states having a New-England-style activist culture and a strong element of early-arriving Scandinavian population. These states' legislatures abolished the death penalty in earlier years, before political factions became entrenched.

Alaska, Hawaii, and West Virginia gained statehood among strong feelings against authoritarian government on ethnic or working-class grounds.

Maine and Rhode Island, not heavily settled in early years, have long done without executions, but Massachusetts and Vermont were able to abolish the death penalty only in 1965. New York followed a similar pattern and has now reinstated the death penalty.

Of America's three major eras of reform, wars brought each to a close—first the Civil War, then World War I, then the Vietnam War.

Some changes in opinion have survived wartime conservatism, but the change of mood was as palpable then as it is now as the United States conducts another war. In 1866, one year after the end of the Civil War, death-penalty abolitionist Marvin H. Bovee wrote at length to Governor Oglesby of Illinois requesting clemency for two condemned murderers, the young Barney Vanansdell and James Lemon. Bovee had led Wisconsin's repeal of the death penalty, and advanced arguments in his letter similar to those used by abolitionist legislators in Michigan. But Bovee's closing point concerned the effect of war on respect for human life:

> However glorious and patriotic the cause for which war may be prosecuted, the demoralizing effect upon the public mind is ever apparent. Ours has been no exception. Since the breaking out of hostilities, the general respect for human life has been very much lessened, while the debasing effect upon the minds of very many who were immediately engaged, is noticeable by all. The killing of thousands is not well calculated to inspire feelings of reverence for human life, but, on the contrary, often stimulates the worst passions of man ... [Vanansdell and Lemon may not] be sufficiently skilled in that branch of governmental science by which an individual is enabled to draw that *very nice distinction* between the *laudable virtue of killing* by national authority, and the *reprehensible criminality of killing* upon individual responsibility.

Most reform movements nationally died with the Civil War. Before the war, reformers could argue that the state didn't have the right to demand a citizen's life. But this point was settled when both Union and Confederacy introduced the draft, sending soldiers to their deaths whether or not they had volunteered. The conflicts leading to the Civil War provided first a set of social tensions that provoked violence, then an object lesson in the use of violence to resolve social tensions.

Two Union soldiers posed in captured Ku Klux Klan "uniforms" (1868).

6

Legacy of Conquest
Civil War, Slavery, and the First Ku Klux Klan

I grew up in New Orleans, Louisiana, without knowing for sure that the Civil War had ended.

Never mind that the war began eighty-something years before my birth, and eighteen years before my grandmother's birth. My grandmother still sang me to sleep with the camp song she learned from her father, a Confederate veteran:

Shoo fly, don't bother me
Shoo fly, don't bother me
Shoo fly, don't bother me
For I belong to Company B.

"Bee"—get it?—wins out over fly.

When I was eleven years old, I found myself at the cemetery on Confederate Memorial Day wearing a party dress and officially excused from school in order to recite an embarrassingly bad poem of many stanzas called "The Sword of Lee." The poem was written by long-dead Confederate army chaplain Father Abram Ryan. Before me was an audience of the elderly, mostly women. Perhaps they were daughters of veterans but, like my grandmother, they couldn't have been old enough to have their own memories of war.

It was supposed to be a joke that, for Southerners, the war hadn't ended. But not everyone was kidding. According to Father Ryan and other authorities (such as my sixth-grade teacher), the South was "defeated, yet without a stain." Father Ryan was wise enough to suggest

that our "conquered banner," the Confederate flag, be folded permanently, but—as we all know—140 years later, some Southerners have
never wrapped it up and put it away. Even those who placed the Civil
War in the past believed, like Father Ryan, that the South's was "the
cause of Right." And if we were right, then wasn't losing the war ethically superior to having won it? We (in this case, the white, Anglo-Saxon
Protestants, plus Father Ryan) were better than others because we had
had the moral refinement to risk everything in defense of a principle.

I'm sorry about the years of childhood I wasted trying to swallow
such guff. But I've come to think it could have been worse. I could have
grown up in a place or time where people really didn't know the Civil
War ever happened. Some might even think the past doesn't matter.
Bone deep, I know it does. The past is the grandmother who sings you
to sleep, the Confederate flag on sale at a gift shop or tattooed on the
arm of the man sitting next to you on the bus. The past is all around
you, making you who you are by telling you where you came from.

I got a big helping of the past when I got love and admiration for
reciting a poem about the tragic glory of the Confederacy.

The Civil War was a big helping of the past for America in a short
four years' time.

Contrary to the wishes of some of my ancestors, the Civil War kept
the United States one nation.

The war made the Thirteenth, Fourteenth, and Fifteenth constitutional amendments possible, ending slavery, promising the vote (at
least to all men, if not to women) and equal protection under the law.

The war created a whole new set of economic winners and losers—
my mother's parents' families among the latter.

Another thing the Civil War did, both North and South, was to give
white and black people a new level of grievance against each other. The
Civil War made it inevitable that slavery would end, and from 1865 to
1870 the U. S. Constitution began to define African-Americans as citizens. I know white Southerners weren't ready (putting it mildly), and I
don't think most white Northerners were ready either, for the loss of

their cherished "racial superiority" *or* the perceived threat to their livelihood that a new population of citizens created. I don't think African-Americans were ready for the bitterness and fury that greeted them, or the nearly unending delays and disappointments they would endure, as they stepped forward to claim the status that Constitutional amendments were finally setting forth in words.

Most troubling to me is that our two-hundred-year history with slavery before the Civil War provided all the evil wisdom we would ever need to fight the racial war among ourselves after the official war ended. We had a repertoire of riots, mob terrorism, unequal law, and unequal punishment, and all the justification to discriminate and to repress that an all-white version of the past could afford. I don't think that the distinction between legal and illegal means was ever that important. When the law was available, it was used. When it became unavailable, as it was for a while during and after the Civil War, intimidation and terrorism were used instead. Having learned that both law and terrorism worked, we then applied them simultaneously. Nor do I think the distinction between slaves and free blacks was very sharp in the minds of most European-Americans who felt they had reason to fear or resent African-Americans. After all, Chief Justice Roger B. Taney of the U. S. Supreme Court had stated, in the Dred Scott ruling of 1857, that free blacks "were identified in the public [i.e., white] mind with the race to which they belonged, and regarded as part of the slave population rather than the free."

From day one, the presence of African-Americans had a primarily economic meaning for most European-Americans. For most, the argument over slavery wasn't about the indecency of one human being claiming to "own" another, and asserting the claim by force. A large part of the slavery debate was about competing economic advantages—plantation agriculture with slave labor versus freehold agriculture, jobs for white workingmen versus jobs for free blacks and for slaves hired out by their owners.

Among the many crazy outcomes of treating human beings as property, whites had to contend with their own fear that slaves would free themselves, rob their masters, and take revenge. This was the beginning of unequal punishment for white and black. Looking at pre-Civil-War Massachusetts as an example, I see that around twelve percent of all persons executed between 1676 and 1795 were slaves. In the general population only about one percent were slaves. In New York state, slavery was abolished only in 1827, and thirty slaves were legally hanged or burned alive after supposedly participating in a conspiracy to rebel in 1741.

The state of Virginia around 1820 listed seventy-three capital offenses for slaves against only one—first degree murder—for white persons. This was a more extreme difference than in other states, but slaves in just about every state where slavery was legal could be, and were, executed for a greater number of offenses than whites.

In the years leading up to the Civil War, discrimination in citizenship against free blacks went along with discriminatory punishment of both free and slave. Some examples of pre-Civil-War discriminatory laws that whites made to target free blacks *outside* the South:

- forbidden to serve in militia, vote, give testimony in cases involving European-Americans (Illinois, Indiana, Ohio; 32 discriminatory statutes in all);
- forbidden to vote or belong to the state legislature or militia by the Iowa and Michigan constitutional conventions (33 statutes);
- forbidden to marry European-Americans in Illinois, Indiana, Iowa, and Michigan (36 statutes).

Of states in this region, Wisconsin might be seen as liberal, since laws in this state forbade *only* the vote to African-Americans. Discriminatory laws were all about making newly formed states and territories unwelcoming to free African-Americans. Meanwhile, more and more in Southern states, "free" blacks could be enslaved for a period of years if they were convicted of one of a variety of offenses.

Racism was already institutionalized in the South as slavery, slave codes, and laws discriminating against freedman. But the legacy of racism created by laws outside the South has been as lasting, if less intense. It carried into lynching in the North as late as 1930, and can still be seen in the rolls of those being executed today.

Effects of laws passed before the Civil War were worsened by the war itself. In the North, the Emancipation Proclamation implied that white citizens of the Union would be risking their lives for African-Americans whom the white working class already looked on as economic competitors. Only two months after the proclamation went into effect, Congress enacted a draft law. The law's worst feature was that it allowed potential draftees to get out of service by paying three hundred dollars or hiring a substitute—a blatant act of coercion against the poor, who would have to offer their own lives while the prosperous escaped danger. Workingmen in a number of Northern cities took out their otherwise helpless rage on African-Americans, but a three-day riot in New York City brought about the greatest number of casualties. Starting on the day that new draftees' names appeared in newspapers, white mobs estimated at up to 50,000 went berserk. When the riot seemed to have ended, President Lincoln sent in watchdog troops he could ill spare from the Army of the Potomac. By then the rioters had hanged, burned, or beaten to death eleven African-Americans, burned down the Colored Orphan Asylum, looted the Colored Seamen's Home, razed whole city blocks, torn up railroad tracks, cut telegraph lines, and forced factories and shops to close.

In the Natchez area in one year during the Civil War, a Southern researcher writes, forty African-Americans were hanged and forty more imprisoned for supposed insurrection.

Today we'd call these acts atrocities. But they didn't prevent the Union leadership at the close of the Civil War from embracing and empowering their former enemies.

The Thirteenth Amendment guaranteed the end of slavery, and in effect allowed African-Americans to act as legal persons—for example, by entering into contracts for marriage and property transactions. Hardly had Lee surrendered, however, when the legislatures and courts of Southern states set about subjugating the African-American population in every way except the Constitutional minimum of outright slavery. Under the new Southern "black codes," with many more prohibitions in addition to the examples I give, African-Americans couldn't vote, serve on juries, or act as witnesses except in a case involving an African-American. Black occupations, ownership of weapons, use of liquor, and their very presence in towns were all regulated. The obvious intention was repression—to guarantee docility and maintain a work force of cheap labor.

Within a year of the end of the Civil War, according to reports gathered by the Freedmen's Bureau, there were 33 people openly murdered by whites in Tennessee, 29 in Arkansas, 24 in South Carolina, 19 in Kentucky, and for two years in Louisiana, 70 victims. Freedmen were killed or injured for attempting political leadership, even for trying to farm or to vote, or for trivial acts that whites liked to call "insubordination." In Georgia, as an agent of the Freedmen's Bureau reported, an African-American was hanged for killing a mule, another stabbed for refusing to enter his dog in a dog fight, another stabbed for not bringing a cup of coffee quickly enough. In the last case, the white man who did the stabbing was fined fifty dollars. The longest sentence that the civil authorities gave any white man for a crime against an African-American was twenty days' jail time. The totals of casualties may be exaggerated or undercounted. But, as they stand, the numbers are equal to those murdered at the height of the so-called mob lynching era that began fifteen years later.

In effect, Southern white governments were working toward a legal state between slavery and freedom, and as close to slavery as they could get.

Southern white intransigence led directly to the Freedmen's Bureau Acts (1865) and Civil Rights Act (1866). When these had little effect in the South, Congress passed the Reconstruction Acts the following year, and these acts led directly to the Fourteenth or equal protection amendment.

Those who ratified the amendment intended to enforce it, as the Civil Rights Act was meant to be enforced, through temporary military protection for African-Americans followed by long-term civil protection. But the military rule under which the Reconstruction South supposedly lived was impotent. Violence quickly became organized and, by 1867, European-American vigilante groups were common in the South under the name of "regulators," "rangers," "moderators" or, bluntly, "n****r killers."

As in the West, newspapers commonly abetted vigilante terrorism. Their editors, hand in glove with vigilance groups, not only saw to it that hatred of African-Americans filled every newspaper page, but also goaded local whites to acts of violence—conveniently listing the names of local white and black Republicans who would make suitable targets. All the while, vigilantism was justified much the way it had been on the frontier, by the Big Lie technique: in this case, that the courts did not punish crime by African-Americans.

<hr />

The first Ku Klux Klan, which gave its name to nearly all Southern terrorism thereafter, began as something very like the college fraternity from hell.

As far as is known, six bored young Confederate veterans formed the Klan around May of 1866 in the small town of Pulaski, in central Tennessee. Greek fraternities along with other secret brotherhoods had been multiplying since the end of the American Revolution, and one writer speculates that the KKK's ritual, disguise, and clandestine way of operating were based on that of a well known antebellum Southern fraternity, Kuklos Adelphon, or the first Kappa Alpha Order.

In researching the Kappa Alpha Order, I find that it still exists. I read on its website that it seeks to give its members a lifetime experience based on the example of "Robert E. Lee, our spiritual founder." Well,

Lee certainly did what the Order invites its recruiters to do today: "Have fun, Travel the country, Meet great people, Make an impact!" Even my grade school, the one that sponsored my appearance at the cemetery on Confederate Memorial Day, was named Robert E. Lee. Eventually New Orleanians elected a predominately African-American city council, who decided that public buildings shouldn't be named after slaveowners. But that wasn't very long ago.

Supposedly, the early Ku Kluxers—whether or not they had anything to do with Kuklos Adelphon—intended to start a social club. But it's hard not to wonder whether the KKK began as a kind of orchestrated shivaree—a case of "the community" co-opting its still-unsettled young males to enforce its standards.

Or were the Klan's activities even taken from community standards? In retrospect, after the written organizational document was revised in 1868, it sounded a lot like a political prescription that wily elders administered to the more aimless, perhaps more self-interested and more easily manipulated, young.

Certainly, the history of the Klan reveals how easily a political agenda could be fitted to the long-familiar shape of shivaree. Less than a year after its founding, the Klan was reorganized to serve the ends of Tennessee Conservatism against the Unionists under Governor Brownlow. The enmity between Republicans and Conservatives, or proto-Democrats, was extraordinarily bitter, and an appeal to racism was a centerpiece of the Conservatives' takeover strategy. They knew there would be white voters to hear them if they threatened that the African-American vote would carry the Unionists to political victory.

The Conservatives' strategy backfired in the short run when Klan violence led to Governor Brownlow's calling out the militia and gave him an excuse to disenfranchise all former Confederates. But disenfranchisement was brief for those who were white, and the long-run success of terrorism in the South was spectacular.

The Klan's "Prescript," or organizational document, as revised in 1868, affirmed "the inalienable right of self-preservation of the people against the exercise of arbitrary and unlicensed power." In pursuit of "self-preservation," the Klan, led by Nathan Bedford Forrest and aided by several other former Confederate generals, spread across entire the South during the first four months of 1868. In Kentucky, for example, where freedmen hadn't received the vote by 1868, Klan persecution served to drive African-American owners and even tenants from their land. This motive for persecution was common where small-farm agriculture predominated over plantation agriculture, since it was in these regions that African-Americans were most likely to acquire land. Throughout the South, the Klan drove off European-Americans as well as African-Americans who tried to conduct schools for freedman, and Klansmen retaliated against blacks who tried to take "white" jobs. The factional aspects of Klan terrorism perhaps reached their culmination in Louisiana during the presidential election in 1868. A combination of the Klan in northern parishes and the "Knights of the White Camellia" in southern parishes instigated violence resulting in 1,081 deaths. Victims, when not shot or hanged outright, were given whippings as high as 200 lashes with whips, ropes, switches, or tree limbs. In one case the victim, who died, was given 900 lashes with the stirrup from a saddle. Another who died had crosses cut into the flesh of his entire body including the soles of his feet.

The Klan's founding statement is a classic example of blaming an opponent for the severity of one's own tactics. The document's language reads as if the power of the Reconstruction government and the new status of African-Americans were visited from nowhere—and this upon a Southern people who favored "Constitutional liberty, and a Government of equitable laws instead of a Government of violence and oppression."

Equitable laws, it seems, would allow the reigning members of power structures based on property rights to formulate their society's lifeways unopposed. With such a civic agenda, it's no surprise that the Klan set about restoring equitable laws through violence and oppression.

Major General John Pope, who commanded the third Reconstruction Military District including Alabama, Georgia, and Florida, wrote to President Grant about his fear that Southern politicians would undermine ostensibly fair laws. Injustice on the part of Southern courts, Pope predicted, would "render justice impossible and establish discrimination against classes or color."

It's interesting to me that Pope identified not only color but social class as targets of discrimination. Again and again in the 140 or so years since Pope wrote that letter, Southern class conflicts that went along with slavery have gotten buried. Instead, researchers and writers play the race card exclusively in assigning causes of collective violence. The first or post-Civil-War Klan charted a campaign of terror that marked out both African-Americans and any European-American who might try to assist a freedman. Conservative loyalists in Tennessee, whether white or black (and there were black conservatives, just as there are today), weren't molested. Like vigilantism in San Francisco or on the mining frontier, Klan actions both neutralized specific political opponents and terrorized those who supported or depended on them. The difference between the West and the South was that, in the South, the rank and file weren't being intimidated into leaving the area. African-American labor, like that of the white working class, was as much needed after Emancipation as before. The racist strategy of the Conservatives fulfilled two objectives—spurring poor whites to solidarity with rich whites, and conquering by dividing when it came to labor's wages and conditions among the working class.

Much Klan violence was carried on under the influence of alcohol, much by young European-American males who had just returned to the tame world from a life of socially approved manhunting and pillage. Their social place and economic future under postwar conditions—at least if Republicans maintained control—were in question. The Klan's leadership tried to take a moral high ground for their power grab, but their messages were ambivalent at best. "Ordinary Klansmen," one researcher wrote, "may have found it hard to draw a logical distinction" between mass rallies featuring a lynching and attended by a hundred members, and a night of drunken bullying done on impulse. Leaders approved of threatening African-Americans, but may not always have approved of carrying the threats through.

Internal contradiction reached the point that leading citizens began to oppose the Klan, if not often publicly. Because African-Americans sometimes retaliated violently against Klan oppression, white opponents could cite their fear of "race war." But effective opposition to the Klan depended on the backing of local and state law enforcement— backing that seldom existed. Only in Tennessee, and in Arkansas where KKK members burned a third of the town of Lewisburg, was the Klan forced to disband. In these states, and in parts of Texas, Alabama, and Louisiana, the Conservative leadership probably severed relations with the Klan by 1869 or 1870.

By this time, or at a slightly later date in other parts of the South, the political objectives of the gentry class had begun to be achieved: effectively disenfranchising freedmen, preventing their owning land, and discouraging their education for anything but farm labor. Further intimidation that would result in African-Americans' leaving the South, as they did in an initial migration of 1879-1880, was not in the elite's interest.

What's more, well-backed Southerners—like well-backed Northerners—were becoming involved in railroading and other forms of industrial capitalism. It couldn't have been lost on many boards of directors in the South that Klan members at a rally could turn into a mob, and a mob could riot—burning their buildings and goods as in Lewisburg, Arkansas, or tearing up railroad track as the New York draft rioters had done in 1863.

New York rioters protesting the draft killed at least twelve persons (1863).

7

Shivaree
Punishment by Mob

On an evening in March of 1834, on the grounds of his widowed mother's plantation south of Natchez, Mississippi, James Foster, Jr., took his wife Susan on a walk to the edge of the bayou and beat her to death. Susan was fifteen years old. Foster claimed he had "switched" Susan for "being unchaste" and that she had subsequently "had a fit." Foster carried his wife's body to a slave cabin before summoning his sister and niece and begging them to "resuscitate" Susan. When Foster's uncle inspected Susan's body the next day, he found signs of an extensive beating, including bleeding from the nostrils. But he cooperated with other family members in privately burying Susan's body less than twenty-four hours later. James was not present. Possibly, he was still sleeping off an alcoholic binge that triggered his murderous attack.

Four days later, Susan's injuries were confirmed when coroner's officers dug up the corpse. They found a broken arm as well as whip marks from head to toe. Foster had left the area but, when the arrest warrant for murder was issued about two months later, he was easily found and did not resist returning to be jailed. Foster was soon to be punished, not by the law but by his neighbors.

Binge drinking and wife-beating were not uncommon in James Foster's social world. His neighbors might have overlooked or tolerated one or two incidents. But Foster had killed a helpless individual who was both under his protection and a member of his family. More, he was a compulsive gambler who had previously been arrested for fraud in Louisiana, then forfeited his honor by jumping the bail posted by his friends. Foster's untrustworthiness was both moral and economic. In

judging Foster guilty of murder, his neighbors seem to have concluded, "A man who would rob his friends and deny responsibility for his
debts would murder his defenseless wife."

The community was not pleased by what happened when Foster
came before the court. Judge Montgomery declined even to prosecute
Foster on the charge of murder. The crime was potentially a capital
offense, but the judge had already dismissed similar cases because of
questions about how the grand jury was convened. Foster's case came
on the last day before Montgomery's retirement, and it seems he just
didn't want to rock the boat.

But the crowd was waiting outside, and they saw Foster as a symbol
of all that was spurious and shifting in their social world.

When Foster emerged from court, the hostile crowd gave him a
kind of sporting chance to outrun them. But the demoralized Foster,
who had been confined in shackles for six months, was immediately
captured and marched to a ravine. There he was tied to a tree. Over a
period from about noon to sundown, the mob beat him by turns with
a cowhide whip. Then, while tar was being heated, Foster was partially
scalped, this penalty having been chosen instead of alternative penalties still on the law books at the time, namely branding or ear-slitting.

Soon tarred and feathered over his fresh wounds, Foster, though he
fainted several times, was led and carted back to town. The festive
nature of this sinister procession was signaled not only by the crowd's
having gotten drunk but by their banging pots and lids, whistling, and
drumming as they accompanied Foster. A mass of blood, tar, and feath-
ers, Foster, by several eyewitness accounts, was scarcely recognizable as
human. "The mob believed he was a monster at heart," said the editor
of the Natchez *Courier*, "and were determined that his external appearance should correspond with the inner man."

———◦═◦———

Were they the community, or were they a mob? The crowd's actions,
half-Mardi Gras and half lynching, have been known for centuries as

shivaree—a collective gesture of mockery toward a community member, carried out in the festive atmosphere of parading, dancing, masking, dressing in costume, singing, and drinking. In its European origins, and often in America, the charivari or shivaree was sometimes just a celebration of marriage. If unfriendly, it was humiliating more often than harmful to the victim. The luckier offenders were simply hanged in effigy, or made to throw coins from their window or invite the mob inside for refreshments. Typical offenses related to marriage customs—choosing a much older or younger partner, abusing one's partner, or failing to provide for the family. James Foster's beating his wife to death, when it became known to the community, may be what signaled his punishment by shivaree.

Shivaree asserted the authority of ordinary members of the community in the face of acts by the few who defied their standards. But when the most serious issues are at stake, shivaree-like public demonstrations in our own time get out of control just as James Foster's beating did. The 1992 acquittal of four police officers after they beat Rodney King was followed by a protest in south central Los Angeles that escalated to copycat beatings, looting, and the burning of stores—a six-day riot that left 54 known dead, 2,383 injured, and 13,212 arrested, with $700 million in property damage around the county. The riot, stopped by National Guardsmen and federal troops, spread to several other cities including Atlanta, Georgia, where 300 were arrested. The protest led to federal prosecution of the police officers for civil rights violations, and conviction of two of the four.

James Foster's offenses invited harsh punishment because the crowd felt his escape from legal penalties was unjust. Once the mob formed, it seemed to take on a life of its own. The real question is why Foster wasn't killed.

The three hundred or more bystanders who gathered outside the courthouse to wait for Foster were usual for a frontier settlement of the day—farmers and laborers, slaves, and Choctaw Indians, all come to town for Saturday court day and market. Some were there to ply their trade, like the riverboat gamblers and prostitutes. Others, like the half-grown, self-indulgent young sons of nearby plantation owners and the idling children of the town, were there to get some excitement or pass the time. Some had strong feelings about Foster's misdeeds. They expected Foster not to be punished legally, and they whipped up their indignation while they waited in the company of the like-minded.

Witnesses reported that few members of the gentry were to be seen. But they were represented, and in no minor role. When Foster came out of the courthouse, he was accompanied by both his own defense attorney and the lead prosecutor. Both were men in their early 30s. On the rough frontier that was Mississippi in the 1830s, both had participated in fistfights over politics. But they were also members in good standing of the establishment. The prosecutor, Spence Monroe Grayson, was a rising young lawyer from an aristocratic Virginia family. The defense attorney, Felix Huston, had the best-paying law practice in town and had acquired a plantation—and a measure of gentility—by marriage.

In court, Felix Huston saved James Foster from a death sentence. Afterward, Huston delivered his client to the crowd while prosecutor Grayson, symbol of the power of law, stood by with arms folded. This paradox spoke volumes about the relations of elite and hoi polloi in the community. Landowners and members of the bar like Huston and Grayson stood at the apex of the community power structure. They were among those with the most to gain when established authority was preserved, because law and order protected their wealth. The jobs and trade they generated indebted others to them. But these leaders couldn't exercise political and economic dominance over the community if they couldn't make good their claim to the moral high ground. Foster himself, though morally fallen, came from a well-to-do plantation family. In protecting Foster from death, Huston and Grayson came to the defense of one of their own. Yet, when the offender so publicly mocked ethics and law as Foster did, his fellows could not let him go lightly punished.

Witnesses said that Huston and Grayson themselves led Foster to his punishment but also kept it within some kind of limit.

At first, however, the crowd did not fall on Foster pell-mell but, in near silence, formed a line. When the procession reached the place of punishment, a customary spot for such acts, it was probably Huston or Grayson who "reasoned" with the crowd, saving Foster from the full scalping that would have killed him. But by the time the crowd brought Foster back to the jail, they were drunk and calling for what was left of his blood. It was Grayson, Foster's prosecutor only hours before, who mounted the steps of the jail and pointed out to the crowd that it had already done its duty. Most then left. The sheriff helped Foster up the steps to the jail and locked him in for his own protection against the stragglers muttering vengeance outside. It was the middle of the night by the time two mounted men appeared, leading a third horse, and found the coast almost clear at the jail. Still fending off a few members of the mob, the two mounted men got Foster onto the spare horse and, despite a shot from a lookout that grazed Foster's hat, spirited him away.

One of James Foster's mounted rescuers was his sister Sarah's husband, Daniel McMillan. The other was probably McMillan's son. The two led Foster home to the senior Mrs. Foster's plantation where the whole story had begun. It took Foster a full five months to recover. But he wasn't able to disappear forever from Natchez, to a fate still unknown to this day, without paying one last penalty. Public records show that Foster signed over his share of his father's estate to his nephew, his sister Sarah's son The boy's father, it seems, would not have rescued James Foster without this reward. Foster's degradation at the hands of both community and clan was complete.

————◆————

In the minds of many, historically and today, deviance from accepted morals and customs threatens the public safety and should be punished accordingly. We hold to certain doctrines: *The young*

must be socialized, the family must remain intact, people mustn't repre-
sent themselves falsely. The shivaree wasn't so much a deliberate action
as part of a half-spontaneous vocabulary of public gestures—one of
several means that some members of the community, acting as a
group, used to express their moral judgments.

Legal judgments didn't necessarily take the place of the shivaree.
The Puritans, taking the Bible as law, were able to express moral judgments by legal means. We know that they also carried on the shivaree,
at least in connection with marriage. After Americans became a nation,
we formally separated religion and state by adopting the first amendment to the Constitution in 1791. When the laws of American states no
longer punished fornication or the excessive drinking of alcohol, these
kinds of offense went on being censured by American communities.
But offenses that *were* punishable in law—like the murder James Foster
committed—also went on being punished by shivaree. Mobs like those
whose members punished Foster protested the light punishments and
acquittals the legal authorities sometimes handed down.

As early as the years before the American revolution, the shivaree
also turned political. The Stamp Act passed by the British parliament
required colonists to pay a tax on every government and business document they created. Under colonial government, the act was taxation
without representation, and it was part of Britain's policy of managing
its colonies' trade for maximum profit to the mother country. To the
cry of "Liberty, Property, and No Stamps!" opponents of British policy
raised scaffolds on which they hanged dummies representing provincial officials and ransacked officials' houses. Especially popular was the
burning of carriages, symbol of wealth and upper-class standing—to
the point where one wealthy Quaker, though not a British sympathizer,
took to calling his coach a "leathern convenience."

Such events could be called riots, but they weren't without organization, as when placards and broadsides mysteriously papered colonial
towns, warning the populace not to make use of stamped paper.
Intimidation was a tactic, both against non-complying merchants and

against government functionaries. Mobs marched by torchlight in the streets in Boston, New York, and other communities. Some of these actions were encouraged if not arranged by the Sons of Liberty, founded in Boston in 1765 and quickly spread throughout the British colonies. The Sons were a semi-secret organization of tradesmen and artisans who opposed the Stamp Act. Merchants and printers, who would have been hardest hit by the tax, were especially active in the group. There is no doubt that more prominent colonists as well, such as John and Samuel Adams in Boston, covertly contributed their organizing skills, influence, and money. Arrayed against the Sons and their sympathizers were colonial governors, officers of the military, and a wealthy few among the colonists who stood to receive paid commissions as distributors of stamps.

What happened to the spirit of patriotic opposition, born in part of mob activism, when an oppressive colonial government gave way to self-government of Americans by Americans? During and after the Revolution, the shivaree turned uglier as both occupying British troops and Whig crowds engaged in acts of collective violence up to and including murder. Worse, representative government was established and public disorder still did not cease. Now lethal in effect, the shivaree as riot began to be applied to private, partisan resentments. Burning, looting, and multiple murder of bystanders, based on ethnicity or religion, reflected the tensions of an increasingly diverse and divided society.

At a certain historical point, when the main objective of a mob was to kill one or more persons, the mob's actions began to be known as lynchings. "Lynching" didn't originally mean lethal punishment, only whipping offenders outside the law. The name came into use around 1790 for a Virginia justice of the peace who was known for the practice. But during the nineteenth century, even before the Civil War, shivaree-style acting out combined with so-called civic reform and punishment of crime to result in murders by "vigilance committees," "whipping bands," and then the Ku Klux Klan.

By the late 1800s, mob lynchings were openly directed against victims on the basis of their race or ethnicity. Only forty years ago, in 1964,
when the bodies of three Civil Rights workers were found shot execution-style in Mississippi, the state's courts did not prosecute anyone for
the killings. It was clear only from federal civil rights prosecutions that
at least fourteen white persons from the community carried out the
killings. Seven defendants each received six years or less in federal
prison time. But only in 2000 did prosecutors in Mississippi begin pursuing murder charges.

The United States is unique among developed nations in that *extralegal execution has scarcely been punished throughout our history.*
Among Americans, sometimes nationwide and sometimes only in
local communities, lynching went on being passed off as "popular justice." Further developments from about 1850 on show that both these
words were a misnomer. Rather than "justice," vigilante and mob
lynchings were repressive and self-serving acts. Rather than an out-
pouring of general sentiment on the part of a whole "population,"
lynchings were instigated by, and served the interests of, a relative few.

Even when the shivaree became deadly, it continued to be justified
as a gesture of social enforcement between equals. But it isn't clear that
only "ordinary" citizens, otherwise powerless, participated. Mob action
was a way for even the influential to intimidate their opponents without a legal grievance.

Some historians have flatly stated that the shivaree in its "police"
function couldn't have existed as a custom without the approval, even
support, of a local elite. After all, it was gentry who had the most access
to police power. By directing the crowd's energy, whether openly or
behind the scenes, the gentry underscored their own power in the
minds of others. A bargain between commoner and gentleman could
be struck because both parties fundamentally shared the same interest
in social order and agreed on its administration. As in the case of James
Foster, a few leaders also used mob action to keep a member of their
own class, even their own clan, in line. The bargain was a good one for

Foster's rescuers, enhancing their position at the expense of a potential rival from their own world. Using Foster's payoff of land, Daniel McMillan established his son as a landowner without McMillan's having to make his own estate smaller by dividing it.

When the Natchez crowd returned James Foster alive, if barely, they may have been drawing an accepted line between torment and execution. Foster would surely have met his death at the hands of the crowd if he had been a man of the people. Especially if he were an outsider—someone from another community, like many gamblers and prostitutes in Natchez, or a foreign immigrant, or an Indian or African-American. In such a case, the town elite wouldn't have had a reason to intervene. They might, in effect, have conceded the right of ordinary citizens to "execute" a moral offender at or below their own social level. Avoiding execution was a privilege of rank and station, and most executions outside the law would take place either when hoi polloi mobbed a scapegoat from their own world, or when local factions of about equal power and authority took each other on. The punishment of moral offenses would not have been half so deadly if it hadn't become entangled with contests over property and politics. We must look to these contests to understand how and why America came to use extralegal executions, and sometimes the legal death penalty as well, as tools of economic and political repression.

TREMENDOUS EXCITEMENT !

Samuel Whittaker and Robert McKenzie rescued from the authorities, and hung by the Vigilance Committee, on Sunday August 24th at 3 o'clock P.M. in the presence of Fifteen thousand People.

Two men "rescued from the authorities" by the vigilantes.

8

"Let Each Man Be His Own Executioner"
Rise of the San Francisco Vigilantes

San Francisco 1851, and power was up for grabs.

Two men stood trial before a mob for assaulting and robbing merchant C. J. Jansen, who lay wounded in a hotel room.

The suspects, Robert Windred and Thomas Berdue, had two strikes against them:

First, police had persuaded merchant Jansen, though he was half-delirious, to identify the two as his assailants. Second, the suspects were Australian—among the many who had been arriving in San Francisco that year.

The *Daily Alta California* of March 13, 1851, commented with self-righteous hypocrisy, "Much as we desire the extension of liberal principles and their enjoyment by the oppressed of all nations, we do not wish to stand side by side with the escaped felons of England." Australia had been partly settled by convict transportees from England. The newspapers equated "Australian" with "ex-convict" or, it was darkly hinted, "escaped convict." A few Australians appeared during the summer of 1849 after news of the first gold strike reached their country. But the majority—a total of only 1,648—reached San Francisco between January and May, 1851. Estimates place the number of convicted felons among them at 300 or fewer within the city's population of at least 25,000.

No doubt the suddenness of the Australians' arrival as much as their reputation simply made them visible and therefore available for blame. But what about the other 23,000-plus residents of San Francisco?

There's a striking contrast between the actual number of Australians and the amount of crime that newspapers alleged they committed. Most San Francisco newspapers were supported by advertising revenues from businessmen, and the newspapers' campaign against the Australians had the effect of misdirecting public attention away from the more questionable activities of businessmen. It's not unlikely that some fires, for example, were started by merchants themselves in order to receive insurance payment for stocks of goods they couldn't sell.

The history of the San Francisco vigilantes illuminates the financial turmoil that can motivate vigilante acts. San Francisco's history is also a classic example of the way that a vigilante past, no matter what its reality, comes to star in a city's history of good and evil. To this day, some San Francisco families are proud to have had vigilante ancestors. "Pioneer" museums and libraries preserve membership certificates, badges, and other memorabilia. The version of history in which vigilantes rescued the city from disorder was first promulgated in newspapers of the 1850s. But the real story most newspapers didn't cover was the shaky finances of the merchants who became vigilantes. These businessmen needed to gain control of local government in order to direct its policies and expenditures to serve business interests. Forming a vigilance committee to overturn San Francisco's elected government by force allowed the few to assume almost unlimited authority over the many.

Those who became leaders of the vigilantes could also become leaders within a new elected government. They positioned themselves to receive the lion's share of financial benefits such as insider access to real estate deals and the awarding of contracts. Vigilante acts in 1851 served as a trial run for a second vigilance committee in 1856. Because they attracted so much attention—being reported even by newspapers in other countries—they also became the pattern for vigilante power grabs in other locales. Since then, the rhetoric of the crime wave and the immigrant menace has been successfully repeated. In effect, the vigilante committee's power to carry out trials ending in execution shaped the development of American local governments and, later, national government as well.

The Australians, arriving with little money, formed part of the working-class majority of the city. Many, if not most, of San Francisco's laborers came directly from other countries. It's not unlikely that the city government elected on the laborers' vote engaged in some dishonest practices, but the number of working people in the city meant that even a strictly honest election probably would have favored their interests rather than those of business people. However, the vigilantes' public appeal to anti-foreign resentment also rallied native-born laborers.

The daily lives of incoming "Americans" during the California gold rush were as raw an example as can be had of the xenophobia that faced most immigrants. A face-off between one set of newcomers and another had been brewing in the boom town for most of its short American history. United States military forces had occupied the formerly Mexican port since 1846, but the nearby discovery of gold in 1848 made San Francisco a magnet for prospectors and speculators from all over the world. A few brought savings or were even backed by outside investment, but many had little more than the clothes on their backs. Most were young and male, unaccompanied by family. Besides the Australians and migrants from the eastern United States, new arrivals included Europeans of several nations, Mexicans, South Americans, and Chinese.

San Franciscans held their first local elections and adopted their first charter only in 1850. Like many new frontier governments, San Francisco's was vulnerable enough to be all but toppled by those who opposed its policies. The tone of politics was set by a competitive free-for-all in which those white "Anglo-Saxon" Protestants who came from the eastern United States attempted to use their status as native-born against all other newcomers. Their claim to advantage was particularly transparent in the gold fields and frontier towns because they weren't an already established population. Beginning with gold-seekers, the competitive bitterness of migrants from back east couldn't be contained for long. The gold in California "plainly" belonged to American citizens, they claimed, even if the future state itself had been snatched from Mexico only three years before. "The gold-mines were preserved by nature for Americans only, who possess noble hearts, and are willing to share with their fellow-men more than any race on earth, but still they do not wish to give all." So wrote a gold-seeker stranded in Panama because seventy-five Peruvians had had the presumption to book steerage class on a ship for San Francisco.

The city, both world port and miners' supply depot, was the only real destination for many who thought themselves bound for the gold fields. It was the place where penniless newcomers labored to earn a stake on the docks, in construction, or in bars, restaurants, stores, and brothels. It was also the point of return for disappointed miners whose stake ran out. In a forerunner of vigilante strategy, some resorted to intimidation to give themselves an advantage, organizing themselves into quasi-military organizations such as the "Hounds."

The self-named Hounds were New York military volunteers who had come to California as part of the American occupation of 1846. Now, finding themselves discharged and idle, they presented themselves as original settlers. The Hounds established a tent headquarters from which they spread out to pilfer from merchants and assault any person of color they could find. On Sundays they paraded in fancy dress with colors, fife and drum, and leaders in military uniform.

If the Hounds were an extraordinarily unpleasant pack of bullies, they were not alone. Similar groups had formed throughout the mining districts by spring of 1849, and they used a special handshake and password. Secret fraternal orders were to arise again and again in connection with vigilantes. Some, like the Hounds, called themselves "Regulators." The new "San Francisco Society of Regulators" announced their objective of driving out all "foreigners." The Hounds or Regulators may also have served as bill collectors for the San Francisco County sheriff. Whether because of this unpopular activity or because of generally terroristic behavior, the organization provoked the founding of not one but two counter-organizations. One was a quasi-military unit with four companies of 100 men each. The other group petitioned the sitting judge to enroll them as police officers. One of these two—which one is not clear—took certain members of the Hounds prisoner and brought them to trial in a "popular"—i.e., non-legal—court. In one of the many inconclusive endings associated with San Francisco's early days, the nineteen Hounds members who were convicted were sentenced to terms of imprisonment, but the sentences were never actually imposed.

Once an elected government gained some ground in San Francisco law enforcement, the war of interest groups began to be fought in the newspapers. How much crime did the city really experience? San Francisco shared a relatively high rate of property crime with other American cities of the time. But even Mary Floyd Williams, a later researcher who was pro-vigilante, couldn't find evidence of a crime wave when she tallied crime-report totals in newspapers of 1851. William Tecumseh Sherman, of Civil War fame, said in his memoir of early days as a San Francisco banker, "As [the vigilantes] controlled the press, they wrote their own history."

San Francisco's first major fire, Christmas Eve 1849, caused an esti-mated one million dollars' damage to property and goods. Three more fires followed in 1850 to a total loss of over nine million dollars. Newspapers regularly blamed "an organized band of incendiaries," even before the fire of May 4, 1851, caused greater loss than the previ-ous four combined. Given the limited investigative techniques of the time, it was impossible to know whether anyone had deliberately set any of the city's fires. Still, for journalistic purposes, and perhaps those of some residents, if there were fires, someone must be setting them. The arsonists' "fixed determination," the *San Francisco Daily Herald* declared, "is to desolate our city and ruin it beyond redemption." A few weeks later, the *Daily Alta California* was calling for the hanging of everyone who deserved it, even if that meant fifty executions.

Who better to lead the fight against crime than "the best known men of the city"—if only people could agree about who these men were.

For a year, prominent businessmen had been trying to consolidate their financial position by gaining political control. But first they had to defeat competition from within. Half to two-thirds of merchants dependent on the gold rush may have failed, but San Francisco's atmosphere in those years was like that of a much advertised lottery. The temptation to speculate on a potentially growing market proved irresistible, and it seemed that everyone who was not in the gold fields set up as an entrepreneur for as long as funds lasted. Commerce was based on imported goods purchased on credit from the East and abroad. With most news and goods conveyed by ship, considerable lead time passed between perception of demand and fulfillment of an order. Prediction of sales was almost impossible owing to the seasonal nature of trade and the ever fluctuating size of the mining camp populations supplied from San Francisco. Permanent oversupply and falling prices were the dreaded, often-realized result, and even outside investment was no guarantee of success. Some merchants, like Levi Strauss, would go on to make enduring fortunes. Throughout the 1850s, however, the big importing and merchant houses had only one successful business year. Bigger businesses were vulnerable because they depended on smaller operators' ability and willingness to cooperate in holding back goods and fixing prices. Smaller operators hoped to make a killing by selling their consignments before others' goods could be released onto the market.

Both fires and robberies, the press said, were enemies of commerce. But fire, if it wiped out the investment of some and contributed to high interest rates, also reduced overstocks of merchandise and helped keep prices high for others. Fire also provided an avenue for budding merchants to seek distinction. Volunteer fire patrols carried out "the noble duty of assisting to save the property of others" and incidentally made it possible to enter San Francisco's merchant-dominated hierarchy at leadership level. William Tell Coleman was typical of aspiring merchants who made their way to the top in part through serving as a firefighter and fighting San Francisco's war on crime. Coleman and a number of other young merchants were men originally of upper-level social background. After their families became impoverished, they made their way west. The attack of the "Australians" on merchant Jansen on February 19, 1851, described at the beginning of this chapter, provided Coleman with one of his first opportunities to become a public figure.

"Let each man be his own executioner"—this was the message on a handbill passed to the crowd outside city hall the day after the two Australians were captured. No one ever learned who was responsible, but the handbill did its work. Becoming more and more agitated, members of the crowd rushed the courtroom where police had taken the prisoners. The situation must not have been unexpected, since a company of California militia—precursors of the National Guard—was already present on parade. Militiamen with fixed bayonets cleared the courtroom and prevented the crowd's capturing the suspects, who were spirited away to not very secure imprisonment. For their pains, the militia were followed back to their armory and challenged to fight before they were finally able to break up the crowd.

An unorganized mass of residents gathered for the second time that evening to appoint a steering committee. The steering committee, asked to decide what to do next, at first disagreed among themselves. Some committee members, including large-scale property owner Sam Brannan, contended that the meeting should try the prisoners forthwith. Having been argued down by others, this contingent afterward passed out a signed handbill. They claimed to have unquestionable evidence that the two suspects were guilty.

The mysterious handbill also called for all citizens to assemble on the Plaza next day to organize against crime. Five to six thousand appeared. San Francisco's first, non-partisan mayor had nearly convinced them to disperse, and pertinently recommended they apply for jury duty, when William Coleman stepped forward. The courts are not to be trusted, he said. The people should try the prisoners at once. Cheering, the crowd again rushed city hall. This time they could not be resisted; instead, they were embraced.

Certain of the "better citizens" hastily convened a tribunal complete with judges, counsel for the citizenry and the two accused, and a jury with foreman. William Coleman, who had no legal training, allowed himself to be persuaded to act as prosecutor. The defendants, who were not admitted to "court" to confront their accusers, were probably fortunate that professional attorneys volunteered to defend them. The defendants' few acquaintances had disappeared out of fear of the mob. To complicate the case, many thought that defendant Thomas Berdue was actually the notorious James Stuart, already wanted for murdering someone elsewhere in the state. In an amazing but not unusual breach of due process, Coleman and others claimed that time was too short to find the potential defense witnesses.

Twelve of the mob, having turned into a jury, apparently considered the evidence with some care. The injured Jansen's testimony was shaky, and three of twelve jurors persisted for several hours in refusing to convict. At 10 P.M., the announcement of a hung jury seemed certain to provoke violence from the crowd. Just then a citizen, E. S. Osgood, came forward to claim that witnesses for Berdue could be found.

Osgood set out at once. But, while he ventured through the dark of night down to one of the wharves, potential tragedy was turning into farce. Osgood managed to locate two witnesses, persuaded them to attend the trial, and returned to court after midnight. When he arrived, Osgood found that the crowd—previously ready to hang both the defendants and all jurors who agreed with them—had dispersed and the tribunal adjourned. Osgood is supposed to have found the remaining citizenry holding an impromptu political meeting, all but unable to say what had become of the trial and its defendants. The anticlimax came only much later when a legal jury found that the defendant thought to be Stuart was a victim of mistaken identity.

Up to February 1851, the story of law and order in San Francisco is about what could have happened, but didn't. It's a strange argument for vigilante justice that, as even apologists for the vigilantes tell us, a legally convened court was quite able to convict Stuart's codefendant and sentence him to the penitentiary. This man was later declared innocent and released. Three months later, despite this evidence that the legal process was at work, San Francisco's first Vigilance Committee was formed.

Some justified the elite-led lynching spree that followed as "the better citizens" working for a social order that would last. Others heartily endorsed illegal executions as "popular sovereignty"—that cherished American doctrine that a citizen's duty was to take direct action in the face of unjust or ineffective laws. In all the talk about the "work" of the vigilantes, no one bothered to mention that no clear-cut reason can be found for establishing a vigilance committee at all. In the nine years from 1850 to 1859, officials legally executed eight persons—a total exactly equal to that of San Francisco's vigilantes, and higher than the county would reach again until its population had increased manyfold. Lynch mobs and vigilante forces, in fact, often wrested their victims from police custody. During lynchings in some towns and cities police may have cooperated, but accounts of the San Francisco lynchings suggest that officers were overwhelmed by a greater number of armed vigilantes.

By the time the Vigilance Committee of 1851 disbanded, these were their claims to fame:

• Hanging four persons by August, including the real Stuart who was supposed to have assaulted merchant Jansen in February.

Since the vigilantes never made the evidence in their "trial" public, it will never be known whether Stuart was guilty of the assault.

- "Examining" ninety-one suspicious persons, "deporting" fourteen, and intimidating fourteen more into leaving.
- Passing the following resolution:

> Resolved, that we, the Vigilance Committee, have the right to enter into any person's or persons' premises where we have good reason to believe that we shall find evidence to substantiate and carry out the object of this body.

What *was* the real objective of these self-appointed enforcers led by a contingent of San Francisco's businessmen? The 1851 vigilance committee didn't reduce crime, take the place of legal executioners, or even end non-vigilante popular violence. In fact, a wildcat crowd attempted to lynch a suspected incendiary on June 31 at the height of vigilante activity. What the committee actually accomplished was to set the precedent for abolishing civil liberties in the name of order. In the short term, they intimidated Australian immigrant laborers, and probably other foreign laborers, who voted an anti-merchant ticket. Equally significant, the vigilantes made themselves into an organization that could bring off a takeover from legal law enforcement.

Vigilantism rallied an out of office interest group, kept them organized for several months, and created a lasting network. Fewer than one in ten of the 1851 rank and file formed part of the 1856 committee, but this was not true of the vigilantes' 1856 governing Executive Committee, headed by the ubiquitous William T. Coleman. The acts of the 1851 committee, and the leadership it created, meant that San Francisco's business community had begun to define itself as a power. It had also begun defining the enemy as outsiders, meaning foreigners.

Five years later when another group of ethnic newcomers actually became elected officials, they and the businessmen would virtually go to war for control of the city.

The paramilitary vigilantes of 1856 boasted their own "troops."

9

Takeover
Return of the San Francisco Vigilantes

In 1854, another of San Francisco's economic downturns was already under way when city council member Henry Meiggs—a prominent lumber merchant and real estate speculator—left suddenly for South America with a large sum of public money. At least half the resulting chorus of mutual accusation was run by the public in the pages of the *Daily Evening Bulletin*. The *Bulletin* was founded in 1855 by James King, a vigilante veteran of 1851 who had been ruined financially the previous year after some dubious banking maneuvers. King's outspoken partisanship, and his attacks on elected officials who he claimed tolerated or encouraged prostitution and gambling, resulted in his being shot down in the street on May 14, 1856.

King, dying, identified his killer as James Casey. Casey was a county supervisor, a rival editor, and a former convict in New York state. As soon as the shooting was known, William T. Coleman of the 1851 vigilantes quickly formed a vigilance committee.

Had history repeated itself within so short a time as five years? The manifesto of the 1856 Vigilance Committee stated that no "thief, burglar, incendiary, assassin, ballot box stuffer, or other disturber of the peace" should go unpunished. This time, the vigilantes formed a paramilitary organization, creating a spectacle of authority that mimed the real government. The vigilantes also used the existing network of leaders developed in 1851 and, with this strategy in place, were able to take over city government while state and federal officials stood by and did nothing. Even California's governor J. Neely Johnson—a member of the vigilantes' political party but obliged to oppose them because of his office—came to vigilante headquarters to negotiate for their non-interference in James Casey's trial. The state militia summoned by the governor fell over one another in their haste to defect to the vigilante organization.

On May 18, four days after the shooting of editor King, the vigilantes carried out their first public act. This was the seizing from jail of King's assailant Casey and another prisoner, Charles Cora, being held for the killing of a U. S. marshal. The executions that followed, like any non-legal executions, can—and, I believe, should—be called lynching, because they resulted from a non-legal trial and weren't carried out by a legally constituted, representative government. But the vigilantes and their supporters made much of their premeditation and the show they put on to claim that their acts differed from so-called mob lynchings. The twenty-four vigilante companies, about 100 each in number, had previously been drilled. The vigilantes' first maneuver "was made an imposing spectacle," as Josiah Royce told the story. "Many were old soldiers themselves; all were used to arms; and a large number of Frenchmen who had joined the organization were especially noteworthy for their fine appearance as soldiers. The movements of this body were skillfully directed, all the detachments into which the force was divided converging to the vicinity of the jail on Broadway, without any mistakes or confusion."

At the jail, "houses all about were covered with spectators, and the streets in the rear of the committee's force were thronged." Under the eyes of these watchers, members of the executive committee entered the jail. Officials, faced with 2,400 vigilantes and a potential mob, had little choice but to give up "first Casey, then Cora."

King died on May 20, and public bulletin boards posted the news at once. That afternoon "the public excitement was tremendous. All the church bells were tolled; the prominent business houses were closed, their doors being draped in black; the flags on the numerous ships in the bay were run up at half-mast; vast crowds gathered in the streets near the committee rooms."

The crowds left, but soon had a reason to return. On May 22, while King's funeral was going on, the vigilantes hanged Casey and Cora publicly from the front windows of their offices on Sacramento Street.

The outcry that followed the hangings split along factional lines, both revealing and reinforcing competition between the merchants and those Josiah Royce dismissed as "politicians and lawyers." These leaders—vigilantes and their office-holding opponents—sought and attracted opposing constituencies divided along occupational and ethnic lines.

Businessmen led the coup. Thirty-three of thirty-seven members of the executive committee can be identified. Of these, fourteen were importers, eight were merchants, and four were bankers. Vigilantes' own membership records show that ethnicity, religion, and politics were coded into the organization. The vigilantes' ultimate strength was enough to suggest widespread popular support—about 6,000 mostly young men (of a population of some 50,000) who were large and small business owners, their clerks and other employees, and artisans. Applicants for vigilante membership were required to state their occupation and place of birth as well as supply two references. Not all were American born, but foreigners came from the northern European countries of France, Germany, England, and Scotland. Americans came from the Northeastern states. Membership records show that laborers and the Irish born were conspicuously few.

Most vigilante merchants belonged to the Know-Nothing coalition, and they were soon to run for office on a platform of opposition to the foreign-born and to Roman Catholics. California's most prominent Irish-American Catholic and leader of the Democratic party was state senator David Colbert Broderick, born in Washington, D. C. After his father moved the family to New York, Broderick entered politics and joined a volunteer fire company. He didn't succeed in New York politics to his own satisfaction, and moved to San Francisco in 1849. Soon he was doing much better, organizing San Francisco's first volunteer fire company and making use of his connections to gain election to the

California senate. Broderick's ultimate ambition was the U. S. senate. Politically he embraced workers' causes, opposing the foreign miners' tax and supporting immigration of free blacks into California. But in business Broderick was much like other get-rich-quick artists of gold-rush San Francisco. He went into a business partnership minting gold coins for profit, he invested in real estate, and he consistently voted state legislative bills that protected his property interests.

No doubt Broderick abused the ballot box. He treated government as a means of generating the jobs, contracts, and favors that also helped keep his party in office. But Broderick's faction also represented and served an otherwise neglected constituency—San Francisco's laborers, many of whom were recent immigrants. Those who endorsed the vigilantes attacked the Catholic Irish, especially, for their noisy drinking and gambling. Such moralizing may have been sincere. It also hid a position of self-interest just as Broderick's populism did. The vigilantes' Know-Nothing party lined up those who had capital against those who did not, and suggested that money should govern. The Know-Nothings invited their audience to focus on the presence of ethnic outsiders such as the Irish who could all too easily be identified and targeted. In this way, the vigilante party courted laborers who had been born in the United States and feared the Irish as aggressive job competitors. From 1851 to 1856 the merchant vigilantes weren't very successful at dominating the electorate from their platform of budget-cutting. But they may have become more persuasive once they added anti-Irish, anti-Catholic insinuations to their arsenal.

When James Casey killed editor King, Casey furnished the Know-Nothing vigilantes with a made-to-order villain—an Irish Catholic Democrat. Casey made King a martyr to fearless journalism and garnered ample public support to get himself hanged by the vigilantes in May. During all the clamor of the next few months, the Vigilance Committee went forward with the action that mattered most to them: forcibly deporting Senator Broderick's key operatives. By the end of August 1856, Broderick's political regime had been dismantled. Even

San Francisco's former mayor saw fit to be away from town for a time. Broderick himself, invited to vigilante headquarters for questioning, chose to leave for the California interior where he could continue his political career in safety. Broderick achieved his great ambition, election to the United States Senate, in 1857. Two years later, he was killed in a duel with yet another character in the drama of gold-rush San Francisco—Justice David S. Terry of the state Supreme Court.

But what exactly were the interests of the businessmen that vigilantes forwarded by their activities? John Nugent, an Irishman and *San Francisco Daily Herald* editor who had supported the 1851 committee, opposed the committee of 1856. In spite of canceled subscriptions and advertising losses that cut the size of the *Herald* down to half, Nugent went on accusing the vigilantes of abuses that mounted month by month during 1856. The vigilantes' reform goal, said Nugent, was no more exalted than to replace existing elected officials with members of the committee. But business had been disrupted, and Eastern investors would stay away from a lawless city.

Or, Nugent went on, was that the vigilantes' real aim—to disrupt shipping so that fewer goods, at higher profits to themselves, would go to market? Even worse, were the merchant vigilantes trying to distract attention from their own unpayable debts? Another opposition newspaper labeled the committee "The Sour Flour and Soft Pork Aristocracy" for what many believed had been their speculations in flour during the winter of 1852-1853.

Still, New York and Boston editorials of 1856 were approving. San Francisco city council member Meiggs had appropriated and even forged municipal securities as collateral for risky investments. Meiggs's dishonesty helped bring on San Francisco's slide into financial overextension. In the eyes of merchants, the municipal budget was taking much more than its share of fiscal resources. Eastern financiers might stop issuing credit if they thought their San Francisco connections had lost control of city politics. San Francisco merchants may have intended not only to take control but to demonstrate to the outside world that they had done so.

———◆———

Thirteen days after the execution of Casey and Cora, California's governor J. Neely Johnson declared San Francisco to be in a state of insurrection. In this step the governor was encouraged by the "courageous and violent" Justice Terry of the California Supreme Court, who "could not bear to see the law set at nought." Governor Johnson attempted to raise a militia force under Major General William T. Sherman, then a San Francisco banker. But few citizens responded, and Sherman soon became so unenthusiastic about his position that he resigned his militia commission. Governor Johnson began petitioning the United States government for arms and ammunition. The vigilance committee built a wall of sandbags in front of their headquarters on Sacramento Street and installed a new alarm bell on the roof. Just as Governor Johnson was awaiting arrival of the state's annual statutory delivery of munitions from the U. S. Army, vigilantes intercepted the schooner *Julia*. They boarded the ship and took several California militiamen as their prisoners.

Meanwhile Justice Terry had gone to the city intent on taking action against the vigilantes. On the same night that the *Julia* was boarded, June 21, Terry attempted to prevent an arrest by the vigilante "police" and stabbed one Hopkins of the vigilantes. The vigilantes took Terry prisoner, and kept him under constant threat of execution for seven weeks.

While Terry was being held captive, a new and more deadly issue complicated the standoff between governor and vigilantes—states' rights. The trouble began when the President of the United States, Franklin Pierce, denied Governor Johnson's request to bring in militia from other states. Political divisions that would lead to civil war in five short years were already looming—in fact California, partly because of a strong Southern population, had discussed secession. President Pierce may have been afraid that forcing the San Francisco issue would bring on a showdown. Pierce undoubtedly oversaw the message of the U. S. naval secretary, who wrote to San Francisco's senior naval officer that "the powers delegated to [the federal government] are well defined and limited. A strict observance of them within their prescribed limitations and restrictions can alone save our Union from the dangers which would inevitably imperil it in the event of a rash conflict between the federal and State governments." Intervention was limited to stationing federal gunboats in San Francisco Bay. This was a less controversial move that could be justified as protecting federal property, not infringing California's independence as a state.

The vigilantes continued to keep Justice Terry captive, but ultimately could not nerve themselves to execute a justice of the state Supreme Court. This loss of face may even have led to the vigilantes' hanging their last two victims—whose guilt of capital murder was doubtful—on July 29. Justice Terry's victim, Hopkins, recovered soon afterward from his knife wound and the vigilantes, perhaps with some relief that the situation had resolved itself, released Justice Terry.

Strengthened by the presence of the gunboats, anti-vigilante forces used the boarding of the *Julia* to charge two vigilantes with piracy, a federal crime. The presiding judge of the U. S. Circuit Court was none other than M. Hall McAllister—a player in the extralegal trial of merchant Jansen's accused attackers five years earlier.

Judge McAllister, who had become an outspoken opponent of the vigilance committee, conducted an aggressive case against the two vigilante defendants from their indictment on September 1 through the conclusion of attorneys' summations on September 10. Observers were nonplused, therefore, when McAllister, in his charge to the jury on September 11, unexpectedly directed for acquittal. Those in the courtroom "stamped and cheered" as the jury acquitted after three minutes of deliberation.

What had become of McAllister's fixed opposition to "the associated mobites styling themselves a Vigilance Committee"? The explanation of this about-face evidently lies in a short but pithy correspondence between Judge McAllister and Major General John E. Wool, Army commander for the Pacific division. On September 9, Judge McAllister reported to Wool that the U. S. marshal, who had custody of the two vigilantes on trial, was uncertain whether he could keep order if "an attempt shall be made to nullify the process of the court"— that is, vigilante intervention by force.

This is what the U.S. marshal may have feared. Judge McAllister somewhat strangely added that "it is impracticable for us to ascertain in advance the issue of the trial." McAllister then inquired whether General Wool had any orders that would allow the Army to extend aid. On September 10, Wool replied to the judge's letter, "this instant received," "I have no orders whatever applicable to the subject in question." McAllister could expect no further help from the U. S. military.

This final, federal-level engagement of the Vigilance Committee of 1856, who disbanded on August 18, ended in stalemate. The vigilantes were no doubt encouraged by the presence of gunboats to release Justice Terry. On the other hand, the anti-vigilantes were not able to obtain conviction of the vigilante pirates. The federal government, in playing the role of reluctant referee, revealed the limits of its own ability or willingness to intervene. No principle of the dignity or sanctity of law mattered as much as avoiding a challenge to popular sovereignty in the troubled decade of the 1850s.

Those whom Justice Terry had referred to as "damned pork merchants" took over from the scattered Broderick faction, sweeping the election of 1856. The vigilante party's ticket was determined by a secret committee instead of a primary, insuring the continuing influence of the former vigilantes. In 1856, the police chief, police-court judge, sheriff, treasurer, and mayor were all former vigilantes. Annual elections were abolished, minimizing party influence and the chance of further rapid political change.

The new officials made much of their economizing. In fact, the state legislature had already put a spending ceiling into effect the previous spring when merging county and city governments. The city government the previous year had already cut the budget by 68 percent. In 1856 the new party cut the budget by another 59 percent and kept it low through the rest of the 1850s, causing even vigilante apologists to comment on the detriment to utilities, street improvements, and schools. In the long term, government expenditure depended most on the city's prosperity, which began only in 1860. Machine politics like those of David Broderick resurfaced when the vigilantes went out of office in 1867.

Results of the Vigilance Committee's actions resembled those of the 1851 committee—the authority vigilantes gained through intimidation was used less to punish crime than to gain political control of a city and its resources. The vigilantes concentrated their energies on "deporting" Broderick adherents they accused of election fraud. Actual law enforcement was left to San Francisco's police force as usual, and the evidence suggests that police had their job well in hand.

The benefit to the vigilante faction was considerable and immediate, but finally it was limited. Their influence was local; the economy was becoming national. The ex-vigilantes' later fortunes, like those of many first-generation San Francisco merchants, were mixed. They never attained the wealth of corporate robber barons such as Leland Stanford, a brother vigilante in the rank and file of 1856. Leadership belonged to the local merchants, supposedly, because they had the community's long-term welfare at heart. This claim is debatable. The vigilantes were young, unestablished men who used the committee to raise themselves to a more secure position. Through organized coercion, they drove out their competitors and acquired the political power that made it worth their while to remain in San Francisco.

———◆———

"Another terrific 'Lynching' took place at San Francisco on the 31st of August last." This is the way the *Illustrated London News* of November 15, 1851, tardily heralded the beginning of San Francisco's vigilante epoch, 1851-1856. For the *News* and its constituency of investors, the meaning of the event was chiefly financial. "We trust this will prove a timely warning to the public," the article continued, "and prevent the mania from spreading of giving 200 percent premium on certain Companies formed for the ostensible purpose of working [gold] mines in California." Distant speculators in the gold market felt freer than Californians to point out the economic stakes of the power struggle in San Francisco.

It was a struggle repeated many times in frontier towns and cities as business interests squared off against elected officials. Businessmen sought minimal taxation and minimal public spending. Elected officials sought high levels of public spending that benefitted not only themselves but the majority of their electorate—the laborers who also strived to make their fortunes in the Far West. Most of the first-arriving miners and other early immigrants, because of their lack of capital, soon drifted from independent enterprise to transient labor in the employ of others. Public works and other government jobs were the most secure to be had—and they could sometimes be had in return for party loyalty.

San Francisco was a prototype, but vigilante committees quickly appeared in Montana, Wyoming, and other frontiers. Vigilante hands were at work, for example, when a committee lynched four officeholders in Laramie, Wyoming, in 1868. The lapses and delays of infant local governments made it easy for out-of-office interest groups to take political issues to other, dirtier arenas outside the electoral process—even to vigilante terrorism.

Again and again, and not only in San Francisco, federal government also played a critical role in keeping local authority weak. Strategic inaction in the face of vigilante lawlessness retarded the development of electoral politics. What developed in its stead was a political culture of dog-eat-dog factionalism. The factions that contended for control of resources called themselves political parties, but they were divided as much by ethnicity, religion, and class as by differences over issues.

Often enough, the object on both sides was simply spoils. By the 1850s, combatants had learned to justify illegal execution and other lawless acts in the name of a moral crusade, a demonstration of popular sovereignty, or both. Organized terrorism was becoming as American as apple pie.

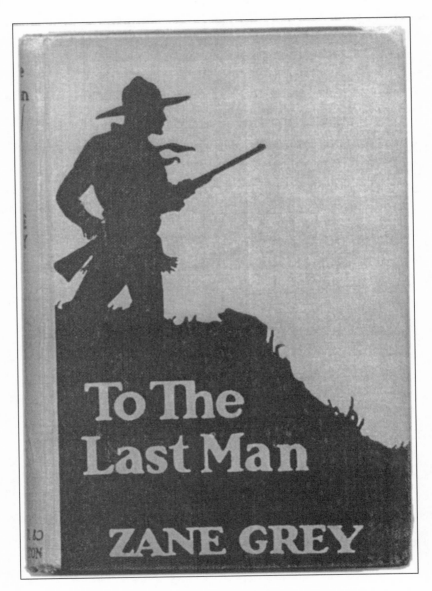

Western novels romanticized the vigilante as an avenger.

10

Boots, Bullets, and Big Bucks
The Vigilante Myth

On a website called Fucked Up College Kids, I find that one original thinker has contributed this idea: Catching the bad guys, punishing crime, would be a lot easier if we could "skip through the paperwork and procedures." Each police officer, Original Thinker suggested, would be empowered to "track, capture, judge, and execute."

Today we often use "vigilante" in this way—a lone avenger. The avenger may be a civilian who takes the law into his or her own hands, like Clint Eastwood's Dirty Harry, but sometimes the avenger is a law enforcement professional. We've romanticized the avenger until we're able to believe, like Original Thinker, that a vigilante is someone who upholds something vaguely referred to as "the laws," and does so effectively because he or she skips the paperwork.

I already know who the bad guy is: that's vigilante thinking. Call it the Rush to Judgment. Anyone can do it—the lone avenger, the vigilance committee, the police officer, the prosecutor, the juror, the reader or writer of a newspaper, the TV viewer watching a true crime story. No need for unbiased evidence-gathering, arguing both sides of the case, making your deliberations public. No need to hesitate over choosing the punishment because "we all know right from wrong." That, I suppose, is what some people mean by "the laws," never guessing that laws and records of judgments are written down in mind-boggling detail for the very reason that right-minded people disagree so regularly when judging a particular case. In spite of such complex realities, Americans' simple faith in vigilantism got off to a strong start on our frontiers. It became entrenched for good as a fair and equitable way of meting out justice when vigilante acts were endorsed by the likes of Theodore Roosevelt in 1911. Industrial capitalists carried vigilante tactics to industrial workplaces and, even more sinister, to courtrooms where convictions were railroaded through.

"A life for a life, what could be fairer than that?" one indignant letter-writer asked. She wrote to a newspaper to protest Governor George Ryan's exchange of 156 Illinois death sentences in January 2003 for imprisonment—for either forty-year terms or life without parole in a five-by-twelve-foot cell shared with another convict.

Imprisonment unfair? Oh, really? Let's hope that Indignant Letter Writer never gets a death sentence for killing someone with her automobile, or finds that her son or daughter in military service has been executed after capture by the enemy. I'm sure she would say, *But that's not what I meant.* Yet she's confident that five words are enough law to go on when taking the lives of 156 people.

Original Thinker, at the Fucked Up College Kids site, suggested that we uphold "the laws" by operating outside the laws. No need for due process derived from our Constitutional amendments—"everything" would be handled by "Internal Affairs"! Now why didn't the original vigilantes think of that?

They did.

The agenda and method of vigilantism haven't changed since before the Revolutionary War. Vigilantes have always acted as a self-appointed Internal Affairs Agency combining police officer, prosecutor, judge, and executioner. Eighteenth-century vigilantes often called themselves "regulators," using the name to imply that they were bringing order from chaos. And so they were—if government by a single interest group is order, and electoral democracy is chaos. In the cases I've researched, a closer look at local history shows that vigilantism arose when two factions were competing for control. Like the San Francisco vigilantes, other "committees" used extralegal force against relatively helpless opponents as a show of the vigilantes' right and might to run the community, the mining camp, or the cattle range. It's typical that, when the first mayor of San Francisco suggested that more business-men might consider volunteering as jurors to strengthen the existing legal system, those renowned supporters of "law and order" made no response at all.

The word "vigilante" gained wide popularity starting in 1866. Thomas Dimsdale, a schoolteacher raised in England, wrote up the activities of the mining-camp vigilance committee in Bannack and Virginia City, Montana, only two years after the first of their twenty-two killings took place. *The Vigilantes of Montana*, as the only full-length, contemporary account of the vigilance committee, was enormously successful in validating the vigilantes' side of the story.

Congress, through sheer inefficiency, had recently allowed territori-al criminal codes to expire in the Idaho territory, including the future state of Montana. The lack of criminal courts under law was a strong point in the case for vigilantism, but it was almost the only one. In December 1863, before the Montana vigilantes began operating, an extralegal but elected miners' court working with an armed posse had already captured and publicly tried three suspects for murder. Based on testimony by one suspect, the court convicted the other two, banishing one and hanging the other. Moments before dying on the scaffold, the unlucky George Ives claimed he was innocent of the crime and named another man. Using Ives's statement as justification, the prosecuting attorney from the Ives case and five other men organized the Montana Vigilance Committee. By the end of February 1864, the vigilantes had killed twenty-two persons, including the elected sheriff of the Bannack Mining District, Henry Plummer. The vigilantes accused Plummer of using his position to run a band of robbers, or road agents—the story on which Plummer was hanged, and the one that legend has handed down to us. Until recently, this unchallenged legend chiefly consisted of the accounts of Dimsdale and his imitator Nathaniel Langford, who wrote *Vigilante Days and Ways* in 1890.

Modern historians have found little evidence either for or against Plummer and the other accused robbers, but have made a case against the vigilantes by questioning Dimsdale's claims and the later statements of a few vigilante veterans and their supporters.

The Bannack vigilantes chose their victims from a list supposedly made out at the dictation of one captured bandit bargaining for his life. However, there are three differing versions of the list. The discrepancy suggests that vigilantes tailored the list after the fact to match the list of their actual victims. Moreover, Plummer and his henchmen supposedly ran a highly organized, highly profitable operation whose members each signed an oath in the blood of a previous victim (kept handy in a bottle for the purpose) and used hand signals, passwords and horseback messengers to communicate. The gang's goal was claimed to be an armed takeover of Virginia City by spring of 1864. But two researchers later investigated the robberies that took place at that time in the district. Only three of the robberies were profitable, and the researchers couldn't connect the perpetrators of the three robberies to each other. Two of the crimes, holdups of stage coaches said to be carrying gold dust, yielded $3,300, and the murder Ives was convicted of yielded $200. The vigilantes claimed that all robberies in the wider area were connected, and they named about 150 individuals as gang members. If these individuals had split their $3,500 in takings, they would have earned $23.33 each for a year's work in setting up their vast, armed conspiracy of crime.

As in San Francisco, Montana and other mining areas were prey to fears of robbery. Unsupported newspaper commentary coupled with rumor elevated the theft of gold dust, in particular, to mythic heights of frequency and conspiracy. Years afterward, the vigilantes' version tended to become the official story because the vigilantes either always were, or became through their acts, the most persuasive—and most feared—citizens around. It isn't just that many frontier vigilantes were in a position to win control by force. Over time, they reached a position to legislate history by influencing state and federal policymakers, officials, and the courts. They also bought history—both by writing it themselves and by patronizing newspaper owners and book writers.

Sheriff Plummer and his alleged gang members had long since been executed—the declared goal of the Montana vigilantes—but there always seemed to be a new set of bad guys on the horizon. Vigilante executions continued for about thirty more years in Montana and other frontier states from Arizona to Washington. As outside investors began to work the frontier cattle business on a grand scale, vigilante episodes got more and more spectacular—none more so than the Johnson County War.

These events in Wyoming in 1892, near the present-day town of Buffalo, on the Powder River, spotlight the heavy hitters and escalating stakes in later vigilante violence. The Johnson County "range war" supposedly pitted big cattle interests against the homesteaders or nesters, small landowners who were attempting to raise sheep or farm. But a more likely trigger for vigilantism was differences among the cattle interests themselves. Some operations were big, but others were bigger. In the 1880s the cattlemen with Eastern financial backing argued that American owned rangeland in the public domain should be leased or sold to cattlemen. But only the biggest firms could have afforded to lease, while smaller firms depended on the open grazing system prevailing on public lands. The tension of this and other issues came while cattlemen were fighting for financial success in an overactive, unstable market.

This situation may have pushed certain members of the Wyoming Stock Growers' Association to demonstrate their strength with a raid on an easily targeted third group—the cowboys and small ranchers. On an open range, the ownership of stock, unbranded calves especially, could be a matter of dispute—rustling itself was in the process of hotly debated legal definition. The middle-sized ranchers chose this moment to bring on a showdown. In 1892 they formed their own cattlemen's association and announced, in spite of a law to the contrary, that they would hold their own roundup to gather and brand cattle. In the eyes of the Stock Growers' Association, the roundup was defiance and many of the cattle were undoubtedly stolen.

Among the committee of "regulators" who formed an expedition against the accused rustlers were the two Harvard-educated partners of the Teschemacher and deBillier Cattle Company, which had been in financial straits since 1887. Some evidence indicates that a show of control over the cattle range would place the company in a beneficial light with Eastern interests, thus giving Teschemacher and deBillier more favorable terms as they liquidated their firm and prepared to bail out. Teschemacher, deBillier and other members of the Stock Growers put together a hit list of seventy persons, combining known stock rustlers with small ranchers, the sheriff of Johnson County, and three county commissioners. The newly formed vigilante committee then purchased horses in Colorado. The committee recruited local henchmen plus twenty-two gunfighters from Paris, Texas, hired with the story that they were to serve warrants on a gang of wanted persons. The Union Pacific Railroad provided a special train to carry men and arms from Cheyenne to Casper. The state militia was put under special orders that prevented the county sheriff from getting their help. Wyoming political leaders, including one of the state's U. S. senators, the acting governor, a former territorial governor, and a former justice of the state supreme court, more or less actively supported the expedition plan.

Drama followed drama in early 1892 as the Stock Growers' expedition rode overnight through a spring snowstorm to the KC Ranch to capture two men on their list. One of the men was shot from ambush within two hours but the other, Nate Champion, lived from morning until late afternoon, writing a last diary under the rifle-fire siege of a dozen or more men surrounding the ranch house. Finally the besiegers set the house alight with burning hay and drove Champion out to his death by rifle and revolver fire. But another enemy whom the attackers had intended to kill escaped to the town of Buffalo to organize a retaliatory force. Two days later, as many as thirty men surrounded the ranch where the Stock Growers' expedition members were staying. The surrounded expedition was rescued after two more days by three troops of U. S. cavalry. Apparently the U. S. senators from Wyoming prevailed on President Benjamin Harrison, who sent the troops at the request of Wyoming's governor.

The cavalry commander assured the besieging force of indignant smallholders and their supporters, apparently in all sincerity, that the stockmen's expeditionary force would be brought to a fair trial. In the end, after supporters of the expeditionary force attempted to get President Harrison to declare martial law in Wyoming, the cases were dismissed.

In fact, in all the cases of vigilantism I've investigated, I'm unable to come up with any case where successful legal action was taken against a vigilante. In later years, Western vigilantism even become respectable enough that a law enforcement agency, the Montana Highway Patrol, could put a vigilante inscription on its insignia. The inscription, "3-7-77," is so mysterious that no one has shown evidence of what it means or can demonstrate that the original Montana vigilantes of 1864 made use of it. I'm sure that the highway patrol has no vigilante intentions—it seems that a zealous captain added the inscription to the patrol's insignia back in the frontier days of 1956.

Given our American tradition, is it any wonder that vigilantes are still with us? Don't take my word that they are—visit the website of RanchRescue.com or one of its chapters. On the main site, the publisher of the Arizona newspaper *Tombstone Tumbleweed* recruits private individuals, as part of a "Civil Homeland Defense Corps," to patrol the Arizona-Mexico border in search of illegal immigrants.

Sorry—the exact dates and locations of Ranch Rescue's current patrolling operations will be revealed *only* to full members.

If you're out there, Original Thinker, and considering a group experience instead of individual "enforcement," I have to warn you: there's more than one side to life in today's vigilante corps. Your first mission with Ranch Rescue is free—except for travel expenses, camping gear, regulation clothing, food, and firearms—then it's a $30 annual membership fee, or $50 for your and your spouse. Only $45 for a life membership! Ranch Rescue claims chapters as far away as Virginia and Oregon. According to the New Mexico chapter's website, a property owner in a county on the U.S.-Mexico border has offered to serve as host for "security volunteers,"who are asked to carry firearms and camp out. Your duties? "To secure the properties, observe and document the passage of trespassers, drug smugglers, vandals, and theives [sic] over private property, and to perform repairs to ranch property and facilities."

Wait a minute! Perform repairs? I can't find my post-hole digger. I must have loaned it to a vigilante. When you get back, let me know how your mission turned out.

I don't find it hard to understand that vigilante action makes a good fantasy. Or that we live in scary times that make us willing to listen to scary scenarios, to imagine terrorist conspiracy everywhere among those who don't seem to share our interests. Or that it's tempting to look for a scapegoat when you discover that being white, male, and a U. S. citizen may not be enough to get you (or your spouse) a job. There's nothing new about the fears of treason, of economic competition from newer immigrants than ourselves, which go all the way back to the beginning in American history. There's nothing new about the fantasies, either. Theodore Roosevelt, as a young gentleman rancher, tried to join the Montana vigilance committee in its 1884 campaign to eradicate certain accused horse thieves. The rancher vigilantes considered Roosevelt a tenderfoot and turned down his application. As for Ranch Rescue, if it's like other right-wing movements whose activities I've researched, most of those who pay their thirty dollars will find themselves contributing to the lifestyle of someone who owns more property than they do.

I think many vigilantes act in good faith, telling themselves they're defending a principle or a way of life. Vigilante thinking will always be around, because we all have fears and fantasies, and we all see others through a set of cultural filters and self-interest that we're usually not even aware of.

But the United States is different from other countries of the developed world in that Americans in high places have served as vigilantes themselves and encouraged the rest of us to think the way they did. Their precedent, I can't help thinking, has done something to our humility and perseverance and faith in law. How could we help being influenced by the noble impatience of the mighty? Especially over the sixty years or more from the 1850s to the 1910s, leading office holders who swore to uphold the U. S. Constitution continued to boast of their vigilante killings. A few examples among many:

- Alexander Mouton, a Louisiana sugar planter who became a vigilante leader in 1859 after serving as governor and U. S. senator;
- William Pitt Kellogg, Chief Justice of the Nebraska Territory in 1861 and later U. S. senator from Louisiana;
- Granville Stuart, merchant, cattleman, and Montana vigilante in 1884, later minister to Uruguay and Paraguay;
- Francis M. Cockrell of Missouri, Democratic nominee for the U. S. presidency in 1904;
- Miguel A. Otero II, a second-generation vigilante and New Mexico governor from a merchant family whose interests were closely tied to the building of railroads.

The younger generation of frontier businessmen who were vigilante leaders, such as Cockrell and Otero, went to Washington, D. C., as Progressives. One connection among them was partnership in a New Mexico law firm to which a son of Francis Cockrell also belonged. Some, like Otero and his fellow New Mexican governor and vigilante George Curry, also had direct ties to Theodore Roosevelt. Curry became provincial governor of the Philippines after the Roosevelt-directed American takeover there.

———◆———

To bring law to California and Montana, Theodore Roosevelt once wrote in a letter, "the Vigilantes had to be organized and had to hang people."

Roosevelt's statement was a self-serving one, defending his part in American acquisition of the Panama Canal Zone in 1904 on the grounds that Panamanians couldn't govern themselves. Roosevelt's statement about frontier law was also a half-truth—or less. But Roosevelt never analyzed these extralegal executions by committee as injustice, unconstitutional meddling with the law or, simply, strong-arm coercion. Years after trying to join the Montana vigilantes, Roosevelt became a patron of the writer Owen Wister. Among Wister's many books was a western novel called *The Virginian* (dedicated to Roosevelt) in which a leading character justifies vigilante hanging as "the code of the West." Wister himself, in the best groupie style, once sat next to an indicted Wyoming lyncher at the elite Cheyenne Club and pronounced the man a solid citizen. Later, Roosevelt went on record approving a vigilante-led lynching in New Orleans, during which the vigilantes removed eleven Italian-Americans from jail and hanged them for allegedly murdering the police chief.

Roosevelt became known as "the Trust Buster" because he used the Sherman Anti-Trust Act to break up a conglomerate of railroads in the Northwest. But in supporting vigilante violence, Roosevelt supported the robber barons. These industrialists in railroading, mining, and textiles expanded vigilantism from a relatively isolated triumph over law to a national force of coercion. The power of industrialists to hire their own police force, like the immunity from prosecution enjoyed by their frontier vigilante cousins, made the United States different from other developed Western countries in the same era. Industrial capitalism, stimulated by settlement of the West but national in scope, provoked sixty years of acute labor conflict. Eventually businessmen no longer did their own enforcing, as the Montana vigilantes had. They simply hired others to do it.

This is what miners or railroad workers meant, from the 1870s on, when they referred to vigilantes: hired goons of the corporations. The purpose of these hired vigilantes was to defeat workers' attempts to organize and strike for better wages or better working conditions.

Allan Pinkerton, admirer of vigilance committees and founder in 1850 of the famous detective agency, pioneered the use of heavily armed "protective patrols" of his agents to be hired by corporate employers. The Pinkerton Protective Patrol operated as a paramilitary unit to spearhead confrontations with striking laborers. Robert Hunter, writer and socialist, described the corporations' private police as "thugs, thieves, incendiaries, dynamiters, perjurers, jury-fixers, manufacturers of evidence, strikebreakers and murderers." In the 1930s, the heirs to this tradition of paid vigilantism brought Woody Guthrie to sing, in "Vigilante Man," "Why does a vigilante man carry that sawed-off shotgun in his hand? Would he shoot his brother and sister down?"

It was a pretty safe question, since it had already been answered in the affirmative sixty years before.

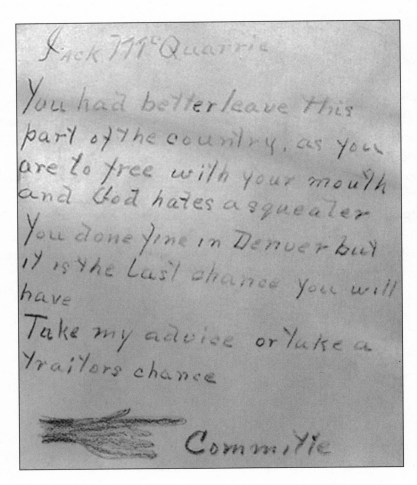

Corporation "enforcers" threatened some who testified against them.

11

"Beaten All to Smash"
Labor, the Robber Barons, and the Law

In many of his best-known songs, Woody Guthrie portrayed the corporations as Goliath and the workers as David. In the case of the labor movement, however, Goliath won.

Something I'll never understand is the opposition of American business to the labor movement, from organized labor's beginnings before 1800. Was it greed, paranoia, self-righteousness, overweening pride, or just a staggering failure of imagination?

From 1800 until 1935, it didn't seem to have occurred to anyone in power to negotiate with workers.

Or maybe they didn't negotiate because they understood from the beginning that they didn't have to. The David of labor had the equivalent of a slingshot, but the Goliath of big business had money, the law, troops, and machine guns. American laborers failed to get and hold a strong position in the workplace partly because of political and social stresses among themselves. Equally important, big employers had bottomless pockets. By hiring spies and armed enforcers and purchasing newspaper opinion, employers overwhelmed workers' efforts to determine their wages, working conditions, and job security.

But the coup de grace was that American governments regularly threw their legal and police muscle behind the economic weight of employers. Government and commerce had indistinguishable interests at times. The hiring of private mercenaries was an extension of the use of city police, county sheriff's officers, militia, and federal troops. Paid vigilantism couldn't have been put to deadly effect if courts hadn't viewed force as a right of management in the name of prosperity and the American way.

The era of the Robber Barons drove a wedge between justice and the law that lasted, conservatively, until the National Labor Relations Board was founded in 1935. From the 1870s to 1930s court decisions, the use of police and military forces, and vigilante actions all represented and promoted the concept that employers, not workers, had the rights that mattered. Through most of American history, laborers did without a legal arena in which to bargain with their employers. Once the law favored business over workers, governments and employers maintained dominance by being better armed. Employers seized public attention and directed it away from their own violence—and away from any questions about justice that labor conflict could have raised. All they had to do was emphasize that collective bargaining and labor demonstrations technically constituted breaking the law. Moreover, big business tactics helped set the tone of American ethnic and racial relations. When employers made use of paid vigilantes in the guise of private police, they created a model for citizens' vigilance committees and ethnically targeted lynchings. I believe these forms of collective violence provided an enduring, tacit approval for vigilante judgments based on contempt for process and prejudged guilt even in legal trials.

The long lasting labor-management struggle built institutions of violence against whole classes of American citizens—not just a small number of short-term opponents as in 1850s San Francisco or other frontier towns. San Francisco vigilantism of the 1850s sprang from a similar division of interests between business and the working people. But in San Francisco the contest was local, the amounts of money and power at stake were relatively small, and the federal government pointedly didn't intervene.

After the Civil War, railroads, mining, steel, and other industries began to be nationwide in scope and corporate in form. The struggle between labor and management became nationwide as well. The mixing of public and private armies, open contempt of industrialists for workers, and rhetoric against immigrants by other immigrants created a lasting definition of who could be repressed and who was to do the repressing. Labor conflict contributed to an impersonal vigilantism of bigotry and class that included goon squad murders and ethnically targeted lynchings. Government-approved hiring and forced emplacement of ethnically identifiable non-union workers also tarred newer foreign immigrants and African-Americans with the brush of disloyalty and even criminality. Conditions of labor conflict also led to high rates of execution among the Italians, Chinese, and other identifiable groups—and executions and lynchings of African-Americans outside the South—which I'll talk about further on.

It's hard to imagine now, but in 1877 the railroad strike that spread from city to city across the United States must have signaled to many Americans that the end of the world was near. The railroad was central to people's lives for traveling and the delivery of goods to markets, and the 1877 strike paralyzed the country. The strike was as much social movement as labor demonstration. The strike came at the end of a four-year economic depression brought on by speculation and industrial infighting. A previous strike of coal miners in 1875 had ended with the miners, as one of their songs said, "beaten all to smash." Reacting to the strike, the Philadelphia and Reading Coal and Iron Company hired armed mercenaries and brought in strike breakers to work the mines. Goaded strikers then began to damage mine and railroad property, losing public support in the process. Union leaders were unable to stop the violence, which continued and escalated throughout the starvation strike and into the post-strike era of ten-hour days in the mines at a twenty percent wage decrease.

Workers began their 1877 protest in Martinsburg, West Virginia, after the Baltimore and Ohio Railroad announced a second wage cut within the year. About one hundred railroad workers blocked the tracks and commandeered engines, stopping all freight trains (but not passenger trains) entering and leaving the city. Strikers also prevented other train workers from operating freight engines. Without hesitation, the B & O company's vice-president telegraphed the governor of West Virginia. Seventy-five militia men were immediately dispatched to take back control of the trains. According to one account at the time, a striker fired at a soldier attempting to board a train, and the soldier fired back. Shortly afterward, an angry crowd surrounded the militia, and the company colonel ordered the soldiers back to the armory to disband. The crowd of protestors grew to an estimated one thousand.

Only one day later, the president of the United States, Rutherford Hayes, issued a proclamation of "domestic violence" and ordered federal troops and artillery to Martinsburg. The sight of these heavily armed U. S. soldiers made the crowd disperse almost immediately. Martinsburg police began arresting accused ringleaders of the strike, and non-striking train workers under military protection soon got some trains moving again.

But word spread. Strikers marched along tracks from city to city. The strike extended to Baltimore and Pittsburgh, then to other cities as far away as St. Louis, Chicago, and even San Francisco, where anti-Chinese riots broke out. Workers in other industries staged sympathy strikes and formed crowds as large as 20,000. Governors in some states attempted to quell the demonstrations with police and militia. In Baltimore, militia did battle with protestors and killed ten.

In Martinsburg, Pittsburgh, and other strike centers, police and National Guard troops refused to fire on the crowd of labor demonstrators. Governors began requesting U. S. soldiers—the first time since the 1830s that federal troops were used against strikers. These troops, rushed from city to city, were able to end the strikes within a few weeks. In reaction to the strikes, state legislatures passed more conspiracy laws, formed new units of militia, and constructed numerous

National Guard armories. For the next fifty years, corporations would wield the double-barreled shotgun of military force and law.

The legal handwriting was already on the wall in 1806. A landmark court decision against Philadelphia shoemakers ruled that banding together to raise wages was criminal conspiracy.

It was a classic in the technique of blaming the victim. Adam Smith observed in 1776, "People of the same trade hardly meet together even for merriment and diversion but the conversation ends in a conspiracy against the public, or in some contrivance to raise prices." Putting it mildly, the court's 1806 ruling against the shoemakers reflected a conservative economic view that permeated the law of developed nations in the early 1800s. Adam Smith is often credited with the idea that economics is a nearly natural force, but he was one of the first to notice in print that business interests were going to need some watching. His warning went unheeded.

Under the guise of defending a free market, conservative law-makers and judges consigned workers to low wages so that they wouldn't "interfere" with the "natural" operations of capitalism. But laws supporting the position of capital against that of labor weren't seen as interference. Individual bargaining was natural, collective bargaining was not. Critic of big business Henry Demarest Lloyd wrote, in an article in 1884, "Last July Messrs. Vanderbilt, Sloan, and one or two others out of several hundred owners of coal lands and coal railroads... agreed to fix prices, and to prevent the production of too much of the raw material of warmth, by suspensions of mining. In anticipation of the arrival of the cold wave from Manitoba, a cold wave was sent out all over the United States, from their parlors in New York, in an order for half-time work by the miners during the first three months of this year, and for an increase of prices. These are the means this combination uses to keep down wages—the price of men, and keep up the price of coal—the wages of capital." The gist of Lloyd's report was that big operators in nearly all trades were engaged in the same stampede to cut competition at the expense of the consumer, small operators, and laborers alike.

As for the courts, they seesawed back and forth in their position toward labor throughout the nineteenth century, but courts of the early 1890s applied anti-trust laws to organized labor as much as to corporate monopolies. At the turn of the century, workers could lay down their tools, shut off their machinery, and walk out, but persuading or stopping others from taking their place, even if it was done non-violently through speeches, leafleting, or picketing, was a criminal offense.

Some say that labor lost the war in the strikes of the late 1880s and early 1890s. In 1877 and 1886, two murder trials of labor activists showcased the enmity between labor and capital. After the second trial, however, I believe, industrial capitalists realized that force combined with legislation, rather than an open forum such as a criminal trial, was the most dependable means of subduing organized labor.

From the point of view of industrialists, the time was ripe. Skilled workers, who had led most earlier strikes, were caught in the bind of technologies that allowed management to hire less skilled, more easily replaced labor. "Vertical integration" within corporations meant that extractive industry, processors, the railroads, and banks could be owned by one conglomerate, cutting off smaller operators who might be alternative sources of employment. At the same time, some industry in the late 1880s was experiencing lower profitability, and managers could keep up their dividends to investors and salaries to corporate officers only by hiring fewer workers or paying them less. In 1889, Andrew Carnegie's workers at his Homestead plant worked twelve-hour days, seven days a week. At nine dollars per week, immigrants were making less than their former wages in Europe. Even after the strike that year, unions were forced to accept a sliding wage scale based on profits.

When the iron and steelworkers' union contract at Carnegie Steel came up for renewal in 1892, Carnegie departed for Scotland leaving his second-in-command, Henry Clay Frick, to lock out union workers and replace them with scabs, or non-union labor. Two days later, the union formally struck, picketing the plant. Before Frick could bring in non-union replacements, he had to provide for their protection from striking union members. Frick built a three-mile barrier around the factory equipped with barbed wire and slots for rifles. He hired three hundred Pinkertons specialized in strike breaking. The force boarded barges and set off down the Monongahela River with the plan of entering the plant in the dead of night.

But the strikers, armed with guns and dynamite, detected the Pinkertons' approach. The gun battle lasted most of the next day, and the outnumbered Pinkertons surrendered. Miners and their wives formed a gauntlet, forcing the Pinkertons to walk between the two long rows while unionists beat and taunted them. No one number has been accepted for casualties in the gun battle and beatings, with estimates ranging from about nine to twenty dead on both sides and several hundred wounded. Union members took over the plant. But less than a week later, the governor of Pennsylvania sent eight thousand state militiamen. They quickly occupied the plant, allowing strikebreakers to begin work.

Anarchist political naivete reappeared at this awkward moment, snatching defeat from the jaws of victory. Immigrant anarchists Emma Goldman and Alexander Berkman—previously uninvolved in the strike—decided to assassinate Henry Frick as an act of revenge. Berkman made his way to Frick's office in Homestead and fired a gun. Frick, though wounded, quickly subdued his attacker. By returning to work in bandages among great publicity the same day he was shot, Frick turned public opinion against the strike. It went on for another three months but finally ended as winter approached and morale sagged. The union never recovered, and workers accepted both lower pay and longer hours in order to be rehired.

Such were the beginnings of the labor wars. The Populist party had been formed in the previous year, 1891, and their candidate James B. Weaver ran a strong third in the Presidential race in 1892. In the next fifteen years, Americans came as close as they ever would to common cause among the working class, including tenant farmers, of all races and ethnicities. The financial panic and depression beginning in 1893 was like a trial run for the Great Depression of the 1930s, making a wider public aware of how easily one could become poor. But the events of 1893 and after also hardened the line between workers and bosses.

In May 1894, workers struck the Pullman Palace Car Company south of Chicago. Pullman had cut workers' wages an average of twenty-five percent, but he didn't lower already above-market rents on the company houses workers were forced to live in. When American Railway Union workers supported the strike in late June by refusing to handle Pullman cars, Chicago was paralyzed. But Pullman was adamant, and government went along. The U. S. Attorney General issued an injunction against strikers based on the Sherman Anti-Trust Act and Interstate Commerce Act.

The next day, President Grover Cleveland sent federal troops to the city—the first time troops had been sent against the wishes of a state's governor.

When some six thousand strikers saw the troops, they began building barricades and toppling railroad cars off their tracks. Meanwhile, because of the federal injunction, American Railway Union leaders couldn't communicate with strikers. Burning and pillaging over the next few days ended by consuming seven buildings of the World Columbian Exposition, destroying seven hundred boxcars, and causing six-figure damage to rail yards. Both strikers and troops used weapons, and twelve persons from both sides were shot and killed. Ultimately, one hundred thousand workers struck. One researcher estimates the workers lost wages totaling over $1.3 million.

The government brought in 1,936 federal troops, 4,000 national guardsmen, about 5,000 extra deputy marshals, 250 extra deputy sheriffs, and 3,000 Chicago policemen—in all, 14,186 armed officers and military. Seventy-one persons, including Eugene Debs and other A. R. U. leaders, were convicted under the federal indictment and given prison terms. The Pullman strikers never got their rent lowered.

Violent mine strikes of 1892 as far apart as Lattimer, Pennsylvania, and Coeur d'Alene, Idaho; an 1895 trolley strike and rioting in Brooklyn, New York—based on their experiences with management intransigence, workers were becoming radicalized at the same time that they were losing ground. Nor did they consistently hang together. Some locals of the Western Federation of Miners, formed in 1894, excluded Mexican-Americans and southern European immigrants. The W. F. M. used force almost from its origins. When a mine owner at Cripple Creek, Colorado, lengthened the work day without raising wages, W. F. M. members won the strike by administering beatings to non-union workers who wouldn't join them, and by dynamiting company property, until the company yielded. Strike violence led by the W. F. M. continued in both Idaho and Colorado—with federal troops occupying northern Idaho for eighteen months in 1898 and 1899—but the tide turned against the union when James Peabody was elected Colorado's governor in 1903. Peabody sent confrontational Adjutant General Sherman Bell of the militia to control the strikes. At this point, the repeated escalation of conflict through scabs, deputies, dynamitings, and militia could have been predicted. The bombing of a train platform in Independence, Colorado, killed thirteen strikebreakers and wounded more. Troops soon "deported" two hundred twenty-five union members and broke the union in Cripple Creek.

The ultimate disaster of the Colorado labor wars was the Ludlow massacre. National Guard troops, their salary paid by the Rockefellers, mowed down not only miners but thirteen of their wives and children. The intransigent attitude of John D. Rockefeller, Jr., was a main driver leading to the Ludlow killings. Since Rockefeller and many like him escaped unpunished—were in fact rewarded—for their irresponsibility, it shouldn't be surprising to anyone that big business in our own time shows contempt for civil rights and the law. At an early date, the government enforced the boundless authority of employers by appointing them executioners.

In 1913, management of the Rockefellers' Colorado Fuel and Iron Company expected a strike. The company used the Baldwin-Felts detective agency to recruit three hundred forty-eight operatives. The county sheriff cooperatively "deputized" the entire force so that they could intimidate and coerce in town as well on company property. The mining company also shipped weapons months in advance of the strike. As a first move, two Baldwin-Felts agents gunned down a union organizer on the streets of the town of Trinidad. Three months later, miners killed one of the killers near the same spot where the organizer had died.

As the strike began, Rockefeller testified before the House Committee on Mines and Mining that, in effect, he would rather lose all his property and kill all his workers than "allow outside people to come in and interfere with employees who are thoroughly satisfied with their labor conditions."

Maybe Rockefeller was referring to the three hundred detectives he had hired. As for mine workers, they lived among company spies, company property, and the company store in the smothering atmosphere of the company town of Ludlow. "Outsiders," including both tradespeople and unauthorized workers, weren't allowed in town. Workers could be paid in scrip redeemable only at the company store. Anyone who joined a union could be fired. The company paid the town marshal and controlled the sheriff, who in turn chose jurors who sat on labor-management disputes. Owing to mine fatalities, Colorado's death rate in the 1910 U. S. census was twice that of the nation as a whole. Safety measures were minimal and fatal mine accidents frequent. With county government in the company's pocket, the coroner almost never assigned liability for miners' deaths to management practices.

Everyone was armed and, even outside the immediate cause of the strike, the air of the county was saturated with violence. In 1913 Baldwin-Felts detectives attacked the strikers' tent camps in Ludlow and Forbes with an armored car equipped with a machine gun. Five persons were killed in the month of October—a total of ten, including casualties on both sides, during the year. National Guardsmen made it possible to bring in strikebreakers. But, as the strike wore on into 1914, the home guard began to be replaced with a mix of company guards, company employees, and Baldwin-Felts men. In this chaotic atmosphere, at nine A.M. on the day after Orthodox Easter in 1914, the Colorado National Guard, or what passed for it, began a barrage of machine-gun fire on the Ludlow tent colony. Previous attacks had led the strikers to build covered pits inside their tents where women and children could hide, but the colony was caught unawares. The strikers, firing back with rifles, ran out of ammunition at about four-thirty P.M. According to one source, at the end of the day, five strikers, including Greek-American organizer Louis Tikas and one eleven year old boy, were dead. Other sources say there were more. One guardsman was also dead.

Guardsmen entered the colony at dusk, looted the tents of their few valuables such as musical instruments, and burned the colony to the ground. Only the next day did a telephone lineman uncover one of the safety pits to discover that two women and eleven children had burned to death. The mother of two of the dead children, who regained consciousness and escaped to Trinidad, was the only survivor of the pit. A state of near war in the county, as miners retaliated, was soon quelled by federal troops. Rockefeller's Colorado Fuel and Iron Company still refused to recognize the union.

Four months later, a county grand jury indicted over three hundred thirty miners for homicide. No "sheriff's deputies," and only two company guards, were indicted. All indictments were dismissed except those against two union organizers, who were convicted of first-degree murder. Appeals testimony before the Colorado Supreme Court revealed, among many other irregularities, that a juror had placed a bet on an outcome of guilty. Beforehand, this juror had stated that he would bring about "either a hung jury, or a hung D**o," using an epithet for the Italian-American defendant.

—————————

The avalanche of incidents, anecdotes, and numbers washes over me as I read the history of the labor wars. They went on and on—as late as August 8, 1953, the *New York Times* reported a United Mine Workers organizer shot dead and another paralyzed in ongoing coal-mining violence in non-union Hayden, Kentucky. The first law giving federal legal rights to labor unions was the Wagner Act of 1935, enacted in the depths of the Depression after—but probably not in response to—the deaths of forty strikers in 1934. The law established the National Labor Relations Board, enforced unions' collective bargaining powers, and prohibited hiring and firing that discriminated against union members. This unusual move on the government's part was later somewhat abridged, but over the next several decades it did lead to a dwindling of labor violence.

But I see two other elements of labor violence haven't been much noticed in the record. They stand out to me now as I read it over.

First is the all-pervading use of "citizens' committees" in labor strikes. During the San Francisco dock workers' strike of 1934, for instance, the police department consented to the formation of the American Legion's Anti-Red Committee and other vigilante groups. Similar committees are casually mentioned in other accounts dating all the way back to the Mollie Maguires in the 1870s.

Second is the link of labor violence to lynchings of ethnically identifiable persons. During the 1890s in two Colorado towns, mobs lynched seven Italians. Another four were hanged less than ten years later. "Four Italians"—all that the NAACP's published record shows— were hanged in Washington state in 1892. The NAACP record, though incomplete, is the only nationally compiled record I know of. It shows that at least thirty-eight persons of Italian surname were lynched in three Western states (four incidents), three Northeastern states (three incidents), five Southern states (seven incidents), and Texas (one incident) in the twenty-six years between 1889 and 1916.

For decades, management hired immigrant strikebreakers and deliberately mixed ethnic groups on work sites. These practices played on workers' terror of job loss and physical harm as well as their desire to rise in the American society they had more or less recently joined. Nonstop throughout the era, newspapers titillated and terrified the citizenry with tales of conspiracy by foreign anarchists, socialists, and communists. Following the Irish and Germans, African-Americans, Asian-Americans, and the newer, more "different" European immigrants all fell victim to this routine. To a greater or lesser extent, they played it on each other. The customs of each new set of citizens were contemptible in the eyes of older arrivals, and immigrant labor posed an economic threat; but beyond these issues was the deadly insult to the social status of American labor that each new arrival represented. The corporations, as one newspaper put it, sought "to degrade native labor by the introduction of a class who, in following the customs of their ancestors, live more like brutes than human beings." Working-class Pennsylvanians, like working-class Southerners, were quick to feel their insecurity within the social order when bracketed with those they felt were beneath them; and they responded with violence against the newcomers. American corporate employers didn't begin to exhibit similar hostility until they realized that immigrant labor, far from being docile, was more than capable of organized resistance.

The labor movement has pretty well died over the last three decades. It survives organizationally as the AFL-CIO and other unions, but organized labor achieved real bargaining clout only for the brief years from 1935 to about 1970. Labor's greatest allies were government support and the existence of jobs that couldn't be moved from one geographical location to another. But I sometimes wonder whether most Americans, in our hearts, haven't sided with Goliath since long before the union slump. Even in the 1930s, some small farmers in Oklahoma, Texas, and other states, cleaned out by the Dust Bowl and driven out by the bankers who held their mortgages, moved to California and all lived happily ever after.

No—they didn't really all live happily ever after. Only a few weeks ago the *New York Times* Sunday magazine reported on a California descendant of Dust Bowl migrants who lost her house to unemployment. But still the dream lives on: *Any day now, I'll be just as rich as you.*

I used to think that the United States never had the kind of working-class culture found in some European nations because few Americans have ever believed they'd remain all their lives in the working class. Now I think we were terrified of remaining in the working class. Even skilled workers, who began as semi-independent producers, saw their security and autonomy stripped away as corporations converted to factory-style production. As early as the 1870s, Welsh or English miners who hired the Irish as car-loaders could expect to be replaced by those same Irish, who in turn were replaced by the next arrivals. Last of all came African-Americans.

World without end. No more than any creature trying to survive did these human beings want to stand out as different. To be "foreign" was to be the lowest paid and first fired, worked under the most abusive and dangerous conditions, unsure of both daily bread and safety from personal or collective violence. Among other ways workers found to beat each other out, literally, were homicide and lynching. Corporate management set the example by resorting to vigilantism— and local governments systematically promoted so-called citizens' committees.

And that was before the workers got to court. "Different" Americans were subject to blatant discrimination and open injustice in legal trials of the labor era, as prosecutors obtained what I would call "vigilante convictions." But more subtle forms of railroading—of unpopular and unprotected citizens such as persons of color and unappealing, indigent, small-time law breakers or "nuisance felons"—appear still to survive in the handling of prosecutions today, including current capital cases like those in Illinois.

The history of labor violence illuminates processes that still make bias in convictions possible. How do we pinpoint the moment when prejudice becomes discrimination? Both in and out of court, certain Americans go on being guilty until proven innocent.

Supporters of the Haymarket rioters wore lapel pins after the execution.

12

"Death and Destruction to the System"
Labor On Trial

On January 11, 2003, Governor George Ryan of Illinois emptied the state's death row.

Ryan commuted the death sentences of 167 inmates. Four were pardoned, three received long prison sentences, and the remaining number were sentenced to life in prison without parole.

Ryan described capital punishment as administered today "one of the great civil rights struggles of our time." News writers and commentators called Ryan's action unprecedented. Perhaps reporters' comments referred to the large number of condemned persons affected—the largest number I know of historically. But gubernatorial clemency follows an American tradition—principled personal judgments that governors have made in order to take the underrepresented side of argument in a pressing public issue. In Illinois it goes back over a century to the era of labor-management conflict and Progressive politics. One hundred twenty years ago, no issue was more pressing than the rights of Labor versus the rights of Capital, and the issue played a formative role in how the death penalty was used. Within ten years of each other, two local governments largely supported by industrial capitalists mounted highly visible criminal trials. The two murder trials were aimed at least in part at discrediting labor. On inconclusive evidence, the Molly Mcguires (Pennsylvania, 1877) and the Haymarket rioters (Chicago, 1887), two groups of labor activists accused of murder, were convicted and hanged essentially for pro-labor activities rather than the crimes of which they stood accused. Only in the

Haymarket case, and only after five of the defendants had died, would labor find a defender in another governor of Illinois.

The Molly Maguires were supposed to be members of a secret Irish terrorist group called the Ancient Order of Hibernians who, in Pennsylvania, were also coal miners and members of the miners' union. It's unclear how much violence the Mollies perpetrated because so much of the record was written by partisans of mining and railroad industrialists. Franklin Gowen, a former district attorney who became acting president of the Philadelphia and Reading Railroad, aggressively pursued a monopoly on coal transportation that indirectly controlled the price of coal by fixing its shipping cost. Gowen also bought up to eighty-five percent of coal properties in several Pennsylvania counties.

Gowen saw his labor force as another problem to be fixed. In 1871 testimony before the state legislature, he began to raise the specter of Molly Maguire terrorism. "Conspiracy rests on the other side," one union representative retorted. But, two years later, Gowen signed his first contract with the Pinkerton Detective Agency to infiltrate the company coal towns and inform on the Mollies.

The first Pinkerton agent was unable even to document the Mollies' existence. But the second agent was the famous, or notorious, James McParlan, who even found his way into a Sherlock Holmes story based on the Mollies case. McParlan created an elaborate false identity as James McKenna and moved among the coal towns for the next three years. Twenty labor activists were accused of conspiracy in the murders of ten persons including a mine operator, managers, white-collar mine employees, a mine guard, a miner, and a policeman. Two of the murders had taken place about fourteen years previously and several took place during a riot. One of the Mollies turned state's evidence to avoid execution; otherwise, McParlan's reports were almost the sole evidence used in the arrest and trial. In a development that I hope seems strange to us now, ex-railroad-president Gowen served as prosecutor.

As a recent commentator pointed out, "A private corporation initiated the investigation through a private detective agency. A private police force arrested the alleged defenders, and private attorneys for the coal companies prosecuted them. The state provided only the courtroom and the gallows." All of the defendants were convicted. Nine were hanged.

"Foreign population easily aroused against the Rich," journalist Joel Headley noted in the chapter summary of his book on riots in the year the Mollies were executed. "This is what has made, and still makes, the foreign population among us so dangerous." The ingenuous Headley went on to comment that "mobs" shouldn't be viewed as American citizens, but as felons and murderers. Headley's view was widely shared (at least by journalists, the rich, and the would-be rich) after the one-sided trial of the Mollies dominated headlines around the country. An account written almost twenty years later described the reduction of wages leading to labor unrest as a "trivial reason." The writer claimed that the Mollies were "bands of armed assassins, defying alike the laws of man and God, and leaving behind them everywhere curses, and tears, and blood," who "committed murders by the score, stupidly, brutally, as a driven ox turns to left or right at the word of command, without knowing why, and without caring."

Propaganda depicting Irish-American Catholics as robotic followers of Rome kept high visibility throughout most of the nineteenth century, and persisted as late as John Kennedy's successful campaign for president of the United States in 1960. During the Molly Maguire scare of the 1870s, the archbishop of Philadelphia had tried to distance the Roman Catholic church by declaring automatic excommunication for anyone known to be a Molly Maguire, and the hanged men weren't allowed a Catholic burial. But their Irish Catholicism was prominent in their public identity as assassins. After the execution of the Mollies, American fear of foreigners and of lawlessness turned next to self-declared anarchist violence.

If we could time-travel back to the 1880s, either in America or in Europe, I think we'd easily recognize the national mood. Terrorism was in the air, and nobody was sure who the enemy was. Tensions went over the top when Tsar Alexander of Russia was killed by an anarchist's bomb in 1881.

Dating back to the 1830s, anarchist thought was driven by resistance to the rise of industrial capitalist power. Anarchist practitioners made up a broad river of humanity including pacifist vegetarians and founders of utopian colonies, naive or disaffected painters, poets, songwriters, and other artists, paid and amateur political assassins, and labor organizers—some violent and some not.

From labor's perspective, it could be unfortunate that they really weren't as well organized as their more paranoid critics claimed to believe. When violence broke out, the press and government leaders were quick to brand nearly everyone who voiced political questions a threat—a conspirator in an overarching world anarchist plot. Management and government used violence with impunity, but its use by strikers almost always alienated public opinion—or so it was said. Equally possible was that newspapers, supported by business advertising and investment, led public opinion as much as they served as "the public's" self-appointed representatives. Unions that succeeded in the long run were those who flew beneath the radar of implacable employer-sponsored opposition. Unlike many unions in European labor movements, long-lived American unions stuck to job-related demands, represented mostly skilled labor, didn't seek political party identity, and fought only the battles that could be won in the newspapers.

In the 1870s workers had begun to stage large, highly publicized strikes, and some labor activists embraced anarchist positions. Anarchist trade unionists formally organized in the United States at a meeting in Philadelphia in 1883, and editor Albert Parsons soon publicized their cause in his newspaper *Chicago Alarm*. Parsons questioned why laborers had to work ten and twelve hour days, with months-long layoffs at the employers' convenience, in order to make barely enough to live on. But he also advocated that workers learn to make and use dynamite, and he engaged in an inflammatory rhetoric of "death and destruction to the system and its upholders, which plunders and enslaves." Labor's main demand in these years was for a shorter working day—which had been legislated as early as 1867 in Illinois, then in other states, but was ignored by employers everywhere. Strikes continued intensively during the early 1880s, culminating in the Chicago May Day, or May first, strike of 1886.

On May third, police killed two unarmed strikers at the McCormick Reaper plant. The next night, protestors held a public meeting to denounce the killing. Toward the end of the protest, 180 police officers marched to the meeting place, which was Haymarket Square, near the Chicago city hall. The officers massed in formation in front of the protestors' impromptu speakers' stand. As soon as the police commander ordered the crowd to disperse, someone threw a bomb.

One officer died instantly, six died later of their wounds from the bombing or from gunfire during the riot that followed. An unknown number of those gathered for the meeting also were shot. No one ever discovered the bomb-thrower's identity.

Police arrested several dozen political radicals including Albert Parsons. Eight of those whom the grand jury indicted—all German-Americans except for Parsons—were brought to trial. The charge was murder, but the only evidence presented was of radical beliefs and speech; the argument made was that the defendants incited, not committed, the act of bombing.

The trial that began on June 21, 1886, generated thousands of pages of transcript, and ended in conviction of all defendants. One received a fifteen-year sentence; the others, including Parsons, were sentenced to death.

Human rights activists and others from around the world called for clemency, but the U. S. Supreme Court denied a final appeal on

November 2, 1887. Two prisoners had their death sentences commuted to prison terms. On the day before the execution, one defendant managed to kill himself by lighting a blasting cap in his mouth. Four other defendants, including Albert Parsons, died next day before an invited audience on the gallows inside Cook County Jail.

Before and during the trial, members of the public could justifiably have felt that the future of the American social order was about to be decided. All parties to the trial, from the defendants to the judge, to the mayor of Chicago who testified for the defense, seemed to take for granted the borderline legality of the Haymarket trial proceedings. Most who participated treated the occasion as a battle between two philosophical and moral opponents, Labor and Capital. Whose version of the story of justice would win? As many as could squeeze into the courtroom attended the months of trial. Newspapers nationwide as well as abroad incessantly covered the proceedings. The defendants lost in court, but not before they and their supporting witnesses and media representatives, as much as the prosecution, used the minutely recorded spectacle of the trial as a chance to speak out. The trial may have been the first time that radical American labor activists voiced their ideas in the hearing of a mainstream audience. After the execution, between 150,000 and 500,000 witnessed the funeral procession of the five dead anarchists.

But the story still hadn't ended. In 1893, Illinois governor John Peter Altgeld pardoned the three convicted defendants who remained in prison.

"Controversial" isn't a strong enough word for public reaction to Altgeld's move. The *New York Times* called him a closet anarchist. The *Washington Post* pointed out that Altgeld, a German immigrant, was an "alien." The *Chicago Tribune* accused him of not reasoning like an American.

Others in the Chicago business community, which had pushed so hard for the anarchists' conviction through the mouthpiece of the *Tribune*, began to doubt the defendants' guilt. These and other prominent persons, like attorney Clarence Darrow, encouraged Altgeld to issue the pardons. When they came, they were more than a simple declaration of executive clemency. Altgeld analyzed the trial transcripts in detail to show that the judge was biased, jury selection was rigged—even allowing friends of the dead policemen onto the jury—and reputable individuals believed the main prosecution witness was a notorious liar. In spite of the nearly deafening opposition of Altgeld's detractors, his searching examination of the trial drew a picture of justice perverted by money and power. The picture was disturbing to many.

Republican governor Ryan defended his commutations on the grounds that Illinois's system is arbitrary and capricious. Three years earlier, Ryan called a moratorium on the state's death penalty after he signed a death warrant for one prisoner who was later shown to be innocent of the crime. Ryan then appointed a two-party commission to study the death penalty and recommend corrections. Of the commission's eighty-five recommendations, the Illinois legislature did not accept even one.

Similar scruples have moved other governors. But, like Governor Ryan, most were at the end of their term when they acted. In 1986, New Mexico's governor, Toney Anaya, also cleared death row—not a top story because "only" five inmates were on the row. Arkansas's governor, Winthrop Rockefeller, commuted the sentences of all fifteen on death row in 1970. Among convicted murders in just one of sixty-four Louisiana parishes, or counties, Louisiana governors commuted three death sentences between 1971 and 1995. Actually, both governors and presidents of the United States have pardoned condemned prisoners and commuted sentences of death throughout much of American history. Maine laws of the 1800s called on governors personally, and at their discretion, to order the execution of those condemned to death. After World War I, President Woodrow Wilson pardoned one convicted murderer in the Alaskan Territory and commuted the sentence of another—who had murdered two persons, including a U. S. marshal—to life imprisonment. These examples could easily be multiplied.

Some states' laws, such as those of Oklahoma, permit a governor to grant even conditional or partial pardons only on recommendation of the state's pardons board. But the system in Illinois law and that of other states draws on the concept of Alexander Hamilton, first expressed in print in 1788 in *The Federalist #74*. The highest executive officer, Hamilton wrote, should be given free rein in pardoning offenders in order to counterbalance the "necessary severity" of laws and their application as decided by legislative bodies and courts. If not for pardons, Hamilton felt, "justice would wear a countenance too sanguinary and cruel." Hamilton applied this element of checks and balances to the federal system, but some states also operate similarly.

In Alexander Hamilton's thinking, the legal system and the legislative system were only parts of something larger—the government as a whole. Hamilton wanted to design a process that would get to a result that could be called justice. I don't think he would agree with those recent commentators who went so far as to label Governor Ryan's recent action an abuse of the legal system. Hamilton assumed that government officials would be self-interested and partisan, but he set out to distribute power so that more than one interest would necessarily contribute to a given decision. In this way, it wasn't as likely that all of those in power would have the same interests. Hamilton and other shapers of our system—who didn't have faith in the law to automate decision making—might not agree with today's voters and lawmakers who support mandatory sentencing and voter referendums.

After the Haymarket bombing case, the next high-visibility trial of a labor activist didn't take place for another twenty years. The defendants were leaders of the Western Federation of Miners. William "Big Bill" Haywood, Charles Moyer, and George Pettibone were indicted in Idaho in 1907 for arranging the murder of ex-governor Frank Steunenberg. Steunenberg had been elected as a Populist and union supporter, but earned the union's enmity by calling for federal troops during one of a series of violent silver mine strikes in Coeur d'Alene.

As in the trial of the Molly Maguires, the prosecution of Haywood pitted labor activists against the Pinkerton Detective Agency. First to be arrested was one Harry Orchard, after bomb-making materials were found among his belongings in a hotel room. James McParlan (now MacParland, and head of Pinkerton's western operations) spent day after day in jail with Orchard, interrogating him for the names of ringleaders and hinting that a confession might save Orchard from the gallows. Ten days later, Orchard had confessed not only to Steunenberg's murder, but to several previous dynamitings and murder attempts on mine proprietors and government officials. Orchard claimed he committed all of these crimes at the behest of mining-union leaders, especially Haywood, and in fear of his own life if he didn't obey them. In his summation, lead prosecutor William Borah, soon to be a senator, attacked Hayward through the Union of Western Miners, saying that he "saw anarchy wave its first bloody triumph in Idaho."

On the defense side, paid for by organized labor, was Clarence Darrow. Darrow reminded the jurors that the world was watching: "If you kill him," said Darrow, "your act will be applauded by many. Where men hate Haywood because he fights for the poor and against the accursed system upon which the favored live and grow rich and fat." After more than twelve hours of jury deliberation, Haywood was found not guilty. Moyer was later acquitted as well, and prosecutors then dropped charges against Pettibone. Harry Orchard was first sentenced to death, but had his sentence commuted by the governor to life in prison, where he lived on until 1954.

The defense in the Steunenberg murder trial presented it as a face-off between Labor and Capital. But in spite of Darrow's rhetoric, the trial broke no new moral high ground. The Haymarket defendants of 1886 were politically naive grass-roots philosophers. Their judge, serene in the support of the establishment and in his own belief that the rich deserved every consideration, had openly and with tremendous public support steered the trial to a verdict of guilty. Twenty years later, defendant Haywood was a man of impressive personal character and sincere political convictions. But he, Moyers, and Pettibone, far from being idealistic amateurs, were career union organizers. On the other side, the murdered Steunenberg and prosecutor William Borah alike had profited by association with mining corporations. Some continued to believe in the labor leaders' guilt, and reputable journalist J. Anthony Lukas recently presented what he saw as damning new evidence. But the most that observers on either side of the trial of Haywood could allege following the trial was that one faction or the other had bribed or threatened the jury. The trial was closer to being an in-house labor versus management quarrel than a struggle between causes.

In reality, by 1906 the unions had lost the war, and the courtroom was no longer the crucial battlefront it had been. Haywood's later career in some ways paralleled that of the labor movement itself. Haywood and Moyers were soon to disagree over the direction of the Western Federation of Miners. Haywood, driven out by Moyers, rose to leadership of the International Workers of the World during that radical union's last good years. Haywood was a spectacularly effective recruiter and powerful strike leader. But, in 1918, the U. S. Department of Justice raided records of the I. W. W. nationwide and prosecuted its leaders. Haywood was convicted under an espionage and sedition act of calling a strike during World War I. After serving a year in Leavenworth, Haywood was released on appeal. He jumped bond and escaped to Moscow, where he lived until his death in 1928. With the help of the U. S. government, he had lost his last courtroom battle.

As for Illinois's Governor Ryan, maybe he thought that life without parole in a five-by-twelve-foot cell with another convicted felon was a lesser punishment than death, even though many death-penalty opponents in the past have disagreed with this perspective. More likely, Ryan responded to the discovery by Northwestern University

journalism students that fourteen of twenty-seven on death row simply *did not commit the crime they were condemned for.* In his view, each
death warrant he signed had become another potential mistake that
couldn't ever be repaired, even partially.

HEADQUARTERS SOUTHERN INDIANA,
VIGILANCE COMMITTEE.
TO THE PEOPLE OF THE UNITED STATES!

"SALUS POPULI SUPREMA LEX."

WHEREAS, it became necessary for this organization to meet out summary punishment to the leaders of the thieves, robbers, murderers and desperadoes, who for many years defied law and order, and threatened the lives and property of honest citizens of this portion of Indiana, and as the late fearful tragedy at New Albany testifies that justice is slow, but sure, we promulgate this our pronunciamento, for the purpose of justifying to the world, and particularly to the people of the State of Indiana, any future action which we may take.

We deeply deplore the necessity which called our organization into existence; but the laws of our State are so defective that as they now stand on the Statute Books, they all favor criminals going unwhipt of justice; a retrospective view will show that in this respect we speak only the truth.

Having first lopped off the branches, and finally uprooted the tree of evil which was in our midst, in defiance of us and our laws, we beg to be allowed to rest here, and be not forced again to take the law into our own hands. We are very loth to shed blood again, and will not do so unless compelled in defence of our lives.

A WARNING,

We are well aware that at the present time, a combination of the few remaining thieves, their friends and sympathizers, has been formed against us, and have threatened all kinds of vengeance against persons whom they suppose to belong to this organization. They threaten assassination in every form, and that they will commit arson in such ways as will defy legal detection. The carrying out in whole, or in part, of each or any of these designs, is the only thing that will again cause us to rise in our own defence. The following named persons are solemnly warned, that their designs and opinions are known, and that they cannot, unknown to us, make a move toward retaliation.

Wilk Reno, Clinton Reno, Trick Reno, James Greer, Stephen Greer, Fee Johnson, Chris. Price, Harvey Needham, Meade Fislar, Mart Lowe, Roland Lee, William Sparks, Jesse Thompson, William Hare, William Biggers, James Fislar, Pollard Able.

If the above named individuals desire to remain in our midst, to pursue honest callings, and otherwise conduct themselves as law abiding citizens, we will protect them always.— If however, they commence their devilish designs against us, our property, or any good citizen of this district, we will rise but *once* more ; do not trifle with us ; for if you do, we will follow you to the bitter end; and give you a "short shrift and a hempen collar." As to this, our actions in the past, will be a guarantee for our conduct in the future.

We trust this will have a good effect. We repeat, we are very loth to take life, and hope we shall never more be necessitated to take the law into our own hands.

By order of the Committee.

Dec. 21, 1868.

Indiana vigilantes justified themselves through handbills posted in towns.

13

White on White Terrorism
After the Civil War

The following notice appeared in the weekly *Corydon (Indiana) Cricket* on August 10, 1878:

> A married man of this place is in the habit of accompanying a young lady, unmarried, home from church, leaving his wife to take care of herself. There is something wrong. *No more of it, please.*

In the tightly bounded world of southern Indiana in the 1870s, the behavior described could easily bring on a visit from the local vigilantes. Between 1874 and 1893, area newspapers and other sources reported on some seventy-six incidents of vigilante terrorism in Harrison County, where Corydon was located, and neighboring Crawford County. It seems that while corporate vigilantes were pursuing coal miners in Pennsylvania, another kind of regulator gang was "vigilant" over the moral customs of small Indiana towns, where the overwhelming majority of residents were white Protestants. The local "White Caps," or whitecaps, punished their own, warning and whipping area residents for offenses such as:

- "obnoxious and vicious character"
- "indisposition to work"
- "selling whiskey and whoring around"
- "general worthlessness"

- "deserted wife and four children; took up with young, unmarried woman" (a different case than the one reported in the *Cricket*)
- "failure to support elderly mother"
- "her life not what it should be"
- "found in bed together"
- "did not keep a clean house"
- "keeping bad company"
- "drunkenness"
- "did not earn his living by the sweat of his face."

Reading these offenses gives me a peculiar feeling—a combination of satisfaction and apprehensiveness. Annoyed by your neighbor's loud music or her dog running loose? Get out your bed sheet and your whip, get your friends and their horses together, make a midnight visit! How often wouldn't I like to see a member of my community brought to book for an obnoxious act that the law doesn't seem to touch? On the other hand, I'm not sure what my neighbors think about me, either. If someone had been observing my behavior at certain less than ideal moments, might I have found myself hauled out of bed in my nightclothes, bewildered and defenseless before a committee of armed men wearing disguises?

It's even less funny when I read that Indiana whitecappers' beatings crippled one of their victims for life, blinded another in one eye, and at the mildest left wounds that took weeks or months to heal. One victim, showing a neighbor the extent of his injuries, was able to embed his little finger in a gash the whip had made in his leg.

Some of these incidents sound like the beating of Matthew Shepherd, an allegedly gay man in Laramie, Wyoming, in 1998. Only two persons were convicted of leaving the unconscious Shepherd to freeze outdoors overnight and die of head wounds five days later in a hospital. If Shepherd's death had been carried out by a larger number of persons, and the community was known to support the act, it would have been a whitecapping. Still, Shepherd's death has an uncomfortable similarity to whitecappers' "morals beatings" because the murderers apparently targeted their victim as a gay man. As media made the case a symbol of intolerance, Christian fundamentalists picketed the trial of Shepherd's accused attackers and also his funeral.

Indiana whitecapping along with a few other white-on-white terrorist movements, such as the Bald Knobbers of highland Missouri, became nationally known in the 1880s when the *New York Times* began reporting incidents. White-on-white terrorism eventually lost local support and was successfully prosecuted in the courts. But Indiana whitecaps did what vigilantes on the western frontier and the first Ku Klux Klan did not. Whatever the reality of their motives, the whitecaps staked a claim to morality so compelling that it justified extralegal punishment—warnings, beatings, and sometimes murder. In doing so, the whitecaps used and perpetuated Klan tactics of secrecy, tight organization, and night riding, and kept the Klan's name alive among the public. Above all, the whitecap legacy was one of validation for the use of force to implement the moral perspective of one group.

On the face of it, whitecapping episodes resembled those shivarees that sometimes got out of hand. It would seem that these community-based vigilantes couldn't be more different than the imported goon squads who threatened and beat union organizers and strikers. Nor did the whitecaps bring about a political takeover as the San Francisco vigilantes did. Rather, whitecappings were a rearguard action, expressed in coercion of individuals, against change taking place from without.

One whitecap letter delivered in Harrison County warned an African-American man to take his children out of the white school and place them in the African-American school. Around the same time, whitecappers beat another African-American for "insolence" on the rumor that he was living with a white woman. Had more African-Americans lived in the area, they might have been the target of more incidents. But their alleged offenses, too, fell into a sphere that could loosely be called breaches of proper conduct rather than the alleged rapes and murders that blacks elsewhere were accused of and lynched for. By far the majority of whitecap incidents were white on white.

Rural Indianians weren't that different from the colonial Puritans who monitored their neighbors with more enthusiasm than Christian charity. Residents of southern Indiana, like most other Appalachian or highland southern people, shared the religious piety of early New Englanders. Unlike the Puritans, though, most highland southerners freely turned to extralegal intimidation to settle their differences. Many Appalachian dwellers' heritage before coming to America was life on the remote Scottish-English border, where government was an outside force mainly associated with paying taxes.

These American highlanders didn't use wealth or education as measures of social status, much less signs of divine favor. Perhaps because of their inability or unwillingness to pay taxes, the illiteracy rate of Kentucky highlanders tripled between 1840 and 1870. Lacking the economic resources of extensive trade or manufacturing, most highlanders lived by subsistence farming. The result was an unusually egalitarian society whose members were prone to feud and who professed to judge themselves and their neighbors—sometimes very narrowly—on behavior alone.

However, just as in Salem during the witch trials, punishable offenses lay in the eye of the beholder. Charges of immorality easily stretched to cover grudges or gain the advantage in a feud. Epidemics of Appalachian vigilantism seemed to coincide with disruptive events and public issues at least as much as with the rate of immoral behavior.

Some vigilante "regulation of morals" and extralegal punishment of alleged lawbreaking took place in southern Indiana between 1854 and 1857, at a time when southern Indiana was a stop on the Underground Railroad, on the one hand, and a stronghold for Copperheads, or Southern sympathizers, on the other. The tensions were already there; the Civil War provided the military training to both Union and Confederate factions. During the war, southern Indiana suffered anti-draft riots, Confederate raids, a battle with the forces of General John Morgan in Corydon, and at least one murder of a citizen.

Ironically, though, the prosperity that came to America after the war may have caused more malaise and factional bitterness in closed societies like that of southern Indiana than the Civil War did. With wide-region trade, a money-based economy, and growing oversight from state governments, communities like Corydon found themselves at a disadvantage. The railroad came later to south than north, leaving the southern counties without a competitive trade connection until 1882. Southern Indiana counties lost population or grew more slowly in the 1870s than central and northern counties, and between 1880 and 1890 the value of farms in the southern counties declined. At the same time, the increasingly powerful state of Indiana exacted taxes for more and more roads, bridges, and other public improvements. The farmers, to whom "a dollar looked as big as a barn door," were forced into the market economy for which they were so ill prepared. Within the community, old residents who had always been able to hold their heads up found themselves mortgaged to the hilt, badgered, and sometimes cheated by a growing variety of public officials. Moreover, state government initiatives like the standard school curriculum attacked the community's sense of autonomy and forced local residents to see themselves in a critical light.

The seventy-six vigilante incidents in Harrison and Crawford counties during these twenty years of economic and political restructuring far exceeded past levels of activity that are known. Hatred of the railroad, as an agent of change, was one trigger. In one of the first vigilante incidents Hall Golden, an attorney, was harassed after he represented the railroad in tax cases against communities along the railroad line. Golden slept in the woods each night to avoid being visited by the whitecaps, but eventually died from tuberculosis aggravated by exposure.

At least some of the incidents involved money and personal disputes, for example, when Henry Long was fatally shot in a courtroom gun battle during his trial for allegedly murdering a local man, Chris Dincklocker. Long's troubles, almost too involved and lengthy to describe, began when he advised Joanna Dincklocker of her property rights while she was divorcing Chris.

Sally Tipton, pregnant out of wedlock, brought a paternity suit against the alleged father. According to Tipton, the father, Cornelius Grabill, was one of the whitecaps in the band who later came to her house to whip her for bearing an illegitimate child.

It's telling that whitecapping decreased in Harrison County as the county's economy improved. But Crawford County, which continued to see bad times, hosted ongoing terrorism as well. After 1890 the Crawford whitecaps became involved in electoral politics as reformers by violence. The county's high annual number of whitecapping incidents began to fall only after a state-level investigation. When cases were brought to court, convictions could not be secured at first because the community supported the whitecappers. But opinion changed as the whitecappers became organized over a wider area and resorted to more and more intimidation to escape legal charges.

In the last incident in Crawford County, a whitecap force of forty confronted two intended victims, farm laborers Bill and Sam Conrad. When Edward Conrad was found murdered, nearly everyone in the county believed that the Conrad sons had murdered their father—because they had physically abused him in the past. But their mother confirmed their alibis, and a grand jury dismissed the charges. Whitecaps and their sympathizers tried to drive the widowed mother, her daughter, and her sons from their isolated land holding at "Conrad Hollow." But Bill and Sam Conrad loaded their shotguns and waited, night after night, for the expected attack of the whitecaps. When the whitecaps arrived, masked men began by dragging mother and sister from the house and threatening to throw the mother in a cistern if she didn't reveal the sons' whereabouts. Unluckily for the whitecaps, they chose to light this scene of intimidation with a lantern. Using the flame as a target, the Conrad brothers, hidden in a corn patch, opened fire with their shotguns. When they killed three whitecaps outright and injured an unknown number, the remains of the force fled pell-mell, leaving behind two others the Conrads had mortally wounded. At this point, the Conrads did pull up stakes, crossing the Ohio River to Kentucky in order to avoid murder charges.

Bad feeling continued in the county as residents took sides. Some still believed that Bill and Sam Conrad had murdered their father. Others waited for what they expected would be the third act—the Conrad brothers' return to take vengeance on their whitecap tormentors. But the truth came out only thirty years later, when the real murderer of Edward Conrad confessed on his death bed. The cause of the murder had been a quarrel ending in the murderer's fatally bludgeoning Conrad Senior with a wooden stave. But no conclusion followed—neither legal justice nor private vengeance.

The Conrad Hollow shootings took place in 1893. That was also the year when the Hatfield versus McCoy feud, across Kentucky at the West Virginia border, ended in the murder trial of eight Hatfields in Kentucky. One was condemned and publicly hanged, the other seven sentenced to life in prison. This outcome too contributed to ending an era of white on white terrorism. The so-called backwoods residents of Indiana, Kentucky, Missouri, and other quasi-Appalachian states found themselves supporting increasingly effective governments whose officers prosecuted them legally for private revenge. The last known Indiana whitecaps were brought to trial in Monroe County in 1912. In spite of the defendants' alibi, provided by supporters, a jury convicted two of the whitecaps after less than twenty-five minutes' deliberation.

Thanks partly to their own organizational powers, and partly to national press coverage, the Indiana whitecapping movement joined the dreaded name of Ku Klux Klan to the idea of punishment for offenses against moral custom. The idea of a connection between proper conduct and criminal offenses still lives in our society, as in former New York mayor Rudolph Giuliani's energetic prosecution of incivility as a strategy to discourage crime. Nor is the idea a new one. The Puritans subscribed to it, and it was part of the rhetoric of San Francisco vigilantism as well. The reverend Mr. T. Dwight Hunt reflected on morals offenses when he preached in San Francisco days after the Vigilance Committee of 1851 carried out their first execution. Hunt related the kind of disorder deserving of punishment by vigilante execution to seemingly milder but equally insidious offenses. Mr. Hunt preached that the citizens

> should, themselves, first set the example of abstinence from even the moderate forms of vice, and then, in a legitimate and determined way, unite in accomplishing needful public reforms. They should then put men into their city council, and on the bench, and into the police, who will discountenance, and put down, and shut up the grog-shops, and the drinking and gambling saloons that infest the city.

Mr. Hunt's influence remained local, and I don't know that his ideas caught hold in San Francisco for any length of time. But the Appalachian morality play started by the whitecaps continued to run, spread by migrants from countryside to town in the early 1900s. It was presented to a middle-class audience nationwide as the second Ku Klux Klan. When the whitecaps first began operations in Crawford and Harrison counties circa 1872 or 1873, they were structured as a fraternal organization called "Knights of the Switch." This name remained as late as 1881, but newspapers also referred to the organization as "vigilantes," "whip-ups," "regulators," or "Ku Klux."

According to a newspaper account, at least one Crawford County group also signed their own threatening letters "K.K.K." Incarnations of the Klan over time may not have been connected by personal or historical ties, organizational structure, or specific issues, but again and again they were able to kindle support. To this end they called on a fear-inciting name, a sense of frustrated entitlement, and the Klan-inspired backcloth image of white-masked horsemen on their nocturnal missions of "redress."

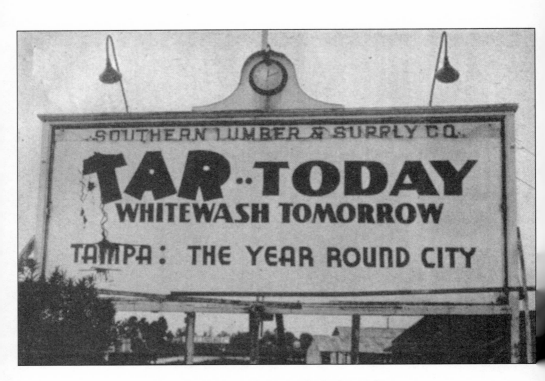

Merchants protested unpunished Klan violence.

14

"Serving Your Racial Needs"
Colonel Simmons's Ku Klux Klan

Some things to understand about the second Ku Klux Klan of 1915-1944: It spread and institutionalized the rhetoric of bigotry nationwide. It justified intimidation and violence against both minority groups and so-called morals offenders. It sometimes pushed labor conflict and community disputes to a deadly conclusion. It provided a continuity of image between the post-Civil War Klan of the 1860s and the "third" Klan that emerged during the 1950s-1960s Civil Rights era.

But, in fact, the second Ku Klux Klan had only an indirect connection to the post-Civil-War Klan. Unlike the Klan's other two incarnations, the second Klan was less about African-Americans, Jews, or Catholics than it was about white, middle-class Protestant entitlement. The second Klan was the creation of one man who hired a professional publicity team to popularize the organization—which they did with spectacular, if temporary, success.

Since things ended badly for the second Klan, the modern-day KKK refers to Confederate general Nathan Bedford Forrest as its founder. Today, the Alabama chapter's slogan, set in moving type at the bottom of their main web page reads: *Serving Your Racial Needs Since 1865.*

In 1915, however, William J. Simmons had a dream—to recreate the moribund, original Ku Klux Klan almost from scratch. Timing his actions to the Atlanta premier of *Birth of a Nation*, Simmons staged the opening ceremony of cross-burning on Stone Mountain, 16 miles from Atlanta. Simmons recruited two original Klan members and Georgia's speaker of the house of representatives to appear with him that night. So was born the second KKK.

Birth of a Nation was perfectly tailored to Simmons's message of white Protestant superiority. The film was an expanded, but near-literal, transcription of *The Clansman* (1905), a novel by North Carolinian Thomas Dixon, Jr. All of Dixon's works glorified the first Ku Klux Klan as the South's "liberator" from the oppression of Reconstruction. *The Clansman* was in part a fictionalized diatribe against Reconstructionist and Pennsylvania industrialist Thaddeus Stevens. Dixon portrayed Stevens as both a Roman Catholic sympathizer and a white man who engaged in sex across racial lines. Above all, the novel invoked "the Aryan race" and set it in opposition to the "barbarism" of the African heritage. *The Clansman* demonized African-American men through a unique combination of paranoiac logic, intellectual vacuity, moral insidiousness, and sexual titillation. With such ingredients, Dixon's works progressed unstoppably from book to stage play to motion picture.

Birth of a Nation, created by Kentucky-born filmmaker D. W. Griffith, was cinema's first full-length epic. Dixon suggested the title—a puzzling choice for a work of neo-Confederate propaganda—at the film's preview showing.

Though the film was a sensational success in the South, it provoked protests elsewhere including riots and official censorship. Author Dixon and director Griffith set about to reverse any negative image by the bold stroke of arranging an official White House showing. For this purpose, Dixon called on the good offices of his former graduate school classmate, Virginian and now United States president Woodrow Wilson. "My only regret," Wilson is supposed to have said after viewing the film, "is that it is all so terribly true." Subsequently, the well connected Dixon prevailed upon another Southern friend, Secretary of the Navy Josephus Daniels, to arrange an interview with Edward White, Chief Justice of the Supreme Court. This remarkable sequence of interventions was completed when Justice White revealed that he had been a member of the original Klan's New Orleans chapter.

Needless to say, White soon prevailed over New York's official objections to showing *Birth*, which went on to gross nearly 18 million dollars. That's when some members of the viewing public wrote to Dixon suggesting that he revive the Klan.

What happened next isn't altogether clear. Some say that the founding of the Second KKK was connected to the 1915 lynching of Leo Frank, a Jewish factory supervisor in Atlanta, for supposedly murdering Mary Phagan, a teenaged worker in the same factory. Only in 2000 did an independent researcher disclose a list of some of the lynching's perpetrators—prominent, well-to-do citizens of Marietta, Georgia. However, Frank's lynchers didn't identify themselves as KKK but as "the Knights of Mary Phagan." Several ringleaders were founding members of the Marietta Country Club, but only one was identified in the list as a member of the Ku Klux Klan.

This mix of social trivia and bland evildoing, followed by incoherent self-justification, is typical of the time when the second Klan began. I'm sure that founder Williams Simmons, like so many other white Southerners, was a Confederate wannabe who felt a mental and emotional kinship to the by-then-legendary Klan. Except for a brief period at the end of the 1860s, however, the real first Klan may never have been a single entity under a single leadership. Simmons had to reinvent the organization with little more to go on than the name and a nationwide, ever thickening atmosphere of bigotry.

The organizational structure Simmons and his employees devised was wildly successful at fund raising and infiltrating state and national politics—suggesting that these were the second Klan's primary aims. Documented Klan incidents don't point to a concerted campaign of intimidation and violence throughout the South, much less nationally. Given the organization's secrecy, the Klan name could be adopted by any local group of string-pullers and toughs with a taste for cross-burning, threatening, whipping, beating, tarring and feathering, and acid-burning.

Some documented episodes, in fact, lead me to see a closer connection between the second Klan and Appalachian whitecapping than between the second Klan and the first Klan. Leaders of the first Klan were southern Democrats who instigated terrorism to gain focused objectives—subduing freedmen and regaining control of state governments in the South. The second Klan varied in its targets and its level of violence from state to state. It achieved political influence largely through rhetoric and lobbying, not violence. Its ideology was backward looking, like that of the whitecaps, directed at "outside" moral and ethnic influences that, in the end, couldn't be excluded. More, some of the worst episodes of violence by the second Klan sprang from factional conflict. As in Appalachian whitecapping, the victims of these episodes were known opponents rather than ethnic or racial symbols. Contrary to what most of us think we know about the Klan of this period, most large-scale Klan intimidations were white on white.

Writers have met frustration in their attempts to measure the amount of violence the second KKK was responsible for. Researchers have made close studies of the Klan by region, but real totals of victims, let alone a breakdown by race and ethnicity, are hard to come by. Obstacles to a reliable total include varying degrees of secretiveness on the part of both Klan members and victims, the fact that most victims were wounded rather than killed, and the lengthy time and intensive labor it takes to research and compile a detailed record for even one city or state.

For Texas and Oklahoma alone, where Klan violence during the 1920s was most public and apparently most frequent, one researcher estimates over a thousand victims injured. Some regions suffered reigns of terror like those that occurred circa 1922 throughout Oklahoma or in Kern County, California. In Kern County, KKK members directed their violence at least partly against local professional men, a campaign of intimidation that ended by creating free-for-all frontier conditions close to those of 1850s San Francisco. In Louisiana, Texas, and Oklahoma, local chapters had explicitly named "whipping bands," who were sometimes actually called vigilance committees. Some whippings of white Protestant women for supposed immorality—such as remarrying or not attending church—turned out to have been instigated by ministers.

Outright murders were few but highly publicized. For instance, the 1922 kidnaping of five men and murder of two in Mer Rouge, Louisiana, ended in martial law and was covered by newspapers nationally for six months. Finally it was found that the kidnapings and murders sprang from a feud, used by the Klan faction to its advantage, between people in the towns of Mer Rouge and Bastrop.

The second Ku Klux Klan was not a product of village or countryside but of urban areas. The year 1920 was the first in which America's urban population exceeded its rural population. From 1910 to 1920, Arkansas, Oklahoma, and Texas urbanized far more quickly than the national average. The population of Louisiana cities such as Bastrop increased by as much as 50 percent. Bastrop was a town populated by recently rural, fundamentalist Protestants who found work in the paper mill and carbon plant. Many who moved to the city for jobs in an expanding economy were those who might have joined the whitecaps in the rural areas they originally came from.

When these brand-new urbanites arrived, they were greeted by an overwhelming clamor of competition in the guise of "people different from, and not as deserving as, me." Their drama of social threat pitted against the sense of entitlement was played out in an atmosphere of economic boom and bust. Corporate capitalist enterprises, such as the paper mill in Bastrop, were important employers. Their ceaseless production of goods, often bought by the same people whose wages and salaries they paid, created a consumer class and brought about professional, middle-management, and small-business opportunities. As the history of American labor conflict shows, industrial capitalism also led to job insecurity tied to profit cycles. Added to economic instability, the home-front paranoia of World War I couldn't have been better designed to increase suspicion of those who were different from oneself. In a postwar economy, the newly arrived struggled to position themselves favorably, and securely, based on their identity as "White Anglo-Saxon Protestants."

Most Klan members were by no means "white trash" but they were middle class, not elite. The middle is the class from which Klan founder Simmons himself came. Simmons was the son of an Alabama physician and farmer who tried a number of careers including the ministry before achieving success as a professional fraternal organizer. For the rest of his life he would be known as "Colonel" Simmons based on his rank in the fraternal order and nonprofit mutual insurance society called Woodmen of the World. During World War I Simmons was not invited to join the government-sponsored American Protective League, endorsed by Theodore Roosevelt. Rather, he settled for membership in the less prestigious branch organization, the Citizens' Bureau of Investigation. However, the Klan, like other vigilante groups, was allowed to carry out semi-official strike-breaking and ferreting out of draft dodgers during the war.

World War I gave the Klan a sense of purpose as well as turned it into a secret organization. But at the end of the war the Klan still numbered only a few thousand and was mainly confined to Alabama and Georgia. In 1920 Simmons hired two organizers to boost the Klan to national stature in return for 80 percent of the profits. Both newspaper advertising and recruiting in Masonic lodges formed the basis of the campaign. After 15 months of publicity and salesmanship, the "Invisible Empire" had about 90,000 new members.

Klan organizers divided the U. S. into sales regions, subdivided in turn into "realms" (states). Sales representatives were generally already members of other lodges, and Protestant ministers were both used on the Klan lecture circuit and approached in most localities as potential organizers. Charters were granted to chapters only when organization and membership had reached a certain point. Organizers at each level received a portion of the ten-dollar initiation fee. Given that the Klan was accepted initially as a tax-free "benevolent and charitable" organization, the ten-dollar initiation fees minus overhead were all profit. A number of spinoff companies manufactured Klan regalia, handled publication and printing, and managed real estate holdings.

Just about every adult American must have become aware of the Klan and its goals in 1921 after a Congressional hearing and "adverse" publicity in a series by the *New York World*. These claims to fame put the finishing touch on the organization's success. During the early 1920s the Klan had chapters not only in highland, Deep South, and border-southern states but in most other states, with particular strengths in parts of California, Colorado, Illinois, Indiana, Ohio, and Pennsylvania. In 1924, estimated membership nationally was 2.5 million. Based on figures claimed by the former Grand Dragon of Texas, Dallas in 1924 had the highest number of Klan members per capita in the country.

So great was the Klan's political influence in 1924 that the national Democratic convention was afraid to denounce the Invisible Empire in so many words. The election of Calvin Coolidge and conservative state-level victories around the nation in this year reflected a high water mark of the Klan's influence. By then, Simmons had been forced out of the organization by a Texas dentist named Hiram Wesley Evans. Two years later Klan membership was declining numerically and deviating increasingly from the mainstream. Citizens who might have joined with no desire to promulgate violence had become alienated by bombings and lynchings that were not confined to the South. Worse perhaps for the Klan's fortunes was publicity over its internal leadership struggles and widespread corruption. The Klan's Indiana leader, David C. Stephenson, went to prison for life as a result of his involvement in the kidnaping and death of a young woman; a 1927 lawsuit against dissident Pennsylvania Klansmen washed other of the Klan's dirty linen in public. The Klan continued into the 1930s with a narrow base of support and an increasing emphasis on repression of African-Americans as well as its existing program of anti-Communist, anti-labor, and moralistic coercion. A federal tax claim against the Klan in

1944 served as a kind of death blow. It was actually splinter Klans, comparable to the dissident Pennsylvania group mentioned above, that revived after the 1954 school desegregation ruling with a single focus on terrorism.

Around 1920, however, probably only ten per cent or so of Klan members joined because of the organization's national aims of opposition to "Catholics, Jews, Negroes, immigrants, and radicals." The 1920s Klan presented a face of ordinariness in its routine activities such as membership drives and rallies, regular meetings, barbecues, and the like. Many members probably didn't go beyond the satisfactions of belonging to an in-group, socializing, and being entertained by the Klan's trademark burning crosses and other showy mystifications, such as the "Kl—" terminology: "Kleagles" for field organizers, "Klectoken" for the initiation fee, "Klavern" for the meeting place, and so on.

The Klan's leading platform nationwide was anti-Catholicism— largely a code word for new immigrants from southern and eastern Europe. But different parts of the Klan message tended to receive individual local emphasis. The Klan's ostensible activity in at least some states centered on "efforts to preserve premarital chastity, marital fidelity, and respect for parental authority; to compel obedience of state and national prohibition laws; to fight the postwar crime wave; and to rid state and local governments of dishonest politicians." In New Jersey and upstate New York, for instance, the hot-button issue was Prohibition. No doubt, as in Indiana whitecapping, stated motives often fronted for private agendas including local power grabs and payback to opponents.

Why did mainstream Americans join the Ku Klux Klan of 1920? In the beginning, a number of Klan leaders were local government officials, university professors, and other middle- to upper-middle-class persons who also took other community leadership roles. These leaders and most Klan members weren't the socially marginal persons we expect to find in today's KKK, its splinter groups and competitors. In truth, Klan attitudes around 1920—and sometimes Klan endorsement for intimidation—weren't far to the right of the beliefs of America's political and intellectual leadership.

In the 19th century, violent bigotry against African Americans spread nationwide. But prejudice against other identifiable minorities tended to focus on whatever ethnic group presented an immediate threat to white Protestants in a particular region—for example, the Australians or the Irish in San Francisco (even as the Irish were carving a political niche in Northeastern states), Chinese and Japanese Americans on the Pacific Coast, or American Indians and Mexican Americans in the Southwest. Until the 1890s, perhaps, riot, massacre, and lynching were relatively isolated incidents stemming from individual cases of economic and political competition.

If any one or two groups can be said to have changed these embryonic expressions of bigotry into a coherent national system, it was America's intellectuals and national political leaders. True, a liberal tradition survived in New York and New England, and was transplanted to pockets in some Midwestern and Plains states—Michigan, Wisconsin, Iowa, and North Dakota, for instance. But, when confronted by masses of immigrants from southern and eastern Europe and from Asia, formerly liberal intellectual and political establishments began to crack at their foundations. From professors and physicians to policy makers and ministers of the gospel, the "Anglo-Saxon" leadership feared losing their dominance in a political culture and economic system that had favored them through American history. Politicians of the Progressive era 1890-1915 had seemed to promise political and social purification—to assimilate newcomers and create more accountable governments. Instead, they delivered bureaucratic politics as a new spoils system. In the eyes of "Anglo Saxons," the new system threatened to be at least as easy for ethnic outsiders to dominate as ward-based politics had been. So-called scientists and other intellectuals provided the ideology, or theoretical fodder, for white Protestant political opposition.

The main tactic was applying pseudo-Darwinism to assert "evidence" that cultural traits were racially based. Italian physician and criminal anthropologist Cesare Lombroso applied racialist theories to the study of criminals by asserting that lawbreakers could be predictively identified by their physical traits, such as head size, noses, ears, and so on. Lombroso's works, written from about 1871 to 1906, were filled with photographs he obtained while doing volunteer work in prisons.

Lombroso's appeal was to "common sense"—that little voice that tells us, "If it sounds true, it is true." Lombroso employed the classically dishonest technique of reasoning from effect to cause: Using populations of prisoners, he matched their offenses to carefully selected details of their appearance as shown in mug shots. He used the appearance of white northern Europeans as a norm, didn't compare the incarcerated with the free, and chose "significant" characteristics without any defensible reason. He even went so far as using a skull said to belong to long-dead Charlotte Corday to explain why she killed Marat during the French Revolution, and analyzed the so-called Oklahoma bandit Belle Starr after reading about her in tabloid journals.

As Lombroso's unsubstantiated theories were challenged, he revised his books again and again and claimed to find new keys to inherent criminality in handwriting, getting tattooed, and suffering from epilepsy. But the key to acceptance for Lombroso's claims was that they were useful and convenient. His books came just as urban dwellers throughout the western world began seeing crime and prison populations as a crisis and fearing every stranger as a threat. Lombroso's ideas were easily reduced to a system of measurements that police departments could use to enhance their credibility and promote the myth of a "criminal type."

I don't know that Theodore Roosevelt subscribed to wacky notions like Lombroso's. But Roosevelt did exemplify the fatal combination of self-confidence and vacillation, good intentions and self-deception, that supported ethnically and racially motivated violence from about 1880 until 1920. Roosevelt went through a variety of stances on the issue of race and culture, but he was far from bigoted by the standard of his times. He repudiated Southern lynching and other kinds of intimidation of African-Americans still prevalent in 1915 and (though he was of course criticized for it) invited George Washington Carver to dinner at the White House. However, as we have seen, Roosevelt espoused vigilante tactics. On one occasion he approved the result of a New Orleans vigilante-led lynching in which eleven Italians were taken from jail and hanged. Allegedly, they had murdered the police chief. Roosevelt commented, "I am, as a matter of principle, sorry to say that the lynching had a most healthy effect in a local situation which was becoming unendurable."

The views of Roosevelt and the frontier politicians who were his associates assumed a high profile at about the time that currents of public policy and public attitude were becoming increasingly national and international. Urban riots, and factional strife like the New Orleans incident, pitted ethnic and racial groups against one another. Winning the Spanish-American War (1898) temporarily convinced "Anglo-Saxon" Americans that they and their democratic institutions could dominate. In the longer term, however, colonialism was probably the final element needed to develop a truly national racism. Governing the Philippines, Hawaii, and Puerto Rico institutionalized color-consciousness among all Americans.

—◆—

Prejudice against African-Americans stands apart from other white American prejudices for having lasted so long and being so widely distributed. Surely slavery is the strongest root of that prejudice.

One thing slavery meant is that Africans came to America from the start in an economic capacity. From the start, just about everyone else perceived them in terms of economic advantage or threat. Slaveholding was a moneymaker for traders, plantation owners, and the urban wealthy. It was an economic menace to non-slave, mostly

European settlers. "Free blacks" never succeeded in separating themselves from the slave identity as an economic factor. Moreover, the luckless identity of slaves as property created a ready-made social hierarchy with black Americans at the bottom. Because black visibility was sustained by color, every other immigrant group before, during, and after the Civil War could measure themselves socially over and against African-Americans. This competitive social ordering grew much more unstable, rather than went away, once slaves became free. Religious, racial, and ethnic prejudice among Anglo-Saxon Protestants has always been a reality. But it was much less an issue for those whose self-definition had long been secured by money, power, and position. Throughout our history, economic elites and powerful political factions have gone on invoking the racial pecking order to jerk the chain of the white working class and lower middle class. The meaning of "white" changed, but it went on being defined against "black."

Outside the South, this definition was cemented during the years before the Civil War. As settlers moved into the Midwest, and then into the Great Plains and Pacific Northwest, agitation over extending slavery worsened both prejudice and discrimination. During the 1850s, varying restrictions on African-American settlement and legal rights were enacted as far west as Utah, Colorado, New Mexico, and Nebraska. This trend was strong in spite of the fact that the U.S. Census Bureau in 1860 reported only 600 African-Americans living west of the Mississippi, with half of these in Kansas. As one researcher notes, Midwesterners were the single largest regional group settling the Great Plains and Pacific Northwest. "Bombarded with antagonistic statements about Negroes from lawmakers and editors, requested to vote for or against restrictive measures, and faced with an almost constant agitation against the expansion of slavery, these pioneers pushed westward with an increased determination to keep the Negro, free or slave, out of the new lands."

Economic and political contests shaped the diatribes and the violence of the Ku Klux Klan in all its manifestations. But the second

Klan's rhetoric of hate was the broadest. The wider range of enemies this propaganda targeted, compared to the Klans before and after it, suggests that the factory was a more crucial arena of struggle than the farm or the plantation. As members of ethnic minorities moved around, so did the sites of violence. But in the 1920s, when the second Klan was strongest, there were only two race riots nationwide. Lynching was taking fewer victims in the South and was soon to stop outside the South. In one way, the rhetoric of the second Klan celebrated an accomplished coup. In 1921 and 1924, Congress passed laws banning Asian immigration and severely cut the number admitted from most "Catholic" and "Jewish" countries of Europe. It could be argued that the Klan declined as the white Protestant public needed it less, and big businessmen came to see publicized violence as bad for their image. By 1930, African-Americans were the last targets left standing.

Thomas Dixon's novel *The Clansman* was made into the first film fully to exploit—to commodify—the negative emotional qualities of the African-American image. *Birth of a Nation* marked a milestone of change—from the nineteenth-century division of Northerner and Southerner to the twentieth-century division of black and white. A sinister note was sounded as the category of "subhuman," long applied to African-Americans in the South, spread and was given sensational sexual content. Although other identifiable groups had been described as animal-like, the predatory sexual image set African-American men apart even within the category of outsiders.

The people who organized and ran the second Ku Klux Klan, like the people who furnished their ideas, weren't mental giants. Especially after 1922 when the leadership changed, the Klan shot itself in the foot by trying to combine broad popular support with giving the public unrestricted permission to use violence. Anything approaching social disorder was anathema to the middle class. They feared not violence, but out-of-control violence. Apparently, they preferred to leave repressive tactics to the government and to corporations whose favor they depended on.

The NAACP hung a banner from their Fifth Avenue office window.

15

"Foreigners and Negroes"
Discrimination, Lynching, and the Penalty of Death

I don't think it's unreasonable to call epidemics of lynching "domestic terrorism" and to wonder why no war was ever declared against them. Except for certain vigilante killings, lynching meant that an accused person was executed without trial—without even the pretext of evidence gathering, legal representation, or judicial argument.

Turn to the dust jacket of this book. Look into the faces of smiling, well dressed men posing for their picture in front of the body of the man they've just hanged from a tree. This is lynching as a community act. It's also lynching as the act of the mob—in some cases 10,000 to 15,000 strong—whose participants delighted in terrifying and hurting its victims before letting them die.

More people were lynched in just ten Southern states between 1882 and 1930 than were killed in the World Trade Center attack—2,805 versus 2,654. Our count of lynchings is so fragmentary outside this one time and place that the total nationwide could be twice 2,805—over five thousand, or about one-third the number of legal executions we know have been held.

The federal government did not—ever—pass a law against lynching. "Social permission to lynch"—including lack of laws and lack of enforcement—effectively robbed whole categories of people of their most basic, moment-to-moment sense of safety. If you belonged to a targeted group you couldn't get through a day, travel, move freely around the community, or reside in your home without fear of imminent and arbitrary death for yourself and your loved ones. Roy Wilkins, former executive director of the NAACP, once wrote that in the lynching era (which Wilkins bracketed as 1889-1939), "No court would listen. Few newspapers would do anything except to egg on the mob spirit. Men of the cloth did not remember a Christ crucified by a ruler and a mob. High and low federal, state, and local officials turned their backs. The president was silent. The U. S. Supreme Court could not hear. There was nowhere to turn."

Is lynching part of the past, something that happened mostly in the 1880s to 1930s and mostly in the South? By the NAACP's definition, lynching was:

- an illegal killing for which there is evidence
- carried out by three or more persons
- who claimed that their act served justice or tradition.

By this definition, you could say that lynching—mob killing supported by community feeling—may have stopped in the United States.

Hate crimes haven't stopped—we had a hate murder four years ago in the town where I live. A self-described white supremacist shot a Korean student in front of the student's church. Unlike lynchers in earlier decades, the perpetrators of hate crimes now don't seem to come from or be backed by the mainstream. The murderers of a gay man in Laramie, Wyoming, or those who dragged an African-American man behind their truck in Jasper County, Texas, weren't the respectable people who flocked to publicly endorse illegal killings in earlier decades. In these two cases, the murderers may not have belonged to any organization larger than a local gang of like-minded, marginalized white males.

Some scholars see the matter differently. They believe that the historical wave of lynching, which was the basis for the NAACP definition, fits into a much longer-lasting pattern of racial violence—of domestic terrorism—against people of color. According to the broader definition, racial violence began in the physical abuse and coercion that went along with slavery. Racial violence continued as lynchings—those that occurred as part of riots and those that occurred apart from riots. Racial violence reached into the present as police brutality and capital punishment, because these penalties disproportionately target persons of color. In the broad view of racial violence, all of these kinds of coercion have been meant to intimidate, to bring about submissive behavior in all who can be put in the same category as the person killed. With racially targeted lynching, it's uncommon to discover the kind of specific grievance or power grab that led to many white-on-white lynchings on our frontiers.

Taking the historical view, I'd say that Americans, in the course of our long career of socially approved violence, embarked on a learning curve.

In earlier centuries, vigilante murder and lethal shivaree usually came out of short-term conditions or an individual, delimited event. The action ended when the enemy, the opponent, was killed or driven away. But collective violence took an ominous turn: it began to be directed against people who could be identified as targets by their appearance alone. This development appeared during the New York draft riots, in post-Civil-War Klan terrorism, and in the massacre and lynching of Chinese and Japanese immigrants on the Far West frontier. These murders too were triggered by specific events. But they went unpunished, they targeted near-random victims rather than real opponents, and they were reinforced by racism at every conceivable level of our social conversation from popular songs to presidential speeches.

In a climate of bigotry, I don't think it was a very big jump from extralegal murder to discriminatory legal execution. This is all the more true when, as often happened, police and sheriffs didn't stop rioters or lynchers, and sometimes attended as spectators—maybe as participants. Racially targeted, arbitrary killings combined with racist attitudes to signal that some people, because of their appearance or manner alone, were fair game. The ideology of bigotry was always ready with a justification—*everybody knew* that persons of a certain appearance and manner were *inherently depraved, lived no better than beasts,* and so forth. Therefore, it was implied, denying such people safety, or punishing them disproportionately for crime, wasn't the same, quite, as harming or punishing a human being.

Racial violence in our nation has gone on so long. It's been so horrific in its persistence and in its effects that many people think of it as a phenomenon apart from the kinds of white-on-white persecution I've been describing in previous chapters. Lynchings took place before and after the years mentioned, of course—for example, around the time of the American Revolution, right after the Civil War, and as late as 1964 when three civil rights workers were murdered in Mississippi. Lynchings happened in most, if not all, of the United States—in Oregon, Pennsylvania, Wisconsin (as in the example on the cover of this book), and other non-Southern, non-frontier societies.

Reading the roll call of the dead whose names and stories we *have* managed to gather, I only wonder why some scholars of racial violence confine their definition of it to the experience of African-Americans. It's not hard to discover that Chinese, Japanese, Italian, and Mexican immigrants and, above all, American Indians, have been massacred, lynched, and legally executed on questionable grounds in multiple-victim incidents over long periods of American history.

One good reason for focusing on African-Americans might be that they go on receiving discriminatory punishments within the criminal justice system even today, from arrest for "driving while black" to being sentenced to death. The total number on death row around the country at the beginning of 2003 was 3,692, and those executed from 1976 to 2003 totaled 850. African-Americans are only about 12 percent of the U. S. population, but make up about 43 percent on death row. They are over 34 percent of those executed from 1976 to 2003. It's hard to know how far they share their predicament with other minority groups, mostly because of debatable census counts and the small number of those executed so far. People known to be American Indians are about one percent of the population, one percent (39) of death row, and 1.5 percent (13) of those executed since 1976. The Latino/Latina population percentage in the U.S. is about 14 percent. Latinos/Latinas are 9.5 percent (350) of those on death row and fewer than 7 percent (54) of those executed. Asian-Americans are also underrepresented—four percent of the general population and one percent or fewer (40) of those on death row or executed (6) in recent years.

European-Americans, of course, are drastically underrepresented on death row and among the executed—about 75 percent of the general population, versus 43 percent on death row (1,662) and 57 percent executed (466).

———

Still, the part of the story of racial violence that jumps out at me isn't only that it's been the African-American experience over their whole history on this continent, as well as the experience of other groups for parts of their history. I also see that we as Americans have *permitted* racial violence for that same long period. We've allowed it to be part, maybe the dirtiest part, of our endorsing "popular justice." We've permitted racial violence along with other forms of persecution by not passing and enforcing laws (sometimes simply out of a desire not to pay taxes), by participating actively in riot, murder, and other acts of revenge, by speaking up for lynching from positions of influence, and also by remaining silent as injustice was done.

If you look at socially approved violence from the perspective of those who've been attacked, it might be possible to say that one group's suffering has been greater than another's—at least that it has lasted longer, harmed more individuals, or more completely destroyed a culture. Also, studying violence from the victims' point of view makes it possible for the victims to tell you that you aren't qualified to evaluate their experience—that you can't control and limit research or make recommendations for the future. Certainly, modern American politics is identity politics, meaning that in order to be heard you have to find others who share your unacceptable circumstances—whether you have a child with a rare illness, rent a mobile home, belong to a disfavored ethnic or gender minority, or have had a loved one murdered.

Then your group must band together to claim redress, representing yourselves as a powerful voting bloc and trying to win an award of recognition, legal privileges, or funding. So there are pressures to present yourself as more difficult for outsiders to understand, more wronged, and to portray your situation as more painful than another's.

Matters are somewhat the same within academic scholarship. Scholars are rewarded for the product called expertise—special knowledge and a special ability to interpret events. When a topic attracts a lot of public attention, the pressure for you as an academic is to make that topic part of your field of training—your scholarly turf. You can't start to assert your authority until you show that the topic belongs in your field—preferably (given the identity politics of academe), that it belongs within your personal history as well.

Maybe this is what we get when we define an issue by its victims— identity politics, in and out of academe. Our acting as identity politicians may be no bad thing, if it's not the only thing that happens.

But I don't see that focusing on the victims helps us to learn why and how violence has been allowed to happen over and over again to so many kinds of people—how it happened that we as a society could place individual opponents or whole categories of people outside the pale of protection. This question connects frontier vigilantism, labor violence, and the kind of lynching and legal execution that has most often targeted randomly chosen members of an identifiable group, such as African-Americans.

Who benefits from the way things are? Who would benefit if changes were made? When and why is it more advantageous to act outside the law than inside it?

"Ours is 'the land of the free,'" Mark Twain wrote in 1870, "nobody denies that—nobody challenges it." And then he added, "Maybe it is because we won't let other people testify." In this passage from *Roughing It*, an account of his frontier travels, Twain was referring to laws that prohibited Chinese testimony against European-Americans in the courts of all Pacific Coast states after 1854. Twain explicitly connected this legal atmosphere to the lack of physical protection of the Chinese, as others have done in respect to African-Americans: "As I write, news comes that in broad daylight in San Francisco, some boys have stoned an inoffensive Chinaman to death, and that although a large crowd witnessed the shameful deed, no one interfered." The Chinese population of San Francisco County at this time was less than ten percent.

To read the history of ethnic groups in America is sometimes to wonder which one you're reading about, because discrimination and its self-justifying rhetoric of bigotry change so little.

Start with American Indians—as the European settlers did, treating them as independent nations at the same time our newly brought diseases reduced their populations up to ninety percent and disorganized their societies. When Indians allied themselves with one European nation against another, or governments reneged on treaties, Indians became a military enemy. Eventually, when the United States government defeated enough Indians militarily, Indians became another minority group with whom European-Americans had a violent history. "For such demons," Patrick Hamilton wrote of the Apache Nation in 1884, "there can be only one treatment—extermination—and the authorities on both sides of the border have at last arrived at this conclusion."

Such talk was common. In Arizona, it amounted to a journalistic campaign of newly arrived European-American settlers against Indians, and it had gone on for at least twenty years before Hamilton's book was written. One observer talked about white settlers in the Prescott area killing the remaining 500 or so Apaches for sport. In 1891, eminent geographer Elie Reclus wrote a book condescendingly entitled *Primitive Folk*, in which he too recommended extermination. Reclus called the Apache "wolves," describing their appearance and eating habits as if they were ferocious, repellent animals.

In spite of this propaganda implying that Indians were inevitably the aggressors, a recent researcher found that violent encounters in

Arizona resulted in nine Indian deaths for every European-American killed. Another scholar studied the rate of indictment and the rate of conviction for crimes in an Arizona county and a Nebraska county. Apache conviction rates were twice those of white defendants—about the same degree of overrepresentation the researcher found for African-American versus white defendants in Omaha. In the Arizona cases, European-American defendants were found not guilty three times as often as Apache defendants. The only Apaches found not guilty were accused of murdering Apaches, not whites. The high number of Apache defendants who entered plea bargains suggests that their defense suffered from defects such as errors in translation, lack of understanding of American jurisprudence, and inability to retain a competent lawyer. At this remove, we can't know how many lies and exaggerations by white witnesses were accepted—but we do know that untruthful witnesses are still a big problem in today's courts.

"Can one throw mud into pure water and not disturb its clearness?" the inventor and artist Samuel F. B. Morse wrote in 1835. The "mud" Morse referred to was Irish Catholic immigrants, and the "pure water" was white immigrants of Protestant origin whose boats had landed a little earlier. About 400,000 left Ireland during the potato famine of 1845-1850. To fuel his rhetoric Morse drew on deep prejudice against Roman Catholicism going back to the Puritans and referred to Catholics as "hundreds of priest-controlled human machines." He also inveighed against the different speech, appearance, and customs that would have made the Irish conspicuous in American cities even if they hadn't been numerous. By 1855, one-sixth of the Irish population had emigrated to the United States, and there were more Irish- than American-born residents in Boston. The Irish dug canals, built railroads, worked underground in mines loading rail cars with coal that was dug by earlier-arrived, better paid immigrants such as the English and Welsh. Many Irish worked at the most menial jobs in mills and factories located, in that era, in urban areas. With the arrival of the Irish just as industry was getting under way, American cities first took on their lasting image as dirty, bad-smelling, crowded, and dominated by foreigners of "filthy" habits who were also seen as elbowing aside the native born.

The Know Nothing or "American" party of the 1850s, which mush-roomed overnight from its beginnings as a fraternal order, was based solely on opposition to Catholics and immigrants. The Know Nothings dominated San Francisco vigilantism against the Irish-American city administration, although African-American slaves and the Chinese were equally resented in California. Slave labor was actually present in the goldfields, brought by Southern slaveowners. European-American miners saw the slaves as a particularly insulting form of competition, refused to work with them, and sometimes drove them away. These white workers were the nucleus of a political faction adamantly opposed to any future population of slave or free blacks, but California's constitutional convention of 1849 also contained a proslavery faction who argued the profitability of slave labor in the mines. One act in effect until 1855 allowed California's pre-constitution slaveholders to recapture escaped slaves, made aiding an escaped slave a criminal act, and prohibited recaptured slaves from testifying on their own behalf. Josiah Royce, in analyzing the Convention debates, speaks of "the Oregon tradition, with its hatred of a free Negro population;" and he went to the length of tabulating the region of origin of the delegates. Although it appeared possible for a time that California would be split into northern and southern halves to accommodate the slaveowners, opposition to slavery proved stronger than support. But the newly formed California legislature, like that of other states, was quick to define a "Negro" and to pass a number of restrictive measures against those who met the definition.

The attitudes of Californian leadership were similar to those in the states from which most settlers came, but California in its demography was unlike other states. The 1860 population stood at two-thirds

"Americans" and one-third Latinos/Latinas, Chinese, and African-Americans mostly of mixed-race parentage. Where in other states the restriction issue subsided because of an ostensibly pro-black Congress after the Civil War, California simply found anti-black restrictions unworkably confusing because residents came from several different non-European ethnicities.

Excluding the Chinese soon became California's dominant economic issue—a struggle to the death between need and resentment. Exclusion was delayed in part because of international trade agreements, in part because of moral objections by Protestant sects (who also had a missionary presence in Asia), in part because the Chinese were profitable workers compared to scarce European-American labor being paid at inflated frontier rates. A lynching-and-looting spree in Los Angeles in 1871 was the first widely publicized incident of mass violence against the Chinese. At this time the city's Chinese population was probably fewer than 1,000 versus more than 31,000 European-Americans. Rioting and the murder of Chinese immigrants occurred in Rock Springs, Wyoming, in 1885, when twenty-three persons were killed and their bodies mutilated. Similar riots were brewing in Seattle during 1885 and 1886 until authorities removed about 200 Chinese from the state under protection of Federal troops.

When Chinese exclusion laws came, they resembled those directed against African-Americans, except that Chinese exclusion could be mandated at federal level. Local and state laws were attempted, but most either proved difficult to enforce or were struck down by state and federal courts. Exclusion came about only when the main railroad lines were mostly built, the vote of Pacific states in the electoral college grew large, and organized labor became a force to be reckoned with in national politics. Between 1882 and 1902 six congressional acts and two treaties went into effect whose provisions, among others:

- barred the immigration of Chinese laborers,
- tightly controlled and later prohibited re-entry of Chinese who left the United States,

- narrowly restricted entry of all Chinese in occupations other than labor, and
- denied citizenship to those Chinese who did manage to attain United States residence.

The Japanese, first welcomed as replacement labor after Chinese exclusion, were soon treated similarly. Two "Gentlemen's Agreements" (1907 and 1920) between the Japanese and American governments restricted immigration. In 1924, a Congressional immigration act barred all Asians and also refused entry to wives and relatives of resident Asians. The Japanese population remained more concentrated in California, and legal discrimination continued when the Japanese were sent to internment camps during World War II.

Between the Civil War and World War I, persons of color and immigrants from southern and eastern Europe became targets of riots, lynching, and massacre. Anti-Italian feeling culminated in vigilante-led lynchings not only in New Orleans but in other cities, especially in the South. Italians were lynched throughout the NAACP's reporting period 1889-1918. Indians were lynched in Oklahoma during white settlement of former reservation lands, and twenty-one Mexicans were lynched in just one Texas county during 1915-1916. At present, researchers have only fragmentary reports like these—poor documentation compared to the record of legal executions.

———

It would be especially dangerous to abolish the death penalty, one Russel Duane argued during the Pennsylvania legislature's 1917 debate on capital punishment, in a state "composed so largely of foreigners and Negroes." Ethnic and racial targeting, so blatant in riots and lynching and in discriminatory laws, has probably always played a part in rates of imprisonment and condemnation to death. The Irish, followed by members of other immigrant groups, were arrested and incarcerated at very high rates. The same kind of research hasn't been done for every city or every immigrant group, but studies of the Columbus, Ohio, jail and the Massachusetts State Penitentiary in the 1800s found that immigrants and African-Americans were overrepresented as convicts compared to their numbers in the general population.

As with Arizona Apache defendants, some of this high rate probably came from language difficulties and misunderstanding of the American legal system. Judging from studies of incarceration today, much of the high rate came from inability to hire a competent attorney. Finally, however, the struggle for order in American society also played its part. The street politics, or shivaree-type demonstrations and riots, that political leaders welcomed and encouraged before and during the American Revolution became frightening to the new nineteenth-century middle class. Police forces developed during these years in part out of middle-class concern for public order and the safety of property. Minor offenses against civility were disproportionately punished. At the same time, police found immigrants an easy source of high arrest totals, for example, through rounding up everyone at the scene of a brawl or riot whether or not the arrestees were actually involved. Seven-eighths of all persons committed to the New York city prison between 1850 and 1860 were arrested for drunkenness, and most of these were unmarried immigrants aged twenty to forty. A few illustrations of riots such as the New York draft riot, drawn not long after the fact, caricature rioters as Irish by giving them snub noses, ragged dress, and straight, bowl-cut hair.

The decade 1901-1910 was the first since the Civil War that the nationwide, average rate of legal execution—crudely estimated as the number of executions per 100,000 overall population—rose higher than the rate of lynching. There were and are big differences in both these rates from region to region. The history of some immigrant groups with the death penalty, either extralegal or legal, is hard to track because no record of nationality was kept, or cases were too few. Records of Mexican-American execution are too sparse to allow much analysis. But the Italians, and the Chinese and Japanese if taken together, were executed in high enough numbers after about 1890 for their rate of execution to be studied statistically.

Italian immigration into the U. S. tripled, at least, in each decade from 1850 until 1910. After 1930, Italians become the most numerous single foreign-born population in the United States, displacing Germans. Still, New York City, with about forty percent foreign-born residents between 1890 and 1920, had fewer than ten percent Italians. It seems that Italians were highly visible rather than numerous, and in the public mind they may have been lumped together with other eastern and southern Europeans as Russel Duane's "foreigners." I searched the execution records for persons of Italian family name, and found that these names started to appear in New York in 1893. Later, numbers of Italian-named persons were executed in Connecticut (1897), Oregon (1905), New Jersey (1907), Ohio (1912), Indiana (1914), and West Virginia (1924). The number of Italian-named persons executed in Indiana, Oregon, and West Virginia is small relative to totals for any one decade. However, Italian-named persons were thirty to forty percent of European-Americans executed in Ohio, New York, and New Jersey from 1911 through 1950. Another way of stating this overrepresentation is that, in these years, Italian-named persons were executed at two to four times the execution rate as a whole.

Lewis Lawes, who crusaded against capital punishment as a result of his experiences as warden of Sing Sing, said that foreign-born Italians accounted for most murder convictions between 1890 and 1928 in New York State. Lawes seems to have felt that language difficulties and poverty were the reason for this large total. But Italian immigration began to be restricted in 1921 and remained that way until 1952. Nation-by-nation quotas were based on 1890 totals, so that new-immigrating groups had very low quotas. Italian immigration was 222,260 in 1921; the 1929 quota was 5,802, and even this low quota wasn't filled during the early 1930s because of the Depression. When I looked at the age of Italian-surnamed persons at the time of their execution, it appeared that most who were executed after about 1937 couldn't have been foreign born or even foreign raised. Nor were appeals as common or lengthy at that time as they are now. Yet Italian-name execution and population percentages only begin to approximate each other after 1950.

Just as we expected from getting to know Tony Soprano and his cronies (and Sammy "The Bull" Gravano), mobsters don't seem to have been legally executed as often as they were killed by each other or by law enforcement. Italian-named persons may have had a Mafia image, but it didn't make them more likely to be executed than Chinese- and Japanese-surnamed persons, or African-Americans. The numbers for Chinese and Japanese are relatively small, but they, the Italian-named, and African-Americans seem to have been overrepresented in execution totals to about the same degree across all groups during the first half of the twentieth century.

———◆———

One of the best recent studies of lynching concluded that, on average in Southern states between 1882 and 1930, an African-American was lynched or legally executed every four days. The study gives a total of 4,291 African-Americans who died during this period. In spite of the evidence that other "visible" groups were executed at discriminatory rates, the numbers of African-Americans illegally and legally executed stands out among the statistics. Our best count of lynchings nationwide is still limited. It appears that the total number of lynchings in the United States, including all races of victim, began to decline after 1894. We can know more surely that rates of *legal* execution declined overall from about 1910 to 1950—in most states outside the South. The Southern rate of execution rose sharply and stayed high from about 1930 to 1950. This increase was almost entirely due to the number of African-Americans who were executed in Southern states.

Southern lynchings became fewer while legal executions of African-Americans remained numerous. Does that mean that one substituted for the other, either as punishments or as means of social control? Researchers are still divided on this question, but I don't think so. If I've learned anything from reading accounts of lynchings—vigilante inspired or mob inspired, white-on-white, within other races or ethnicities, or interracial—it's that lynching allows the persecutor to get at the persecuted in a way that the law wouldn't justify.

But, you may ask (at least, I've asked myself), what about vigilantes and so-called lynch mobs who snatched their victims from jail, where these persons already awaited trial or sentencing?

Lynching was supposed to be a "lesson" to people like the victim, whether the victim was a political opponent or a person of another race or ethnicity. But lynching allowed the people who carried it out to show that *they* specifically, *they* in particular, had the power to execute.

At some times and places through American history, the most powerful group also constituted the official government. Often enough—as in the case of the San Francisco vigilantes, or Southern Democrats after the Civil War—the most powerful group was out of office. That's why I think the audience for lynchings was a double one—both the victim's identity group and the political opponents of the perpetrator. These two audiences weren't necessarily composed of the same individuals. The message of Ku Klux terrorism wasn't only to African-Americans and their local white citizen supporters. It was also to the Republican party at a time when Republicans and Democrats were in critical combat for control of Southern states.

The idea of the double audience for a lynching can be carried over into legal execution. The bureaucracy's decision to prosecute and the jury's decision to convict have both a local, "citizen" dimension and a big-picture dimension. I think more locally based research would show that factional politics and economic conflict can be traced as part of decisions about who, and how many, were executed. When anti-draft mobs containing many Irish immigrants rioted against African-Americans, was that the beginning and end of conflict and mutual resentment? Or, as the descendants of Irish or various other immigrants gained political and economic power, did their prejudices and animosities become institutionalized in the offices of prosecuting attorneys and the minds of jurors? What county, state, or even national power struggles were in progress during the period that Italian-Americans or African-Americans were being executed at high rates outside the South as well as within it?

Looking at the numbers, I don't think that enough Americans are being executed today to justify the idea of terrorism against any one group. Opponents of the death penalty have even argued that capital punishment is "capricious and arbitrary" as defined in the Constitution because the penalty is applied to such a small percentage of murderers. But, given the publicity that certain executions receive, I can easily believe that certain defendants serve as scapegoats whenever one political faction wants to impress its followers while intimidating its opponents.

Scapegoats are chosen from among those who can't defend themselves as effectively as others. It's always been the case that scapegoats were chosen mostly from among the poor. But there's been an ugly synergy all along between poverty and racial discrimination. At least some other ethnic or racial groups, like the Chinese-, Japanese-, and Italian-Americans, eventually stopped being overrepresented in execution totals. But poor African-American defendants haven't yet been able to escape their disadvantage as targets of discriminatory conviction and sentencing.

One way of looking at this position of disadvantage is by way of racial identity, the role that a racial or ethnic group plays in the drama of public life. Prejudice upholds discrimination. The level of discrimination in the justice system, like the rate of execution itself, varies wildly from state to state. But efforts to create a fairer death penalty, even where governments are carrying out their effort in good faith, haven't gotten at the problem of racial disparity. This situation points to the kind of prejudice that flies below the radar of legal procedures and judicial rules. On the evidence of capital punishment statistics, this heritage of disfavor still animates our decisions about what justice should be.

Pursuant to Section 1149 of the Penal Code

The State of Arizona

requests your presence at the execution of

Mrs. Eva Dugan

condemned to die on

Friday, February 21, 1930

at the Arizona State Prison
5 A. M.
Florence, Arizona

Lorenzo Wright
Superintendent

Ruth Snyder's botched hanging led Arizona to use the gas chamber.

16

A Clean, Well-Lighted Place:
Death-Penalty Reform in the Progressive Era

"Dear Sir," Warden J. A. Johnston of San Quentin wrote on April 26, 1916, to Herbert J. McGrath, sheriff of Grant County, New Mexico, who was preparing to conduct his first execution:

> Per request of your letter of April 24, 1916, I am shipping you two ropes by Wells Fargo Express, duplicate of this letter being enclosed therewith.
>
> Answering your request for information I would advise as follows:
>
> Presuming you have your gallows up and your trap ready to spring, measure on the gallows, from the floor up, the height of the man to be executed. Subtract the distance from the top of his head to the butt of his left ear. From *there* down you figure your drop. If you had given the height of each man, I could have told you what the drop would be in each case.
>
> A man that stands 5 feet 7 inches in height and weighs 175 pounds will require 4 feet 11 inches drop. If his height is 5 feet 9 or 10 inches, he requires 5 foot 4 inches drop.
>
> A man 5 feet 7 inches in height and weighing 125 pounds requires a 5 foot 8 inches drop.

When you have figured where the butt of the man's ear will be while standing on the trap, tie a piece of string across the gallows at that height. Then measure from the bottom of the knot (after you make your loop about four (4) inches in diameter—which is the size of a man's neck after he drops through the trap), to whatever the length of drop you are to give him; tie a string on the rope, and when you tie your rope on the beam of your gallows, see that the string on the rope is up to the string across the gallows, and you have your drop.

Strap the man's hands *straight* down on his sides, so his elbows will not strike against the sides of the trap as he drops through.

Strap him on the trap. One man places the noose over his head, the *knot behind his left ear*. Another places the black cap on. Another buckles a strap below his knees. The noose is drawn with a quick pull as tight as possible, and the trap is sprung.

Get your rope working easily through the knot by rubbing a little mutton tallow on it. Avoid getting any kinks on your noose, as they will cause the body to spin around when you drop it.

—•—

By the time Warden Johnston so carefully considered the drop needed to dislocate a human neck, rather than let the victim die by oxygen starvation, he had fallen behind the thrilling pace of technological innovation. Western legislatures continued to demand hanging until the 1920s or later, but other states beginning with New York had long since learned to electrocute. In 1889, Elbridge T. Gerry, reformer, legislator, and grandson of a signer of the Declaration of Independence, published an article in *The North American Review* entitled "Capital Punishment by Electricity." Humanity dictated, said

Gerry, that mental suffering *before* execution was sufficient punishment "even [for] the vilest convict," and the method of execution should be "as rapid and painless as possible."

Gerry included detailed examples of bungled hanging and confidently asserted that electrocution would change all that. Gerry dismissed the alternative methods of beheading and garrotting. True (he claimed), they were instantaneous. But garrotting, which Gerry took pains to point out was practiced only in Spain and its colonies, produced "a ghastly mutilation of the body." As for beheading, Gerry added with a titillating touch of mystery, it "is necessarily followed by the effusion of blood, and is open to many objections unnecessary here to enumerate."

Reformers in America's Progressive era were pretty squeamish, and they largely represented a newly sensitive white-collar sector. These mostly urban, college-educated Americans had grown well-to-do among the spreading ripples of the industrial economy, especially the enhanced standing of professionals, bureaucrats, and middle managers. The time from about 1890 to World War I could be called the Springtime of this new middle class. Their faith in science and technology were fresh. They felt secure enough to want to regulate business, reform government, create healthy living and working conditions for the laboring masses, and make the nation more directly democratic through electoral primaries, public referendums, and the vote for women. The new middle class wanted to fulfill themselves as individuals, worried about bad smells, and deplored events that weren't quite "nice," such as an execution.

Those who wanted badly enough to end the death penalty could look at Elbridge Gerry's ghoulish dabbling in the ways and means of execution—and tell themselves they saw a stage on the road to nationwide abolition of capital punishment.

Optimism didn't feel foolish when the intensity of anti-gallows campaigning and the number who took part in it had never been surpassed. Dozens of reform organizations claimed national status, hundreds of articles appeared in the popular press, and so many governors opposed the death penalty that annual governors' conferences of the decade sometimes resembled reform meetings. Between 1907 and 1916, ten states abolished capital punishment: Arizona, Colorado, Kansas, Minnesota, Missouri, North Dakota, Oregon, South Dakota, Tennessee, and Washington.

But less than a decade later, this ten-state triumph was already turning to ashes. Tennessee, Arizona, and Missouri brought back the death penalty after a year or two, Colorado, Oregon, and Washington after an average of five years. Kansas and South Dakota were to hold out until the 1930s, but their defection left only the two states of Minnesota and North Dakota from what had appeared to be the abolitionists' victory sweep.

I can't help comparing the two records, one of flash-in-the-pan Progressive enthusiasm, the other of low-key but long-term effectiveness before the Civil War. True, antebellum activism brought about permanent abolition in only four states—Michigan (1846), Rhode Island (1852) and Wisconsin (1853), with Maine following up on prewar activism by abolition in 1887—but all four of these states are still without the death penalty today. Since the Progressive years, eight of ten states where abolition legislation passed have gone back to using the death penalty.

※

Before the Civil War, the fight to end execution was David against Goliath—the individual against the state, the newly free American against the oppression of an inherited establishment. By the end of the century, what such ethical support could death penalty abolitionists call on? Their strategy, in essence, was to turn the idea of personal growth into a system of moral values. On this basis, they could say that an execution was an unforgivable termination of human potential.

Abolitionist claims, shared with certain other Progressive reformers, thinkers, and writers, could loosely be called spiritualist. Human potential, they asserted, was grounded in the kinship of individuals with one another through a supreme, harmonious natural order.

Perhaps this view of the world is a matter of faith. I must say, however many explanations of the natural order and spiritual connectedness that I read, I can't make sense of the idea.

A typical American novel in the spiritual vein was the popular *Turn of the Balance* (1907). Author Brand Whitlock, a death-penalty abolitionist, offered his protagonist Elizabeth as the embodiment of a new age. A banker's daughter, Elizabeth lives a life in stark contrast to that of another of the book's characters, the petty criminal Archie. Ultimately, Elizabeth and Archie are connected by their struggle for consciousness. Elizabeth makes contact with Archie when he is falsely accused of murder because, as it just so happens, she is being wooed by both Archie's defense attorney and the prosecutor. Unfortunately, Archie is convicted in spite of his innocence. As his execution nears, Elizabeth passes the time exploring the barriers to individual fulfillment presented by "unnatural" class differences and corruption in the justice system. As the lethal current passes through Archie, the doomed convict struggles "in torture and torment" toward a last second of human awareness. Almost simultaneously, Elizabeth comes to see in the moral bankruptcy of her own class a punishment similar to that they inflict on the hapless poor such as Archie.

Elizabeth sees that "both crime and punishment emanated from the same ignorant spirit of cruelty and fear. Would they ever learn of the great equity and tolerance, the simple love in nature?"

Sounds good—especially if you're still alive after gaining the insight.

Alert readers will recognize that the connection of spirit to the natural world—now called New Age spirituality—is still being preached in some quarters. If we tend to associate New Age thinking with California, we should all notice, as well, that Californians passed a 1976 amendment to the state constitution authorizing capital punishment. Californians also pioneered the three-strikes law in order to imprison repeat offenders, even non-violent ones, for life.

Searching for the wisdom of New Age gurus, I find that one Cory Quirino, Filipina inspirational speaker and author of a guide to beauty and health, advises readers to "connect to the mind of heaven." As a 1993 kidnap victim and now spokesperson for the Prevention of Crime Foundation, Quirino is also looking forward to the execution of her three abductors.

This is what Progressive era anti-death-penalty crusaders needed to know: the quest for personal growth and the thirst for revenge can coexist. Canny politician Elbridge Gerry, not Brand Whitlock's Elizabeth, was the harbinger of things to come. Gerry's—and the public's—curiosity about a new technology turned the execution into a celebration of technical rationality, bureaucratic decorum, and the art of euphemism.

Experts paved the way, and toney words and highbrow venues of explanation took the act of execution as far as it needed to be from any taint of vengeance, butchery, or capricious cruelty. Harold P. Brown explained this new humanitarianism in *The North American Review* only months before New York state's first execution in the electric chair took place. "The preparations necessary for electrical execution are very simple," Brown assured his readers. The convict, "shod in wet felt slippers," walks to the chair and is "instantly strapped into position;" "dials of electrical instruments indicate that all the apparatus is in perfect order." *Really,* Brown seemed to be saying, *it's a science experiment. If you were there—which, don't worry, you'll never have to be—you'd see how perfectly ... well, perfectly conducted it all is.*

Just as self-congratulation was about to be reached, however, a setback took place. It seemed that the joining of Gerry's two great outcomes of progress, electric power and more humane execution, might prove too much for the public mind. In the late 1870s, a patent had been applied for in New York to execute criminals by electrocution, and a similar idea had also been broached in Germany. One electric company sponsored "demonstrations" in which calves, horses, and other chosen creatures were shocked until the killing voltage of alternating current was attained. The company meant to tout the virtues of direct over alternating current. But other electric companies opposed death-penalty electrocution for fear that it would increase public mistrust of all uses of electricity. Not until Gerry and his fellow New York legislators saw the animal experiments did the new execution method find a sponsor. Soon afterward, on January 1, 1889, New York's law substituting electrocution for hanging went into effect.

The first death verdict under this law raised the question of cruel and unusual punishment. Learned discussion in the *North American Review, Scientific American*, and *Public Opinion* demonstrated conclusively, however, that "the majesty of the law would be vindicated and no pain caused." At Auburn Penitentiary on August 6, 1890, William Kemmler became the first condemned criminal to be executed by electric current.

Witnesses were upset by the smell of burning flesh and the "lifelike" straining against the straps after Kemmler was supposed to be unconscious. This was a smooth performance on the part of authority compared to a New York execution three years later—the current failed partway through and the condemned had to be chloroformed until his execution could be completed. But the indignation, though widespread, was short lived. Subsequent botched executions were to raise no serious qualms for the next century. New York had electrocuted 100 by 1906; less than twenty years later, over half of the thirty-four states that would ever replace hanging had done so. Execution by lethal gas had been discussed in print since at least the 1890s in much the same terms as electrocution, and was first used in Nevada in 1924. The Progressive era of death penalty abolition was over.

"The great industry of the world for four long years was killing," Clarence Darrow would later comment bitterly as he tried to explain why so many states rescinded their anti-death-penalty laws after World War I. As the approach of civil war had undercut the antebellum abolition campaign, America's entry into World War I undercut Progressive abolitionism. Wartime brutalization of the public—especially the many veterans who returned from the front—probably played its part. But another role of the war in America was to bare the nation's political fault lines—conservative against radical labor, white against black, the native born against new immigrants such as German-Americans who had succeeded all too well for the taste of some. Political positions for and against abolition went with membership in certain interest groups. They also reflected political advantages that each side expected to gain—this time, chiefly voter approval and a public following.

In this enterprise state legislators proved more insightful than governors, and local newspapers more far seeing than the national press. Once World War I began, scenarios in a number of states ended with the same last act.

- Missouri's governor Frederick G. Gardner was a death-penalty opponent, but he cited public support for capital punishment when he reluctantly allowed its restoration to be considered in a 1919 special session. The session's topic was supposed to be women's suffrage, and the governor hesitated to include capital punishment since the legislature had just voted against the death penalty in a regular session. But a legal majority of the House of Representatives presented Gardner with a petition. Gardner then demanded statistics on Missouri's crime rate before and after the death penalty was abolished. The statistics were never presented, but it was not long until the bill to restore capital punishment passed anyway.
- In Pennsylvania's 1917 death-penalty debate, a wartime circumstance gave the opportunity for one faction to pull the rug out from the other. The Senate passed an abolition bill by so wide a margin, 32 to 12, that the House was expected to follow. But before the House vote could be taken, an explosion at a Philadelphia-area munitions factory killed 150 workers and gave rise to rumors of sabotage. The House then defeated the abolition bill 97 to 83.
- Massachusetts, like Pennsylvania, had been a hub of anti-death-penalty activism since before the Civil War. Massachusetts legislators, however, voted down the 1920 abolition bill by 171 to 20.
- In Oregon, where factional labor tensions raged, the governor called for a capital treason law, citing "IWW-ism and other forms of disloyalty." A special session was convened in 1920 on

the constitutional amendment to restore capital punishment, during which the new governor managed to use the expressions "wave of crime," "criminal blight," "cold-blooded," "fiendish," and "dastardly" within a single speech.

———

Progressive idealists foresaw an American society of the future that would be truly humane as well as seemly and tasteful. They believed that social problems could be conquered by modern management practices such as the destruction of slums and penitentiary reform. Under such an onslaught of virtue, those who clung to capital punishment should have been shamed into renouncing their support. But, as practical politicians understood very well, death-penalty advocates were not convinced and probably never would be. On the contrary, punishment politics was strengthened immeasurably by the "good government" practices of Progressivism such as referendum and recall. Adding weight to these factors was the ever-growing army of law enforcement, judicial, and corrections systems bureaucrats. In hindsight it seems inevitable that government officials would develop vested interests of their own. "Scientific execution" came along at just the right moment to provide a brilliant solution to the dilemma of barbaric punishment versus political expediency. "The chair" was a step in the bureaucratic direction, and it was quickly put to use and kept in use for the large number of executions in populous states through the immigrant decades of the 1890s to 1920s.

What was new—and uniquely characteristic of Progressive reformism—was that politicians on both sides of the death penalty issue relied on experts. These came from the newly created professional categories of criminology, penology, and applied statistics. When proponents of execution alluded to criminals hardened beyond hope and pointed to the newly available disposal system of electrocution, opponents sketched out a program of rehabilitation based on expert diagnosis. In this heady atmosphere of experts' theories, pro-execution

Oregon senator B. L. Eddy, cited Darwin *and* asserted that he believed both Old and New testaments to be the word of God.

As part of the statistical argument, some raised the issue of poverty—did it increase the chance of being executed, as observers from Thomas Paine onward had contended? But the question went nowhere. Wartime rhetoric and wartime self-interest steamrollered considerations of fact.

Brand Whitlock, author of *The Turn of the Balance*, was not only a novelist but also a mayor of Toledo who had been campaigning against the death penalty since 1893. He was never able to effect abolition in Ohio, and as early as 1914 was sufficiently discouraged to give his memoir the weary title *Forty Years of It*. Still, the abolition movement trudged on during the 1920s and 1930s with Progressive Era leaders such as Whitlock and Darrow as well as new recruits like prolific author Lewis Lawes, warden of Sing Sing. All of these persons worked through organizations such as the International Anti-Capital-Punishment League (San Francisco and Los Angeles); the Anti-Capital-Punishment Society (Chicago); the Massachusetts Prison Reform Association; or, in New York alone, the Anti-Capital-Punishment League, the Anti-Capital-Punishment Society, and the League for the Abolition of Capital Punishment.

Collier's and some other wide-circulation periodicals had begun to support abolition, and the formerly pro-capital-punishment *New York Times* again raised the old issue that jurors were reluctant to convict at all when doing so meant the death sentence. Along with these journals, many intellectuals and officials with roots in Progressivism retained their underdog liberalism. But legislatures, governors, and broad segments of the public seemed to become more and more conservative. Local newspaper editorials made their assessment of the future plain by continuing to favor capital punishment. Ultimately, initiatives sponsored by reform organizations were unsuccessful in creating new abolition laws, nor could they block restoration of the death penalty in Kansas and South Dakota during the 1930s.

The Great Depression overlaid the ethnic social divisions of World War I with another category—haves against have-nots. Rates of execution for ethnic minorities remained high. Social critics like musician Woody Guthrie dared to say that poverty and radical views had more to do with criminal sentences than the crime itself. The first national polls during the 1930s did not connect responses to personal characteristics such as race and income. But a fairly broad minority must have felt the death penalty was unfair. Supporters of capital punishment during the Depression were in no larger majority than they are today—61 percent in 1937, with 39 percent opposed.

Still, as has nearly always been the case since national polls were instituted, advocates of the death penalty outnumbered opponents. This not-to-be-removed roadblock to abolition was something that death penalty abolitionists would have to learn to work around. Gradually, they did so—by switching arenas from state legislatures to the legal system.

Adopting electrocution after 1890 was different than earlier reforms to death penalty law. Previous changes—making executions private (1833), allowing jury discretion in sentencing (1838), and moving from county jail to penitentiary execution sites (1864)—tended to be made soonest in states where the death penalty was eventually abolished, at least for a time. But replacement of hanging by more modern methods entrenched execution as the status quo almost as often as it led to abolition. After 1914, humanitarian appeals, that once promised so much in the minds of reformers, were revealed as a double-edged sword. "Spirituality" was an individual quest. It wasn't an engagement with political issues, which relate fundamentally to the life of a community. At its best, spirituality led to identity politics—and, after all, how many people can identify with the doomed? And how many would want to? Once condemned convicts could be removed to the remoteness of the penitentiary and executed in the clean, well lighted place provided by science, humane "disposal" could be marketed as a real alternative to ending the death penalty.

Civil rights and beyond.

17

"Evolving Standards of Decency"
Civil Rights and the Abolition of the Death Penalty

William Henry Furman, with an IQ of 65, was a twenty-five-year old African-American. In 1968, he was convicted of murdering a white Coast Guard petty officer, father and stepfather of ten children, while burgling the victim's home. In appealing Furman's death sentence, his attorneys objected to the fact that Furman's jury had been given unrestricted discretion to choose the death sentence or life in prison. The attorneys argued that because the decision wasn't based on criteria, or on a principle of some kind, it violated Furman's right to due process and also made the resulting sentence cruel and unusual punishment.

In a historic decision, June 29, 1972, the Supreme Court agreed.

Capital punishment was over, ended in all fifty states.

The majority—consisting of justices Brennan, Douglas, Marshall, Stewart, and White—held in five separate opinions that capital punishment was contrary to present standards of decency, offered no deterrent advantage over imprisonment, and was applied capriciously and unfairly, especially against minorities.

Death penalty abolitionists were jubilant. The head of the Legal Defense Fund declared that there would "no longer be any more capital punishment in the United States," and another commentator called the decision "inevitable." At this heady moment the Supreme Court's conclusion must have felt like the culmination of the whole liberalizing trend that had made the Civil Rights era possible. As far back as 1958, then-Chief-Justice Earl Warren had identified the root issue of the Eighth Amendment as "the dignity of man." The amendment could not be interpreted in a static way over time, he suggested, but "must draw its meaning from the evolving standards of decency that mark the program of a maturing society."

The Supreme Court's views, if not society's, had been changing since the 1930s. In this decade, lawyers for defendants condemned to death began to succeed in making court appeals. Their basis was the Fourteenth Amendment. Section 1 of the amendment declares, in part, that no state can make or enforce laws that curtail the "privileges or immunities" of U. S. citizens; "nor shall any State deprive any Person of life, liberty, or property, without due process of law." Due process in a criminal case means:

- being informed of charges against oneself
- having the opportunity through a trial to present a defense
- having access to legal counsel
- having the right to an appeal if one is found guilty

The framers of the Constitution would have been surprised to find these rights applied to cases under state laws. Due process rights originated in the first ten Constitutional amendments, known as the Bill of Rights, but rights guaranteed in these amendments (4, 5, 6, and 8) were meant to protect U. S. citizens against the federal—not state—government. Only the Civil War made it obvious to federal lawmakers that citizens—specifically former slaves and those who befriended them—had to be protected against their own state governments. Court decisions since 1868, when the Fourteenth Amendment was passed, have filled out this protection intention through the legal principle called "incorporation."

From the 1930s to the 1960s, the number of appeals filed in death-penalty cases grew tenfold, from about 3 percent to 33 percent. We don't have historical data on appeals by those on death row who weren't executed, so these numbers are taken from those whose appeals didn't succeed. A series of Supreme Court decisions in this direction began in 1932—requiring that the defendant in capital cases have counsel (Powell v. Alabama), later prohibiting racial discrimination in jury selection (Patton v. Mississippi, 1947) and ruling against coerced confessions (Fikes v. Alabama, 1957). Policy analyses began to appear more frequently in law journals after World War II.

Ironically, stronger protection for capital defendants created another basis for appeals: the length of time between sentence and execution. To some, by the 1950s, the delay was a flaw in the system. But, only a decade later, others would make it into a strategy to be pursued.

These changes took place amid a public discussion of the death penalty that was heating up. European governments began debating the issue shortly after the end of World War II. In November 1952, the American journal *Annals of the American Academy of Political and Social Science* summarized the European trend as part of a special issue on capital punishment. The media began spotlighting American cases beginning with the Rosenberg execution in 1953. The Rosenberg issue was primarily one of guilt or innocence. But another case, that of Caryl Chessman, set off a decade of rhetoric on capital punishment.

Chessman was sentenced to death in 1948 on a technicality that resulted indirectly from the kidnaping and murder of Charles Lindbergh's baby fifteen years before. Famous aviator and inventor Lindbergh and his wife Anne Morrow Lindbergh were beloved public figures—both ultimate celebrities and ultimate survivors of a loved one's murder. After the murder, the U. S. Congress passed a law making kidnaping a federal offense if the victim was taken across a state line or if ransom was demanded through use of the U. S. mail. Twenty states' legislatures rushed to pass similar laws so that kidnaping with bodily harm could be tried in state courts as a capital offense.

Caryl Chessman was sentenced in California under one of these "little Lindbergh" laws, which mandated one of two automatic sentences: life without parole or death. Chessman wasn't accused of murder or rape. But he had terrorized Los Angeles for several weeks in 1948 as the lover's lane bandit who shined a police-type light into the cars of necking couples, robbed them, and sometimes forced the women to perform sexual acts. The patently hostile judge who tried the case construed these acts as bodily harm, and Chessman's taking the women to another site as kidnaping.

In some ways, Chessman was a classical example of the type of defendant who gets condemned in our time—indigent, in prison for previous offenses most of his adult life, and accused of harm to someone whose life was perceived to be much more valuable than his. From the trial onward, however, Chessman didn't act like other defendants. He chose to defend himself rather than employ a lawyer, and he claimed that his initial confession, which he later denied, was beaten out of him by the police. When convicted and sentenced to death, Chessman began to spend his time on death row writing books about his case. He had to smuggle the first manuscript out of prison, but three more books followed. By combining legal maneuvers and publicity, he kept himself alive for a then-record twelve years.

Caryl Chessman's books, such as *Cell 2455 Death Row* (1954), were bestsellers. He articulately portrayed mitigating circumstances in his life and the ways he had changed for the better during years on death row, and he gained worldwide sympathy. A Brazilian petition amassed over 2.5 million signatures for clemency. The plea was also supported by the Queen of Belgium, the Vatican, Albert Schweitzer, and others. But finally, against the will of abolitionist governor Edmund G. Brown, who had no latitude to give clemency in this case, Chessman died in the gas chamber on May 2, 1960.

Reactions to Chessman were almost a litmus test for authoritarians versus liberals. Many elements of his case could have and probably did set up a strong public and official wave of retributive feeling against him—his alleged sexual crimes, his refusal to say that he was guilty or to show remorse, his indirectly blaming society for conditions that made him a criminal, his using technical points of the law (though the judge and jury also did so), his "setting himself apart" from usual prisoner behavior by first defending himself and then writing books, and even his garnering foreign sympathy in the decade of the Ugly American.

On the other hand, many other people considered and were troubled by the fact that he wasn't a murderer, rapist, or even kidnaper in any substantial way. Concerned individuals also pointed to many doubtful points in his trial and subsequent appeals, to massive publicity including many statements contrary to fact, to the questionable deterrent effect of an execution twelve years after the crimes, and to Chessman's evident maturation toward social usefulness during his prison years.

The gap loomed large between public opinion taken as a whole and the pro-death-penalty opinion of vocal minorities, including law enforcement officials.

A Gallup poll taken about six weeks before Chessman's execution showed that a bare majority of 51 percent favored capital punishment. In 1957, one poll had already shown 50 percent opposed to the death penalty, and polls between then and 1966 showed high rates of "no opinion." In 1966, only 42 percent were in favor, with 47 percent actually opposed. Nine states ended capital punishment during this period: Alaska, Hawaii, and Delaware in 1958; Oregon in 1964; Iowa, New York, Vermont, and West Virginia in 1965; and New Mexico in 1969. In 1969, the total stood at 15 states having either no death penalty or, like North Dakota, Vermont, New York, and New Mexico, de facto abolition through a very restrictive use of the death penalty. Massachusetts joined abolishing states in 1984 when their state supreme court overturned a 1982 bill that had been designed to meet constitutionality requirements as outlined in the Furman decision. But a majority of legislatures reaffirmed death-penalty legislation. The California legislature is reported to have refused abolition bills 16 times between 1933 and 1960. Several governors who opposed the death penalty were defeated during these years—Robert Holmes of Oregon, 1958; Endicott Peabody of Massachusetts, 1964; and Edmund G. Brown of California, 1966.

Chessman's case focused the country's attention on a defense strategy based on technical legal points. This plan of attack was the pull factor and the hostility of state legislators was the push factor driving death-penalty battles into the courts. In the new arena, death-penalty defense acquired a strong civil rights context. It also highlighted regional differences in the way capital punishment was applied.

In 1963, attorneys for the NAACP Legal Defense Fund took up a suggestion by U. S. Supreme Court Justice Arthur Goldberg—who thought that the death penalty for rape, still frequently applied in the South and border states, might be unconstitutional. The Fund sponsored a study of racial discrimination in sentencing convicted rapists to death. The study found clear-cut discrimination in the sentencing of convicted blacks whose victims were white, and NAACP attorneys used this evidence in a number of appeals. It would be another fourteen years until the Supreme Court decided that a death sentence for rape was unconstitutional. But NAACP lawyers pressed ahead with new grounds for reversals—for example, that excluding death penalty opponents from juries and imposing mandatory death sentences were also unconstitutional. Defense attorneys took the position that these and other trial measures violated both the Eighth Amendment (prohibiting cruel and unusual punishment) and the Fourteenth Amendment (asserting the right to due process and equal protection under the law).

By 1965, the NAACP team had mounted an all-out attack—defending every death penalty inmate who asked their help and using all their arguments in each case they defended. This case-by-case strategy was meant to dramatize the brutality of execution by creating a backlog of the condemned. The public, the Legal Defense Fund and their advisers believed, would balk at executing hundreds almost en masse. The strategy was also intended to expose the weaknesses of the law in a way that couldn't be ignored. Within two years these abolitionist lawyers had brought executions to a halt.

State legal staffs began to expect that their death-penalty statutes would soon be declared unconstitutional, and they were right.

In 1972, the California Supreme Court and then the United States Supreme Court ruled in separate cases that capital punishment laws as written constituted cruel and unusual punishment. The federal decision in Furman v. Georgia marked the first time that the U. S. Supreme

Court ever set aside a death sentence, and it set aside 629—the number of persons on Death Row on June 29, 1972.

Capital punishment had been rejected by contemporary Americans—or would increasingly be so as public opinion became better informed. So the abolitionists, including some Supreme Court justices, believed. In their rush to see their longstanding hopes come true, opponents of capital punishment seem not to have noticed that the court agreed only by the minimum margin of five to four—and only in part. Dissenting justices Burger, Blackmun, Powell, and Rehnquist disagreed that capital punishment violated the Eighth Amendment. Rehnquist also emphasized the limited scope of the Supreme Court for making policy, Blackmun pointed out the lack of Supreme Court opposition at any past time, and Powell simply brushed aside the objection that the penalty falls disproportionately on the poor or nonwhite.

It would soon become all too clear that the court's decision didn't declare the death penalty itself to be unconstitutional.

At the time, the dissenting justices' most astute observation seemed to go unnoticed—considerable evidence suggested that Americans found capital punishment acceptable. In no time at all, the justices were proved right as states formed study commissions, introduced bills to reinstate the death penalty in conformity to the Furman decision, and passed the bills into law. Members of Congress began considering an amendment to the Constitution. Exactly two years after Furman, 100 persons were on death row in seventeen states. Another two years, and the fragile Supreme Court plurality of Furman came to an end.

In Gregg v. Georgia (1976), Gregg's attorneys made much the same argument used in Furman—that Gregg's death sentence was inherently cruel and unusual. Public standards of decency, the lawyers said, had evolved to the point that any execution was barbaric. The idea of capital punishment itself violated the Eighth and Fourteenth amendments.

A worse argument at this point in history could hardly have been chosen. In only four years, politics had moved on to a brave new world, and the Supreme Court was not slow to point this out.

First, said the 7-2 majority, thirty-five legislatures had brought back the death penalty as quickly as they possibly could. Congress had also re-enacted a death penalty—for lethal aircraft piracy—showing that our elected representatives, both state and national, supported capital punishment.

Second, California voters had approved a constitutional amendment authorizing the death penalty—showing that a broad base of voters in at least one state supported capital punishment.

Third, since the Furman decision, juries were choosing death over life imprisonment—460 persons on Death Row at the end of March 1976. These sentences showed that "the community" considered capital punishment useful, necessary, and appropriate.

What happened? The Gregg decision was not a product of newly appointed, more conservative justices. On the contrary, two justices who had voted in favor of the Furman decision, Stewart and White, cast the deciding votes in Gregg.

Strange as it seems, the Furman decision itself may have galvanized backers. Had Gregg come in the same year as Furman, 1972, the court could not have pointed to great public support for capital punishment. A poll that year showed 50 percent in favor, 41 percent opposed. Even the downturn of public mood in the years following multiple assassinations and the Vietnam war had not created a climate of death penalty support.

Clearly, as shown by the reactions of elected state officials to the Furman ruling, the death penalty was about authority. Georgia's lieutenant governor Lester Maddox labeled the decision to overturn the death penalty a "license for anarchy, rape, and murder." *The New York Daily News* called on legislators to restore capital punishment explicitly to test the Supreme Court's reaction. Legislators and bureaucrats, the media, and eventually the public seemed to feel that something had been taken from them—a measure of power and autonomy. In the four years from 1972 to 1976, public support for the death penalty made a dramatic leap upward—from 50 percent to 65 percent.

Above all, the near-instantaneous reaction of state legislators fueled the rush to reinstate the death penalty. The Civil Rights era, marked by federal intervention, was also marked by resentment of that intervention. In refusing to let the U. S. Supreme Court's "challenge" pass, state legislators may have been responding to their own fear of political powerlessness—and that of special interests such as state and local police forces. Media observers and commentators found a sensational story in the inflammatory comments that constituted political response in some states. Over a four-year period, the public only had to follow.

Court decisions from Gregg forward fine-tuned the revised death penalties that executing states so quickly adopted. Mandatory death sentences were abolished, jury guidelines as proposed by various states were accepted or sent back for more editing. Long overdue, the court's decision in Coker v. Georgia (1977) finally ruled the blatantly racist offense of capital rape unconstitutional.

But all states that wanted a death penalty for murder got one, and the abolitionists' only other argument against capital punishment—the statistical evidence of racial bias—was never accepted by the Supreme Court. They overruled death for rape on the grounds that it was an excessive penalty. Intent to discriminate racially, the justices said, must be demonstrated on a case-by-case basis. This statistics cannot do. With the defeat of their two main arguments, the Legal Defense Fund and its allies saw their strategy for abolishing the death penalty come to a dead end. They had tried to bypass legislative and popular support for capital punishment by going to the courts, and now the courts too turned against them.

With this reverse, the third major campaign to abolish the death penalty was over.

Civil-rights activists generated enough awareness that nine states— almost as many as in the Progressive Era—had already abolished capital punishment voluntarily before the Furman ruling. Of these, a surprising five—one more than in the antebellum campaign and three more than in the Progressive campaign—have never reinstated the death penalty.

Two of these five states, Iowa and Vermont, have a history of previous abolition activism. Before the Civil War, Vermonters led a campaign in which abolition legislation was attempted, though it didn't succeed. In Iowa, capital punishment was outlawed from 1872 to 1878 before being reinstated.

In the other three states, the death penalty became a civil rights issue. Alaska and Hawaii, with large indigenous populations, reacted to a history in which white newcomers forced capital punishment laws and used them against the original settlers. In embracing statehood, these two states rejected the death penalty. Opposition to the death penalty in West Virginia came in part from a populist tradition of sympathy for the underdog. Organized labor kept these feelings alive. And they were shared by the Scandinavian-descended workers of Michigan who carried a 1931 referendum upholding abolition.

Taken together, these five stories share a theme: citizens questioning the extent of a state's legitimate power over them. Opposition to state authority began to be debated at the most effective moment—just when regional identities were forming. Political parties nurtured and embedded certain views because their leaders looked to those who shared their attitudes when choosing candidates and appointees. From the founding of the United States until the Civil War, the question of state authority came up again and again, and it continued to be raised for several decades afterward in a few states such as Iowa. Individualistic or humanistic views, by contrast, were easily taken on and shed by a fickle public of joiners, as most clearly shown during the Progressive era. Institutionalized or party support for abolishing the death penalty lay dormant until the 1960s.

But some things didn't change during the Civil Rights era. Backlash against federal activism whipped up support for authoritarian state governments that supposedly represented local, versus outsider, interests.

The purpose of federal activism in a broad range of issues—education, hiring, and use of public facilities as well as the rights of prisoners—was, presumably, to bring about nationwide uniformity in civil rights law. But the tendency of most post-Furman court decisions of the 1980s and 1990s was to grant leeway to states that might want to cut back again on prisoners' rights. The following examples are decisions that have stood for ten to twenty years and are just now being revisited:

- "Proportionality review," in which state appellate courts compared a given death sentence to penalties imposed in other, similar cases to avoid discrimination, was made optional (Pulley v. Harris, 1984).
- States no longer needed to provide an attorney to the indigent condemned after their one mandatory appeal (Murray v. Giarratano, 1989). Supposedly, many or most appeals are frivolous and this measures eliminates such appeals—for the poor only, of course. In reality, 20 to 30 percent of death sentences since 1973 were overturned through appeals at all stages after conviction, and constitutional errors—not minor technicalities—were a frequent reason sentences were overturned. On the other hand, some persons have been executed on technicalities, such as the expiration of their appeals period before new evidence of innocence was found.
- New evidence potentially proving the condemned's actual innocence is no longer to be grounds for a hearing in federal court (Herrera v. Collins, 1993). Clemency is supposed to substitute for post-appeal court pleas where new evidence could be introduced. Before 1970, governors extended clemency—usually commutation of death to a life sentence—to about thirty percent of condemned persons. The rate over the past thirty years is about one case per year nationwide.

One decision of the "anti-defendant" years has been revisited: the 1989 Penry v. Linaugh finding that executing someone who is mentally retarded didn't violate the U. S. Constitution. This decision made mental retardation a potential mitigating factor to be considered only case by case—because, said the Supreme Court majority, there is no evidence that Americans have reached consensus on opposing execution of the retarded. The Supreme Court reversed itself only in 2002 (Atkins v. Virginia), stating that public consensus has now been reached. Meanwhile, twenty-seven or more retarded persons are thought to have been executed since Furman. One of them asked that part of his last meal be saved "for later." Another, who had "confessed" and been condemned, but hadn't yet been executed, was released after sixteen years on death row when DNA evidence cleared him of guilt in the crime.

Decisions like those cited above have permitted differences in execution law and practice from state to state that are only a little less extreme today than they were seventy-five years previously. Since the death penalty began to be applied again in 1977 (in Utah, against Gary Gilmore, who relinquished his appeals), Texas has carried out more than one-third of all executions in the United States. This total is way ahead of Virginia's, at about 10 percent (87) and the totals of Missouri (59), Oklahoma (55), and Florida (54) at about seven percent each.

It seems pretty likely that these states are those whose elected officials have figured out, based on their state's or county's history, that capital punishment is a leading vote-getter. State governments that lean heavily on the death penalty have successfully tapped into interest-group politics and get-tough-on-crime rhetoric. These trends have shrunk the ability of political parties to mold voter opinion. The change in political tactics was never more clear than in 1988 when the elder George Bush demolished the presidential campaign of Michael Dukakis, Democratic candidate and then-governor of Massachusetts. Bush—who lived in Texas as an oil investor at the time his son George W. was born—made a winning issue of the fact that Dukakis had started a 48-hour "prisoner furlough" program leading to the release of a convicted murderer, Willie Horton, who escaped from furlough to commit an assault and a rape. Al Gore, Dukakis's opponent for the Democratic nomination, was actually the first to question Dukakis publicly for supporting prisoner furlough. Gore's comment attracted Republican interest. Crucially, the word was spread by a so-called "independent expenditure group," who circulated a flyer featuring a photo of the African-American Horton.

Parties tailor their campaign to the most vocal group of single-interest voters at any given moment, and candidates who express the wrong opinion can be blackballed. Most elected officials who can put teeth into opposing the death penalty, like Illinois's ex-governor George Ryan, do so when they don't expect to run for re-election to their current office. As long as this political climate lasts, the leadership ball may be the other court—the state or federal supreme court. For instance, it's real news that, in 2003, the "racial and gender bias committee" appointed by Pennsylvania's highest court, after a three-year study, recommended a death-penalty moratorium.

In 1995 three scholars, in a report called A Broken System: Error Rates in Capital Cases, 1973-1995, used court records to determine that "68 percent of all verdicts fully reviewed in that period were found to be so seriously flawed that they had to be scrapped and retried. Where outcomes are known (for state post-conviction reversals), only 18 percent of retrials resulted in the reimposition of death. Seventy-five percent ended in a sentence less than death for murder, and seven percent ended in an acquittal." If actual innocence is not enough, the poor record of appeals courts in sustaining capital convictions may yet catch the attention of what San Francisco vigilantes liked to call "the law and order faction." In American death-penalty politics, some will go a long way to argue that those who speak up for due process of law are just another interest group.

Coin-Operated Electric Chair.

18

The Endless End of Capital Punishment

As we go about our daily lives now, we run no risk of encountering an official hanging in progress. We won't see a legally executed body dangling from a gibbet placed on the town square or in the parking lot of a suburban shopping mall. Gallows Hill, its ten thousand spectators, and its drawn-out spectacle of suffering belong to the past. But the hangman's knot goes on being tied—in a room within a building within a compound. The room is windowless, brightly fluorescent, divided in two by Plexiglas and a curtain. On one side are a dozen people, on the other side one. We've regularized and sanitized until we're down to white tiles, a gurney, and an intravenous drip. What was an event has been downgraded to an occurrence, then to the parody of a therapeutic procedure.

It's fitting that, in today's execution, the executioner is nowhere in sight. Execution is an act we carry out in common—lethal coercion in the name of all of us, as citizens of a state or the nation. Execution is a use of our political will, whether we bring it about through active support or through indifference. No matter how deeply prosecutors choose to involve a murder victim's loved ones in the pain of the trial and appeals, no matter how much empathy we feel for loved ones' suffering, execution is not a private transaction between survivors and the condemned.

I doubt we can go back to very high rates of execution or to public execution as a live spectator event. I don't think we'll see widespread vigilantism or mob lynching again. Americans came to our present use of the death penalty through a historical learning curve. The nationalizing of public opinion and the growth of government bureaucracies have left violent dissenters—both left and right—out in the cold, whether it's the Los Angeles rioters of 1965 or Timothy McVeigh in 2001. Recent experiences suggest that such dissenters will be stopped without their changing the wider world.

The historian Charles Tilly said, "People seeking to seize, hold, or realign the levers of power have continually engaged in collective violence as part of their struggles. The oppressed have struck in the name of justice, the privileged in the name of order, those in between in the name of fear." Execution is a level of power already attained as well as a bid for more power directed against an opposing faction. It's an end move in the unequal contest of two forces.

American factional contests from about 1790 to 1930 were especially intense: slaveholders against freeholders, capitalists against workers, native born against foreign, European-descended whites against people of color. The spread of Euro-American settlers across the continent was rapid and ugly, taking on all comers, chewing up and spitting out many. Our economic system was and is competitive— not in the sense of being based on a free market, but based on the struggles of factions. Each strives to gain the police and political power to determine a governing economic policy that favors its own interests. Our decentralized government created extra layers of competition. Early reliance on public opinion as the ostensible guide to policy created a broad audience to be played to. Ongoing but not unanimous public demand for the death penalty had to be met. At the same time, anti-execution sentiment and more restrictive definitions of public order, in the interests of large-scale commerce particularly, had to be satisfied—even if they were achieved in part by corporate vigilante violence.

Corporations manipulated and violently suppressed contending elements of labor, skilled versus unskilled, ethnicity against ethnicity, even as these worker factions fought among themselves. Social sorting was taking place along occupational lines as workers sought to join a middle class increasingly self-identified by occupation and mores. Around the same time, historical movements to reform mores through collective violence, from post-Civil-War Indiana whitecapping through the second Ku Klux Klan of the 1920s, easily mixed moral disapproval with economic self-interest. In the case of the Klan, moral inferiority became attached to particular religions and ethnicities. These were placed on a continuum with "real Americanism," a category whose boundaries were hardened by World War I. In the South before Emancipation, every European-American held police power over every African-American. The extent of power was limited only by the rule that he not decrease the value of slaves as property. After Emancipation, white Protestant perception of a common cause—to maintain power and authority—appears to have been strengthened by the institution of lynching, and not only in the South. A final step in the process of targeting occurred at about the same time as the rise of the second Klan—the setting apart of African-Americans. By assigning the very worst behavior primarily to one scapegoat group, European-Americans fused together their separate fears of immorality, encroachment, and violence.

Short of enforcement by martial law—which occurred in the 1850s in San Francisco, in the South after the Civil War, and in company towns between about 1880 and 1930—executions can't be held without the public's granting some legitimacy to capital punishment. In colonial times, public spaces, the presence of celebrity ministers, and a large (but not too large) audience could give the impression that taking a life was the will of the community. The processional road from community to Calvary even mimicked a kind of assent by the condemned, an affirmation of the rightness and necessity of atonement. A similar ceremony, but outside the law, continued to find community support on frontiers, and even into my own day in the South.

After our nation achieved independence from the British, execution became contentious. Our debates over capital punishment both sprang from and affected the nation's crises of political and social identity.

Does taking the lives of our fellow citizens make the rest of us savages, or does it mean we're obeying eternal laws? Is there some principle beyond personal safety and economic convenience underlying our union into a nation? Is there a limit to the consent of the governed? Where does a state's power end and the federal government's begin? Who gets to be an American, who doesn't?

First, debate centered on the identity of the young republic, including the contrast to be drawn between its liberalism and the colonial "barbarism" expressed in earlier criminal codes. Soon the debate shifted to the importance of individual human life. The Romantic movement invoked this emphasis, and the Second Great Awakening added religious expression and a zeal for mores reform. Third was the notion of "social privacy," or seemliness. But the new nation contained elements that could both "reform" execution and preserve it. Outcomes ranged from complete opposition to capital punishment, through support for reduced and privatized capital punishment, to continued support for the death penalty publicly administered.

The historical theorist Michel Foucault wrote that members of the middle class in parts of Europe opposed capital punishment as a means of asserting themselves politically at the expense of the monarchy. By the reform period of the 1820s and 1830s in the United States, an early kind of middle class dominated reform debate. This class was represented by reform leaders among politicians, preachers, and literary figures, and also by enlightened commercial capitalists such as Quaker merchant Thomas Cope, who in 1820 commented so disapprovingly on the ribald, unrepentant, and public last days of the condemned Bennet. Puritans and Quakers shared with other early Anglo-European settlers an enduring practice of appealing to the authority of religion and, related to this, an obsessive concern with mores. Reasoned resistance to authority such as the Enlightenment espoused has been the most effective motive historically for abolishing capital punishment. Deists and other freethinkers who were the intellectual descendants of the Enlightenment increasingly lost their mainstream cultural prestige after the American founding. But some of their descendants found fresh sources of energy and political support in building liberal political identities in newly settled states such as Michigan, Wisconsin, and Minnesota.

After about 1790, the meaning of the execution in the eyes of spectators became an unstable mixture of the authoritarian and the individualistic. Over time, governments resolved this instability by making execution private, then changing its method in keeping with new technologies. Penitentiary architecture at first symbolized reform aspirations and the pride of new governments by evoking periods of might and splendor in the human past. The elaborateness of these styles served as a source of civic pride, then of bureaucratic self-advertisement. External architectural references did not relate to local traditions or conditions or to what went on within the walls. When the penitentiary became the execution site, bureaucrats moved the death penalty decisively into the sphere of procedures, not gestures or debates. Penitentiary execution introduced extra-communal reasons for decisions about punishment. Penitentiary execution also facilitated technical innovations that could be labeled humane. Disappearance from the public forum and the minimization of visible suffering reconciled the irreconcilable. In a pluralistic society whose legal authority is decentralized, division of opinion on the subject of execution cannot finally be resolved. Rather, opposing stances must be accommodated. Execution as we practice it today satisfies its supporters but doesn't impinge on the world of the polity.

In the past, both legal execution and lynching helped to create and to label the winners and losers in a given power struggle. Penitentiary imprisonment may still work in this way. But execution today isn't even repression. It's mere symbolism. The fewer we execute, the more obvious this reality becomes. Lately, it's also become more obvious as we find out how many we've executed are actually innocent.

Opposition to the death penalty began in a fear of government encroachment that has not diminished, yet the citizens of most states are now willing to concede the power of life and death to their governments. From one perspective this is a success story. Americans have come to feel that ours is a government of the people, and in form it increasingly is. In 1846 the Michigan legislature was able to abolish the death penalty with neither yea nor nay from voters; by 1972 members of the highest court in the land appealed to citizen "standards" of acceptable punishment as a basis of judicial decision against death penalty laws as they stood.

From another perspective the continuation of the death penalty in America is a story of the loss of innocence: the lost faith of Enlightenment thinkers in reason, of reformers in redemption, of the citizenry in its own unitary good will. Belief and the loss of belief have been cyclic. But each repetition has tied off a set of options even as it has provided a set of substitutes. Newer ideologies inevitably democratized society by translating into a broader base of political power, leading to the referendum and the opinion poll. In an ironic finale, the act of execution has become both one of the most authoritarian and one of the most direct transactions possible between the individual and the state.

At the same time, the abandonment of public space and the bloodlessness of mandated killing have made the condemned an abstraction. They are a true Other, devoid of any dimension of existence to which we can commit ourselves ethically. "Who killed this man?" becomes a question increasingly easy to shrug off. This situation implies no lessening of political control but rather the compounding and diffusion of control to the point of untrackability. As this process has occurred, it has become increasingly difficult to assign what I can only call "reality" to the gesture of the execution. Where does capital punishment fit into the life of the polity? To what does it connect?

Killing is in part the mental act of severing absolutely our connection to another. We may commit this act while under the influence of drugs or delusions or uncontrolled rage, or we may commit it with premeditation for a perceived advantage. Or we may commit it in the name of justice. In all cases equally, we abdicate the social bond. In the case of capital punishment, what makes abdication of the social bond most suspect is that it is neither random nor clearly merited by the individuals singled out for legal killing. Rather, the condemned are members of particular populations who have been abandoned or sacrificed in other contexts as well—for example, those who have been the most frequent victims of *extralegal* punishments, such as lynching. Execution, no matter how legal or popular, is an instance of the very state of affairs we are so quick to deplore in other contexts. I find it significant that collectively we are no better equipped to heal the families of murder victims than we are to find a productive role or outlet of restitution for murderers.

In 1877, the widow of Benjamin Yost asked to pull the lever that would spring the trap and hang two of the Molly Maguires convicted of murdering her husband. Her request was refused, but family members of some murder victims still ask that the death penalty be applied, and that they witness the execution. The meaning of our losses is also part of our position in the death penalty debate. Both supporters and opponents say they want justice. But what does justice mean? For many death penalty opponents, including myself, justice means a level playing field and protection from the arbitrary use of force. At a more emotional level, I can find in myself that old favorite, rebellion against authority—the child asking why.

One child asks why, the other asks tit for tat. Someone who has lost a loved one to murder may feel that her or his loss has been treated contemptuously if the murderer doesn't receive the ultimate penalty. Execution as a sign of respect. Imprisonment, even for life and without possibility of parole, may be presented to survivors as only a second prize. Some victims' families who witnessed the execution have said that the murderer should have suffered more, should have had to die a thousand times.

I haven't lost a loved one to murder. I have to extend my imagination from the kind of loss I have sustained, suddenly and irremediably losing my trust in a loved one. After this loss I spent years in anger, fantasizing revenge in graphic terms. I don't know whether I could have forgiven in the sense of embracing the one who harmed me. But I know that my thirst for revenge was the thirst of Tantalus, the protagonist of a Greek myth who was condemned to stand in water that shrank away when he tried to drink. No penalty I could invent or dwell on in imagination, no reverse that the hurtful other could or did suffer (including death) could ever become as real or grow as large in my mind as the loss I suffered. Anger made more anger. When I got too tired to uphold my anger any longer, I found that grief had had the patience to wait for me. Anger is to grief as skinning one's knee is to plunging one's bare hand into a fire. I wonder if some who insist on vengeance for their personal losses know intuitively that their anger is staving off a greater pain.

Our overlooking both murder survivors and perpetrators represents at least in part the same kind of self-interested reasoning that Josiah Royce described when he said that California Gold Rush miners preferred to lynch thieves rather than build a jail. As we discover more errors in the legal system that executes, voters in more and more states may face a choice between paying for a real defense for the poor and abridging the rights of capital defendants. And even if we adopt one of these choices at the expense of the other, we won't have come up with a better way to heal the wounded survivors of violence. Will we just go on offering death sentences to "console" a very few of the survivors, and let the rest get on alone as best they can?

What we decide about issues like these will become our next chapter. Punishment is only partly apportioned according to facts, therefore it's an ongoing act of storytelling. Stories, unlike the events themselves, push for closure and have little room for ambiguity. They tell us that it's easy to figure out who did this thing, that it's easy to figure out what the thing is; murder is murder. The climax of the story is punishment, and the most dramatically satisfying punishment is death. Stories don't tell us that a minuscule fraction of those who lose a loved one to murder can ever be offered the choice of witnessing the execution of the condemned murderer, who in any case may be innocent. As we tell the story of capital punishment, we calibrate and assert a value for human life. The ritual of punishment suggests that the value of human life is an unchanging one—even as in political reality we who are safe pick and choose among those who are eligible to die. In carrying out an execution, we use human mortality itself to deny that human meanings are temporary. At times and places where we have had cause to believe most strongly in our own possibilities and worth, we have had the least need to punish. The present in America is not one of those times and places.

Photo Credits

The Hanging of George Woods

An execution in Yuma, Arizona, 1906. Courtesy of the Arizona Historical Society/Tucson (photo #60563).

1. "The Right Type of Case"

Larry Stegall, cover of prisoner-produced magazine *The Angolite*, July-August 1981. Courtesy of the Louisiana State Penitentiary, Angola, Louisiana.

2. The Worst of the Worst

"The Examination of a Witch," painting by T. H. Matteson, 1853. Courtesy of the Peabody Essex Museum, Salem, Massachusetts (photo #134,536).

3. "A Vast Circle of People"

Eliphalet Adams, A Sermon Preached on the occasion of the Execution of Katherine Garret... Pamphlet printed and sold by T. Green, New London, Connecticut, 1738). Courtesy of the Boston Athenaeum Library.

4. "Darkness, Threatening, Ruins, Terror"

Cell block seven, built 1829, photographed 1998. Courtesy of Randall Wise, photographer, and the Eastern State Penitentiary, Philadelphia.

5. The Will of the People

Hanging of Pvt. William Johnson near Peterburg, Virginia, June 20, 1864. Courtesy of the Library of Congress, Prints and Photographs Division (photo #B8184-2355).

6.   Legacy of Conquest

Soldiers in Ku Klux Klan dress, Huntsville, Alabama. Illustration in Harper's Weekly, December 19, 1868. Courtesy of the Indiana University Library Research Collections, Bloomington.

7.   Shivaree

Mob dragging a dead soldier during the New York anti-draft riot of 1863. Illustration in Joel T. Headley, *Pen and Pencil Sketches of the Great Riots* (New York: E. B. Treat, 1877). Courtesy of the Indiana University Library Research Collections, Bloomington.

8.   "Let Each Man Be His Own Executioner"

"Lettersheet," or illustrated letter paper, depicting two hangings by the Vigilance Committee of 1851. Courtesy of the Bancroft Library, University of California, Berkeley (photo #1963.151A).

9.   Takeover

News sheet for sale in San Francisco following executions by the Vigilance Committee of 1856. Courtesy of the Bancroft Library, University of California, Berkeley (photo #1963.2.32A).

10.   Boots, Bullets, and Big Bucks

Cover, Zane Grey, *To the Last Man* (Canada: Hodder & Stoughton, 1921). Author's collection.

11.   "Beaten All to Smash"

Letter from the "Black Hand" threatening a strike sympathizer, c. 1914. Courtesy of the Western History Collection, Denver Public Library, Colorado (photo X-60 379).

12.   "Death and Destruction to the System"

Pin worn in solidarity with executed Haymarket rioters, 1888. Courtesy of the Chicago Historical Society (DIA-1958.420).

13. White Terrorism

Handbill dated from Headquarters, Southern Indiana Vigilance Committee, December 21, 1868. Author's collection.

14. "Serving Your Racial Needs"

Cover illustration of a pamphlet published c. 1935 by the New-York-based Committee for the Defense of Civil Rights in Tampa (Florida), Norman Thomas, Chairman. Courtesy of the Indiana University Library Research Collections, Bloomington.

15. "Foreigners and Negroes"

NAACP Office, 69 Fifth Avenue, New York, c. 1938. Courtesy of the NAACP and the Library of Congress, Prints and Photographs Division (photo #LC-USZC4-4734/LC-USZ62-33793 [6-10B]).

16. A Clean, Well-Lighted Place

Eva Dugan, police booking photo and official invitation to witness her non-public hanging. Courtesy of the Arizona Historical Society/Northern Division, Flagstaff (photo #666-163).

17. "Evolving Standards of Decency"

"White Woman to Be Tried as Black Man," by Ruben Bolling, 1998. Courtesy of the artist.

18. The Endless End of Capital Punishment

"Coin-Operated Electric Chair," by Clayton Bailey, 1984. Courtesy of www.claytonbailey.com.

Notes

The Hanging of George Woods

The interpretations of legal execution that I make throughout this book are based on data compiled by M. Watt Espy, Jr., Capital Punishment Research Project, Headland, Alabama. Espy's is the most complete existing list of colonial American and U. S. legal executions from 1608 to 1991. A slightly less complete version has been digitized as ICPSR 8451, authored by Espy and John O. Smylka, and archived at the Inter-university Consortium for Political and Social Research, Ann Arbor, Michigan. Many researchers, including me, have extended Espy's data by adding cases from additional historical records and by bringing the list into the present. "Death Row, USA," a project of the NAACP Legal Defense and Educational Fund, Inc., online at http://www.deathpenaltyinfo.org/DeathRowUSA1.html, provides quarterly updates of those executed and those on death row.

Though I've done my own historical research and analysis, my thinking about capital punishment owes a great deal to others' hard work. Throughout these notes, I'll try to mention those whose research, experiences, and writing I relied on. A compact, strong scholarly analysis and overview of the American death penalty is *Deathquest* (Cincinnati: Anderson, 1999; also paperback), by criminal justice professor Robert M. Bohm. Peter Neufeld and Jim Dwyer's *Actual Innocence* (New York: Doubleday, 2000) is the case study of how wrongful conviction happened in Illinois. Neufeld and Dwyer's reporting is confirmed by scholarly data from, among other sources, Hugo Adam Bedau and Michael L. Radelet, "Miscarriages of Justice in Potentially Capital Cases," *Stanford Law Review* 40 (1987): 21-179. Still approachable and inspiring in its humanness, yet as even-handed as any account of personal experience I've read, is Sister Helen Prejean's *Dead Man Walking* (New York: Random House, 1993; also paperback).

The fast-changing status of the American death penalty can best be followed on selected Internet sites. A good place to start, although their statistics are a year or two old at any given time, is the U. S. Bureau of Justice Statistics, http://www.ojp.usdoj.gov/bjs/. Information on the international death penalty can be found on Amnesty International's webpage at http://www.amnestyusa.org/abolish/world.html.

Page

2   *Jamestown, Virginia, in 1608 and 1622:* M. Watt Espy, Jr., personal communication.

3   *over 15,000 convicted criminals have been executed:* Data from Capital Punishment Research Project and NAACP Legal Defense and Educational Fund, Inc. quarterly report for October, 2002. Different sources give different exact counts. Espy counted 4,295 executions for the colonial period, bringing the total to 19,365 (1,608 to October 2002). Such an exact number is misleading, given that an unknown number of historical executions still haven't been documented.

1. "The Right Type of Case"

Opponents of the death penalty, because they're the underdogs at present, may have worked harder to make their case. Two good websites are run by the Death Penalty Information Center, http://www.deathpenaltyinfo.org/topics.html and the Campaign to End the Death Penalty, http://www.nodeathpenalty.org/fiveRs3.html.

The Texas Defender Service has an excellent factual website dealing with death-penalty law and process in Texas at http://www.texasdefender.org/study/study.html. Various death-penalty poll results are available at the site of the Death Penalty Information Center, http://www.deathpenaltyinfo.org/Polls.html.

Page

11   *John Lamb was executed, Sammy Gravano was not:* Sources are David Isay and Stacy Abramson, interviewers, "#587: A Death Row Inmate Tells His Own Life Story," and Jeffrey Goldberg, "Sammy the Bull Explains How the Mob Got Made," *New York Times Magazine*, January 2, 2000.

12   *more than two-thirds of those who have their sentences reviewed:* James S. Liebman, Jeffrey Fagan, and Valerie West, "Death Matters: A Reply," *Judicature* 84:2 (2000), 72.

14   *107 condemned persons (and counting):* Innocence and the Death Penalty, Death Penalty Information Center, online at http://www.deathpenaltyinfo.org/innoc.html.

15   *The first argument is deterrence:* Robert M. Bohm, *Deathquest* (Cincinnati: Anderson, 1999), 83-101, summarizes arguments and studies on the death penalty as deterrent.

16   *The second argument is cost:* Bohm, *Deathquest*, 103-124, for studies and numbers.

18   *even if innocent people are sentenced to death:* Gallup Poll News Service, based on a CNN/USA Today/Gallup poll, January 16-18, 1998.

18   *In another poll, respondents were asked:* Gallup Poll News Service based on a poll taken February 14-15, 2000.

19   *persons with household incomes under $15,000 per year:* Crime and Victim Statistics (2001), Bureau of Justice Statistics, U. S. Department of Justice, online at http://www.ojp.usdoj.gov/bjs/cvict.htm.

2. The Worst of the Worst

Thomas Paine's works are online as a project of the Department of Humanities Computing, University of Groningen, The Netherlands, 2002: http://odur.let.rug.nl/~usa/D/1776-1800/paine.

In one year alone, three publishers brought out or reprinted books on the Salem witch trials: Francis Hill, *A Delusion of Satan* (Cambridge MA: Da Capo, 2002 [1995]); Mary Beth Norton, *In the Devil's Snare* (New York: Alfred A. Knopf, 2002); Marilynne K. Roach, *The Salem Witch Trials* (New York:

Cooper Square Press, 2002). Strong on analysis is Paul Boyer and Stephen Nissenbaum's *Salem Possessed* (Cambridge MA: Harvard University Press, 1974). The earliest account from an outside perspective may be Charles W. Upham, *Salem Witchcraft*, originally published in 1867, reprinted Mineola NY: Dover Publications, 2000. Upham's account includes great maps showing the spread of the witchcraft epidemic, and it's and still worth reading. Trial transcripts, some in original handwriting, are online at the website of Douglas Lindner, Famous American Trials, http://www.law.umkc.edu/faculty/projects/ftrials/salem/salem.htm.

Page

23   *The Indiana Supreme Court's commission on race and gender fairness:* Press release, January 17, 2003, David J. Remondini, Indiana Supreme Court media representative, email dremondini@state.courts.in.us, online at www.in.gov/judiciary/fairness/index.html. See Executive Report, Indiana Supreme Court Commission on Race and Gender Fairness, online at http://www.in.gov/judiciary/fairness/pubs.html.

36   *even if the prisoner's case for error isn't airtight:* Linda Greenhouse, "Justices Stress Inmates' Right to Press Appeal," *New York Times*, February 25, 2003.

36   *"even if we find Mr. Amrine is actually innocent":* Quoted in Adam Liptak, "Prosecutors See Limits to Doubt in Capital Cases," *New York Times*, February 24, 2003.

37   *"reveling, frolicking, profane and unclean conversation":* Letter from Jonathan Edwards, December 12, 1743, Northampton, Massachusetts, to the Reverend Thomas Prince in Boston. Published as "The State of Religion at Northampton in the County of Hampshire, About 100 Miles Westward of Boston" in *The Christian History* 1 (Jan. 14, 21, 28, 1743).

3. "A Vast Circle of People"

The case of Amina Lawal is summarized from an insiders' perspective at the website of Women Living Under Muslim Laws, http://www.wluml.org/english/new-archives/nigeria/amina-lawal-summary-0802.htm.

The executions of Chamblit and Garret are told, respectively, in Thomas Foxcroft, *A Sermon Preach'd on Lord's-Day Sept. 23, 1733, Upon the affecting Occasion of An unhappy Young Woman present in the Assembly under Sentence of Death* (Boston, New England: S. Kneeland and T. Green, 1733), and Eliphalet Adams, *A Sermon Preached on the Occasion of the Execution of Katherine Garret, an Indian-Servant* ... (New London: T. Green, 1738). The Foxcroft pamphlet includes the text of "An Act to prevent the Destroying and Murdering of Bastard Children." Also see David H. Flaherty, "Crime and Social Control in Provincial Massachusetts," *Historical Journal* 24 (1981), 339-360, and Daniel A. Cohen, "In Defense of the Gallows: Justification of Capital Punishment in New England Execution Sermons, 1674-1825," *American Quarterly* 40:2 (1988), 147-164. A good discussion of the development of middle class thinking about the death penalty in Thomas Cope's time is Louis Masur, *Rites of Execution: Capital Punishment and the Transformation of American Culture, 1776-1865* (New York: Oxford University Press, 1989). The office of the prosecutor, Clark County, Indiana, offers hundreds of online links to sites making arguments in support of the death penalty today: http://www.clarkprosecutor.org/html/links/dplinks.htmpro.

Page

44 *"absolutely the most vicious and savage individual I know"*: Wesley Lowe, Pro-Death-Penalty Webpage at http://www.wesleylowe.com/cp.html.

47 *"Can this be the best mode of managing such cases?"*: All quotations from Thomas P. Cope are part of his diary entry of July 21, 1820. See Eliza Cope Harrison, ed., *Philadelphia Merchant: The Diary of Thomas P. Cope, 1800-1851* (South Bend, IN: Gateway Editions, 1978), 357.

48 *"Under Ashcroft, Judicial Power Flows Back to Washington"*: Adam Liptak, *New York Times*, February 16, 2003.

4. "Darkness, Threatening, Ruins, Terror"

For the number of those incarcerated on death row, see the NAACP Legal Defense and Educational Fund, Inc., quarterly report for October 2002. For numbers in prisons as a whole, and useful analysis, see the U. S. Bureau of Justice Statistics at http://www.ojp.usdoj.gov/bjs/prisons.htm, and the *MotherJones.com* report at http://www.motherjones.com/prisons/atlas.html.

Michael Steven Hindus, *Prison and Plantation* (Chapel Hill: University of North Carolina Press, 1980), 214-149, discusses the historical development of reform ideas, and the reasons for discouragement, in the two contrasting penal systems of South Carolina and Massachusetts between 1767 and 1868. Also see David J. Rothman, *The Discovery of the Asylum* (Boston, MA: Little, Brown, 1971), and Michel Foucault, *Discipline and Punish: The Birth of the Prison*, tr. Alan Sheridan (New York: Pantheon, 1977 [1975]). A model case study of the process of penitentiary "reform," sufficiently detailed to evoke exactly what went wrong, is contained in Harry Elmer Barnes, *A History of the Penal, Reformatory, and Correctional Institutions of the State of New Jersey* (Trenton, NJ: MacCrellish and Quigley, 1918 [New York: Arno Press, 1974]), 55-234. Also see Harry Elmer Barnes, *The Evolution of Penology in Pennsylvania* (Montclair, NJ: Patterson Smith, 1968, originally published 1927).

Several articles in historical society journals detail the history of capital punishment reform in individual states, and these stories and the public discussion that went with them are summarized in David Brion Davis, "The Movement to Abolish Capital Punishment," *American Historical Review* 63 (1957).

Page

51   *only twenty-five percent of our drop in crime can be accounted for:* William Spelman, "The Limited Importance of Prison Expansion," in Alfred Blumstein and Joel Wallman, eds., *The Crime Drop in America* (New York: Cambridge University Press, 2000), 7-129.

53   *"To reclaim rather than to destroy": The Statutes at Large of Pennsylvania* 12 (1786), 280.

55   *"Darkness, threatening, ruins, terror,"* Francesco Milizia *wrote*: *Principi di architettura civile* (Venezia, Italy, 1785), 2, 227-228, this and following quotations translated by Norman Johnston and cited in Johnston, *The Human Cage: A Brief History of Prison Architecture* (New York: Walker and Company, 1973), 16.

56   *to create "architecture adapted to morals"*: Boston Prison Discipline Society (*Fourth Annual Report*, 1829, 54-55), quoted in Rothman, *Discovery of the Asylum*, 83-84. Also see John Haviland, A Description of the Plan for a New Penitentiary (Philadelphia, no publication data, 1824).

56   *Reporting on New Jersey's original, congregate penitentiary:* Quotations from *Votes and Proceedings of the Fifty-fourth General Assembly of the State of New Jersey*, February 11, 1830, 170-171.

58   *Samuel Gridley Howe could use the expression "the criminal or dangerous class"*: Howe, *A Letter to J. H. Wilkins, H. B. Rogers, and F. B. Fay, Commissioners of Massachusetts for the State Reform School for Girls* (Boston, MA, 1854), 12, quoted in Hindus, *Prison and Plantation*, 234.

60   *When Samuel Mills, a 26-year-old miner, was executed:* All quotations relating to the Mills hanging are from Elmore Whipple, interviewed in 1935 by Ella Shannon Bowles, "Last Public Hanging in New Hampshire," *Yankee* (April 1938), 26-27.

5. The Will of the People

Michigan's abolition of the death penalty is told by Edward W. Bennett, "The Reasons for Michigan's Abolition of Capital Punishment," *Michigan History* 62:1 (1978), 42-55, and Albert Post, "Michigan Abolishes Capital Punishment," *Michigan History* 29:1 (1945), 44-50. Also see H. H. Bingham, "The Abolishment of Death Penalty: History of the Substitution of Solitary Imprisonment for the Death Penalty in the State of Michigan and the Comparative Results," a report from Michigan State Prison, Jackson, on December 1, 1869, in undated issue of *Pioneer Collections* (Lansing: Pioneer Society of Michigan) 6, 99-102. All of these sources contain some biographical information on legislators; also see S. D. Bingham, compiler, *Early History of Michigan with Biographies of State Officers, Members of Congress, Judges, and Legislators* (Lansing, MI: Thorp and Godfrey, State Printers and Binders, 1888) and, for James Van Dyke and William Fenton, *Cyclopedia of Michigan* (New York: Western Publishing and Engraving, 1890), 231-232. The political analysis of Michigan legislators draws on Alexandra McCoy, Political Affiliations of American Economic Elites: Wayne County, Michigan, 1844, 1860, As a Test Case (Ph.D. thesis, Wayne State University, Detroit, MI, 1965), and Ronald P. Formisano, *The Birth of Mass Political Parties: Michigan, 1827-1861* (Princeton, NJ: Princeton University Press, 1971).

The history of the death penalty in most states has to be researched one state at a time. The articles that have appeared in various historical journals are too numerous to list, but examples include J. J. Barbour, "Efforts to Abolish the Death Penalty in Illinois," *Georgetown Law Journal* 9 (1919), 500, Norman S. Hayner and John R. Cranor, "The Death Penalty in Washington State," *The Annals of the American Academy of Political and Social Science* 284 (1952), 101-104, and Albert Post, "The Anti-gallows Movement in Ohio," *Ohio State Archaeological and Historical Quarterly* 54 (1945), April-June, 104-112. More recently, historical death-penalty information has appeared on websites, such as the Justice Center Website of the University of Alaska, Anchorage, at http://www.uaa.alaska.edu/just/death/alaska.html. The cultural history of individual states is diffused through myriad state histories and histories of time periods and influential individuals, for instance Perry Miller, *Roger Williams, An Essay in Interpretation,* in *The Complete Writings of Roger Williams* (New York: Russell and Russel, 1963), vol. 7 (for Rhode Island); Charles M. Andrews, *The Colonial Period of American History,* vol. 2 (New Haven, CN: Yale University Press, 1934); Lois Kimball Mathews, *The Expansion of New England* (Boston, MA: Houghton Mifflin, 1909), 234-247 for Wisconsin; Stanley D. Porteus, *A Century of Social Thinking in Hawaii* (Palo Alto, CA: Pacific Books, 1962), esp. 3-58; Otis K. Rice, *West Virginia: A History* (Lexington, KY: University Press of Kentucky, 1985), 142ff, 281.

Current poll results by state, nationally, and internationally are found online at the Death Penalty Information Center website, http://www.deathpenaltyinfo.org/Polls.htm.

Page

63   *Wisconsin is one of three states, with Michigan:* The Michigan abolition
      law passed in 1846 was signed by the governor and went into effect on
      March 1, 1847.

65   *"imprisonment in the state prison for life":* This wording and its revisions
      are recorded in the *Journal of the House of Representatives, 1846,* 515-
      516, 575-577, 599, 612-613, and *Journal of the Senate, 1846,* 90-92; also
      see the *Revised Statutes of the State of Michigan, 1846,* 658.

65   *it wasn't until 1929 that reinstatement really came close:* For activity
      1929-1931, see Willis F. Dunbar, *Michigan: A History of the Wolverine
      State,* rev. George S. May (Grand Rapids, MI: William B. Eerdmans,
      1980), esp. p. 613; Michigan Legislative Service Bureau, *Capital
      Punishment,* Research Report 4:6 (1989), 4-5; Bennett, "Michigan's
      Abolition," 55 and note 37.

66   *"No law shall be enacted providing for the penalty of death":* Article IV,
      Section 46, *Constitution of the State of Michigan, 1963.*

66   *A poll of Detroit voters in a 1986 primary: Detroit Free Press,* August 3,
      1986, 11A; national comparison poll, George H. Gallup, *The Gallup
      Poll, 1987* (Wilmington, DE: Scholarly Research Services, 1988), 251.

67   *Judging from the record of legislative debate:* Documents of the Senate and
      of the House of Representatives, 1844, nos. 22 and 23.

68   *no more than a "newfangled theory":* Stephen Vickery, representative
      from Kalamazoo County, quoted in the *Advertiser,* Detroit, MI,
      February 1, 1843.

68   *"traitors and pirates, and murderers and robbers":* Hiram Stone's report
      and the minority report are recorded in *Documents of the Senate and of
      the House of Representatives, 1844* (Detroit, MI: Bagg and Harmon),
      nos. 22 and 23.

73   *Marvin H. Bovee wrote at length to Governor Oglesby:* Marvin H. Bovee
      to Governor Richard J. Oglesby, June 14, 1866, collected in Bovee, *Christ
      and the Gallows* (New York: Masonic Publishing Co., 1869), 271-279.
      Italics in the original.

6. Legacy of Conquest

This chapter owes a lot to Daniel J. Flanigan, *The Criminal Law of Slavery and Freedom* (New York: Garland, 1987), and Allen W. Trelease, *White Terror,* 1st ed. (New York: Harper and Row, 1971). The precursor to Trelease's reporting and analysis on the first Klan is Stanley Horn, *Invisible Empire* (Boston: Houghton, Mifflin, 1939). An overview of the era and its violence is Eric Foner, *Reconstruction: America's Unfinished Revolution, 1863-1877* (New York: Harper and Row, 1988).

Extensive records are on file in the National Archives, and available at repository libraries, for both the Freedmen's Bureau (U. S. Bureau of Refugees, Freedmen, and Abandoned Lands) and Congressional hearings on the activities of the Klan (U. S. Joint Select Committee to Inquire into the Condition of Affairs in the Late Insurrectionary States, 1871).

Most influential to my thinking about lynching is Stewart E. Tolnay and E. M. Beck's book *A Festival of Violence* (Urbana: University of Illinois Press, 1995), a statistical and verbal analysis of lynchings in ten Southern states based on verified, case by case historical data. Without minimizing the role of racial hatred in Southern lynching, the authors concluded that economic competition was generally needed to fan ugly talk and ugly behavior into murder after murder over the many years that lynching was a community supported activity in their study states. Tolnay and Beck's time period (1882-1930) is later than the Civil War era covered in this chapter, and their geographic range is regional. They aren't in any way responsible for the way I've applied their reasoning, either within or outside their study area.

Page

77   *identified in the public [i.e., white] mind with the race to which they belonged:* Dred Scott v. Sanford, 19 Howard 477 (1856).

78   *twelve percent of all persons executed were slaves:* Estimated from the Espy data base of legal executions and historical U. S. census data. Indians, whose population size is unknown, were executed in about equal numbers to African-Americans in Massachusetts.

78   *pre-Civil-War discriminatory laws:* Eugene H. Berwanger, *The Frontier Against Slavery* (Urbana: University of Illinois Press, 1967), 59.

79   *mobs estimated at up to 50,000 went berserk:* Joel B. Headley gives a detailed, near-contemporary account of the draft riot, and recounts other historical American riots, in *Pen and Pencil Sketches of the Great Riots* (New York: E. B. Treat, 1877).

79   *forty African-Americans were hanged and forty more imprisoned:* Reported in Bell I. Wiley, *Southern Negroes, 1861-1865* (New Haven: Yale University Press, 1938).

80   *according to reports gathered by the Freedmen's Bureau:* Reported in John A. Carpenter, "Atrocities in the Reconstruction Period," *Journal of Negro History* 47 (October 1962), 242-243.

80   *stabbed for not bringing a cup of coffee quickly enough:* Reported in Flanigan, *Criminal Law of Slavery and Freedom,* 394.

81   *Kuklos Adelphon, or the first Kappa Alpha Order:* See the Order's website at http://www.ka-order.org/ and a history of Kuklos Adelphon at http://www.uta.edu/student_orgs/kao/rbhistory.html.

84   *"render justice impossible and establish discrimination against classes or color":* Major General John Pope to President U. S. Grant, July 24, 1867 (National Archives RG 393, Third Military District).

84   *"Ordinary Klansmen," one researcher wrote, "may have found it hard":* Trelease, *White Terror,* 41.

7. Shivaree

Bertram Wyatt-Brown is the first scholar I know of to take notice of the James Foster case, which he presents at length in *Southern Honor* (Oxford University Press, 1982), 462-495. Wyatt-Brown states that his account was taken chiefly from court records in the case State v. James Foster, Jr., Circuit Court Clerk's Office, Adams County, Mississippi, June Term, 1834. Foster family papers, which might add information to the story, could not be found. Good sources on the charivari or shivaree are Natalie Zemon Davis, *Society and Culture in Early Modern France* (Stanford, CA: Stanford University Press, 1975), and Bryan D. Palmer, "Discordant Music: Charivaris and

Whitecapping in Nineteenth-Century North America,"*Labour/Le Travailleur*
1:1: 5-62. Paul Gilje, *The Road to Mobocracy: Popular Disorders in New York
City, 1763-1884* (Chapel Hill: University of North Carolina Press, 1987),
applies the dynamics of shivaree to political uprisings.

Page

87   *she had subsequently "had a fit":* See Wyatt-Brown, *Southern Honor,*
        464-465 for quotations from the court record.

88   *"The mob believed he was a monster at heart":* January 9, 1835, quoted
        in Wyatt-Brown, *Southern Honor*, 489.

92   *"leathern convenience":* Anecdote told of "a wealthy Quaker named
        Murray" in Joel B. Headley, *Pen and Pencil Sketches of the Great* Riots
        (New York: E. B. Treat, 1877), 52. This mocking name for a carriage can
        be found in various writings of the 1700s.

94   *the bodies of three Civil Rights workers were found shot execution-style in
        Mississippi:* See Mike Boettcher, Unresolved murder cases from Civil
        Rights era finally winding up back in court, Cnn.com, June 20, 2000, at
        http://www.cnn.com/2000/US/06/20/reopening.race.cases.

8. "Let Each Man Be His Own Executioner"

San Francisco's gold-rush history, centering on the vigilantes of 1851 and
1856, inspired argumentative writing almost from the day the original events
occurred. Robert M. Senkewicz, *Vigilantes in Gold Rush San Francisco*
(Stanford, CA: Stanford University Press, 1985), both writes about the vigilantes and gives a detailed, critical account of earlier histories from 1855 to
1974. From the 1850s to 1920s, most writers on San Francisco's gold rush history defended the vigilantes. Two well known, near-contemporary apologists
were Harvard philosopher Josiah Royce, son of a Forty-niner mother, in his
book *California* (Boston: Houghton, Mifflin, 1888 [1886]), and historian
Hubert Howe Bancroft, who was personally acquainted with many ex-vigilantes (*Popular Tribunals of California*, 2 vol., San Francisco: History
Company, 1887). Volume 1 of the Bancroft book is largely devoted to the vigilance committee of 1851. Josiah Royce favorably contrasted vigilantism led

by business interests with "miners' courts," in which a committee of peers tried violators, sentenced them, and carried out the sentences. Miners' courts are examined in Duane A. Smith, *Rocky Mountain Mining Camps: The Urban Frontier* (Bloomington: Indiana University Press, 1967). I base much of the 1851 narrative on Royce (Chapter 5) and Bancroft, but draw different conclusions.

The first study to concentrate on the social context of the 1851 vigilantes was Mary Floyd Williams, *History of the San Francisco Vigilance Committee of 1851* (Berkeley: University of California Press, 1921). The fact that Williams didn't find evidence of a crime wave is significant since she generally approved the 1851 vigilantes' results if not their methods. Senkewicz, *Vigilantes*, treats the 1851 vigilance committee at length, drawing on both earlier scholarship and newspaper accounts from the period. For gold rush economic conditions, see Peter R. Decker, *Fortunes and Failures: White Collar Mobility in Nineteenth-Century San Francisco* (Cambridge: Harvard University Press, 1978).

Page

97   *a total of only 1,648:* Senkewicz, *Vigilantes,* 77-78. Senkewicz analyzes the Australian emigrant population on page 79.

100   *"The gold-mines were preserved by nature for Americans only":* Quoted in Royce, *California,* 238-239.

100   *The self-named Hounds were New York military volunteers:* See Royce, *California,* 407-408.

101   *William Tecumseh Sherman, of Civil War fame:* Sherman, *Memoirs,* vol. 1 (New York: D. Appleton and Co., 1875), 159.

101   *"an organized band of incendiaries":* San Francisco *Daily Herald,* May 17, 1851.

101   *The arsonists' "fixed determination":* San Francisco *Daily Herald,* May 17, 1851. See *Daily Alta California,* June 8, 1851, for the call for executions.

102   *"the best known men of the city":* Daily Alta California, June 8, 1851.

103 *"Let each man be his own executioner"*: *Weekly Alta California*, March 1, 1851. For narrative of the arrest and trial of "Stuart," see Royce, *California*, 407-417.

105 *from 1850 to 1859, officials legally executed eight persons:* Data for San Francisco County in M. Watt Espy, Jr., Capital Punishment Research Project, Headland, Alabama, as digitized as by the Inter-university Consortium for Political and Social Research, Ann Arbor, Michigan (ICPSR 8451).

106 *"Resolved, that we, the Vigilance Committee":* Quoted in Bancroft, *Popular Tribunals*, vol. 1, 323-324.

9. Takeover

Robert M. Senkewicz, *Vigilantes in Gold Rush San Francisco* (Stanford, CA: Stanford University Press, 1985), treating both 1851 and 1856 vigilantism, focuses on the political agenda of the 1856 vigilantes as part of his analysis. Narratives and defenses of the vigilantes' acts are contained in Josiah Royce, *California* (Boston: Houghton, Mifflin, 1888 [1886]), and Hubert Howe Bancroft, *Popular Tribunals of California*, vol. 2 (San Francisco: History Company, 1887). Richard Maxwell Brown, *Strain of Violence* (New York: Oxford University Press, 1975), uses membership records archived at the Huntington Library, San Marino, California, to analyze the vigilantes as part of an American tradition of vigilantism. Brown's perspective in this book is more favorable to the vigilantes than my perspective. For the social opportunities presented by vigilante membership, see Brown, *Strain of Violence,* 111-112, and A. Theodore Brown, *Frontier Community: Kansas City to 1870* (Columbia: University of Missouri Press, 1963). For David Broderick as a leader of the Democrats, see David A. Williams, *David C. Broderick: A Political Portrait* (San Marino CA: Huntington Library, 1969).

Page

109 *shot down in the street*: For a narrative of King's death and the following vigilante actions, see Royce, *California*, 437-453.

109   no *"thief, burglar, incendiary, assassin, ballot box stuffer, or other dis-*
      turber of the peace": Bancroft, *Popular Tribunals*, vol. 2, 112.

109   *The vigilantes' first maneuver "was made an imposing spectacle"*: See
      Royce, *California*, 447, for this and following quotations regarding the
      seizing of the prisoners.

110   *That afternoon "the public excitement was tremendous"*: Royce,
      California, 448.

111   *those Josiah Royce dismissed as "politicians and lawyers"*: Royce, 446.

111   *Thirty-three of thirty-seven members of the executive committee can be*
      identified: For this and remaining information about membership, see
      Senkewicz, *Vigilantes*, 170, and Brown, *Strain of Violence*, 137.

113   *John Nugent, an Irishman and San Francisco Daily Herald editor*:
      Nugent's comments are summarized in Senkewicz, *Vigilantes*, 77-84.

113   *"The Sour Flour and Soft Pork Aristocracy"*: The Democratic State
      Journal, no date, quoted in Senkewicz, *Vigilantes*, 181.

114   *"the courageous and violent" Justice Terry*: Royce, *California*, 462; 462-
      464 for following narrative of Terry's brush with the vigilantes.

115   *Pierce undoubtedly oversaw the message*: J. C. Dobbin, Secretary of the
      Navy, to Commander William Mervine of the Pacific squadron, San
      Francisco, CA, August 2, 1856 (U. S. Senate Executive Document 101).

115   *Those in the courtroom "stamped and cheered"*: John D. Gordan III,
      Authorized By No Law (Pasadena, CA: Ninth Judicial Circuit Historical
      Society, and San Francisco, CA: United States District Court for the
      Northern District of California Historical Society, 1987), 3.

115   *"the associated mobites styling themselves a Vigilance Committee"*:
      Gordan, *Authorized By No Law*, 53.

116   *if "an attempt shall be made to nullify the process of the court"*: For this
      and quotations in following paragraph, see letter of M. Hall McAllister,
      Circuit Judge, District of California, and Ogden Hoffman, District
      Judge, San Francisco, to Major General John E. Wool, United States
      Army, Department of the Pacific, September 9, 1856; letter of General
      Wool to judges McAllister and Hoffman, September 10, 1856, both in

Senate Executive Document 43, 34th Congress, Third Session, February
10, 1857.

116   *"damned pork merchants"*: Royce, *California*, 460.

116   *the state legislature had already put a spending ceiling into effect*: For following budget figures, see Senkewicz, *Vigilantes*, 191.

117   *the evidence suggests that police had their job well in hand*: On crime and
policing 1855-1856, see Brown, *Strain of Violence*, 141.

10. Boots, Bullets, and Big Bucks

Vigilante history of Montana and Wyoming is examined from a modern
point of view in Harry Sinclair Drago, *The Great Range Wars* (New York:
Dodd, Mead, 1970), 216-231, and, for Wyoming, Helena Huntington Smith,
The War on Powder River (New York: McGraw Hill, 1966). An unusually rich
website on the 1864-1865 vigilantes is Louis Schmittroth's Vigilantes of
Montana, at http://schmittroth.tripod.com/mont_vigi. This anti-vigilante
site contains links to full-text articles and books, including an account of a
simulated legal trial of one lynching victim that was carried out by law students and professors in 1993. The site also reprints the nuanced analysis of
historian J. W. Smurr, "Afterthoughts on the Vigilantes," which first appeared
in *Montana: The Magazine of Western History* 8:2 (April 2, 1958), 8-20. Smurr
cites local newspaper articles of 1870 that criticized a vigilante hanging in that
year. On the origins of "3-7-77," see Fredrick Allen, "Montana Vigilantes,"
Montana: The Magazine of Western History 54 (Spring 2001): 3-19. For more
about Roosevelt's support of vigilantism over the years, see Granville Stuart,
Forty Years on the Frontier, vol. 2 (Glendale CA: Arthur H. Clark, 1925), 195-
210; Ray H. Mattison, "Roosevelt and the Stockmen's Association," *North
Dakota History* 17 (1950), 81-85; Carleton Putnam, *Theodore Roosevelt: The
Formative Years, 1858-1886* (New York: Scribner, 1958), 460ff.

Most writings on the Montana and Wyoming vigilantes until the 1900s
were as favorable to vigilantism as were the writings on San Francisco's vigilantes. Thomas Dimsdale's apology for their acts, *The Vigilantes of Montana*,
first appeared as a newspaper serial in 1865 before becoming a book the next
year (Virginia City MT: D. W. Tilton and Co., 1866). H. H. Bancroft presented

what he considered documentary evidence favoring the vigilantes in *Popular Tribunals*, vol. 1 (San Francisco: History Company, 1887), 670-714. Granville Stuart dealt with his career as a vigilante, and with 1880s Montana and Wyoming vigilantism generally, in his memoir cited above.

Page

121   *On a website called Fucked Up College Kids:* "Vigilante Justice," F. U. C. K. File 189, signed "DisordeR," at http://www.attrition.org/~jericho/works/zines/FUCK/fuck0189.htm.

122   *when vigilante acts were endorsed by the likes of Theodore Roosevelt:* I treat this incident in Chapter 14, "Colonel Simmons' Ku Klux Klan."

124   *two researchers later investigated the robberies:* R. E. Mather and F. E. Boswell, *Hanging the Sheriff: A Biography of Henry Plummer* (Missoula MT: Historic Montana Publishing Co., 2003 [1987]).

128   *According to the New Mexico chapter's website:* See "Operation Jaguar" under Upcoming Events on each state chapter's webpage, e.g., http://www.ranchrescue.com/new_mexico.htm#jaguar.

129   *leading office holders who swore to uphold the U. S. Constitution:* Richard Maxwell Brown, *Strain of Violence* (New York: Oxford University Press, 1975), 162ff, lists some office holders and their vigilante connections.

130   *Theodore Roosevelt once wrote in a letter:* Roosevelt to William Rask Thayer, July 10, 1915, in Elting E. Morison, ed., *The Letters of Theodore Roosevelt*, vol. 8 (Cambridge MA: Harvard University Press, 1954), 945-947.

131   *"thugs, thieves, incendiaries, dynamiters, perjurers, jury-fixers, manufac-turers of evidence, strikebreakers and murderers":* Robert Hunter quoted in Stephen H. Norwood, *Strikebreaking and Intimidation* (Chapel Hill: University of North Carolina Press, 2002), 11.

11. "Beaten All to Smash"

I don't think anyone has tried to total the exact number of persons killed nationwide during labor riots and strikes where force was used. Myriad sources exist for each of the historical strikes I describe, and many sources include historical context. Examples that stand out: For the 1877 railroad strike as viewed by a journalist of the time, see Joel B. Headley, *Pen and Pencil Sketches of the Great Riots* (New York: E. B. Treat, 1877), 349-456. For Chicago's Pullman strike, see the website of Lynn Harry Nelson, University of Kansas, Lawrence, at http://www.ku.edu/kansas/pullman/, based partly on United States Strike Commission, *Report on the Chicago Strike, June-July, 1894*, Senate Executive Document No. 7, 53d Congress, 3rd session. Two good sources for the Homestead strike and its background are Paul Krause, *The Battle for Homestead, 1880-1892*, and David P. Demarest, Jr, ed., *"The River Ran Red": Homestead 1892*. The Demarest volume focuses on contemporaneous accounts and photographs. This and the Krause history are companion volumes issued by the University of Pittsburgh Press, Pittsburgh, in 1992. A full history of conflict in the U.S. coal industry, including the Ludlow massacre, is in Priscilla Long, *Where the Sun Never Shines* (New York: Paragon House, 1989). Clare V. McKanna, Jr., *Homicide, Race, and Justice in the West, 1880-1920* (Tucson: University of Arizona Press, 1997), 84ff, 104-112, describes Colorado mining violence from 1903 to the Ludlow massacre of 1914. Though I'm not persuaded by McKanna's "culture of violence" interpretation for murders overall, he took the useful and important step of counting and analyzing coroner's inquests and homicide indictments in one main Colorado mining county during his study period. Idaho strike history and its ramifications are covered in detail throughout much of J. Anthony Lukas's *Big Trouble* (New York: Simon and Schuester, 1997).

Page

135   *"beaten all to smash"*: Unknown author quoted in Joseph F. Patterson, "After the W. B. A.," *Historical Society of Schuylkill County Publications*, vol. 4 (1912), 168-184.

137   *A landmark court decision against Philadelphia shoemakers:* Commonwealth v. Pullis (Phila. Mayor's Ct. 1806), also called the Philadelphia Cordwainers' Case. The defendants were fined.

137   *Adam Smith observed in 1776:* Smith, *An Inquiry into the Nature and Causes of the Wealth of Nations*, vol. 1, ch 10, para 82; text online at http://www.econlib.org/library/Smith/smWN.html.

137 *Critic of big business Henry Demarest Lloyd wrote:* Lloyd, "The Captains of Industry," *North American Review* 331 (June 1884), reproduced online at http://www.fordham.edu/halsall/mod/1884hdlloyd.html.

142 *"allow outside people to come in and interfere":* Reported in the *New York Times* and quoted in McKanna, *Homicide, Race, and Justice,* 106.

144 *Beforehand, this juror had stated:* Quotation from Colorado Supreme Court, Zancannelli v. the People, 63 Colorado 261 (1917).

145 The *NAACP record, though incomplete, is the only nationally compiled record I know of:* NAACP, *Thirty Years of Lynching in the United States* (New York: Arno Press, 1969 [1919]).

145 *"more like brutes than human beings":* Quoted from "a local Pennsylvania newspaper" of 1884 in John Higham, *Strangers in the Land: Patterns of American Nativism, 1860-1925* (New York: Atheneum, 1965), 47ff and note 27.

12. "Death and Destruction to the System"

Most writers who treat labor conflict are partisans of either labor or management, and relatively little of the research on nineteenth century strikes and labor trials has gone beyond oral histories or accounts taken from trial testimony. There probably isn't any unfound evidence that will shed more light on the near-mythic Molly Maguires. Peter A. Weisman, an undergraduate student at Lehigh University, compiled and annotated an extensive bibliography (1999) of sources for the history of the Mollies. The bibliography can be found at http://www.lehigh.edu/~ineng/paw/paw-history.htm. For two viewpoints on the Mollies, Franklin Gowen, and James McParlan, I drew on the narratives of Priscilla Long, *Where the Sun Never Shines* (New York: Paragon House, 1989), 106-115, and J. Anthony Lukas, *Big Trouble* (New York: Simon and Schuester, 1997), 175-187. For the Haymarket trials, the Chicago Historical Society maintains an interpretive site with several pages and links at http://www.chicagohistory.org/dramas/overview/over.htm.

The murder of ex-governor Steunenberg and trial of William Haywood and others is the subject of Lukas's *Big Trouble*.

Page

149 *"one of the great civil rights struggles of our time":* quoted in "Ryan Clearing Illinois Death Row," CBSNEWS.com, January 11, 2003, at http://www.cbsnews.com/stories/2002/12/30/national/main534639 .shtml.

150 *"Conspiracy rests on the other side":* Testimony in Pennsylvania Senate Document 39, 1548.

151 *As a recent commentator pointed out:* Pennsylvania judge John P. Lavelle, The Hard Coal Docket (privately printed, 1994), quoted at http://www.tnonline.com/coalcracker/mollies.html.

151 *journalist Joel Headley noted:* Headley, *Pen and Pencil Sketches of the Great Riots* (New York: E. B. Treat, 1877), 7, 98.

151 *An account written almost twenty years later:* Cleveland Moffett, "The Overthrow of the Molly Maguires," *McClure's Magazine* (1894), 99-100.

153 *the Chicago May Day, or May first, strike of 1886:* For a pro-labor account of May Day's origin in the Chicago strike, see Philip S. Foner, *May Day* (New York: International Publishers, 1986).

153 *The trial that began on June 21:* Excerpts of the trial transcripts digitized by the Chicago Historical Society are online at http://memory .loc.gov/ammem/award98/ichihtml/trialvols.html.

154 *"Controversial" isn't a strong enough word:* For an account of Altgeld's action and quotations from the press, see Robert D. Sampson, "Governor Altgeld Pardons the Haymarket Rioters," *Illinois Times*, July 22-28, 1993, online at the website of the Illinois Labor History Society, http://www.kentlaw.edu/ilhs/prisoner.htm. The text of Altgeld's pardon can be obtained from the Illinois Labor History Society.

155 *President Woodrow Wilson pardoned one convicted murderer:* See William F. Duker, "The Presidential Power to Pardon: A Constitutional History," *William and Mary Law Review* 18 (1977): 475-538.

157 *he "saw anarchy wave its first bloody triumph in Idaho":* Borah and Darrow are quoted, respectively, from the transcript, State of Idaho v. William D. Haywood, and from the *Idaho Daily Statesman*, July 26, 1907, in Lukas, *Big Trouble*, 719 and 711.

158 *J. Anthony Lukas recently presented what he saw as damning new evidence:* Lukas, *Big Trouble*, 750-754.

13. White Terrorism

For the story of Indiana whitecapping, I draw on Madeleine M. Noble's carefully documented account of Indiana vigilantism, The White Caps of Harrison and Crawford County, Indiana (Ph.D. thesis, University of Michigan, Ann Arbor, 1973). Noble completed her thesis when living residents had childhood memories of whitecapping. Josiah Royce, philosopher and son of a forty-niner, defended the T. Dwight Hunt morals argument at length in *California* (Boston: Houghton Mifflin, 1888 [1886]), his history of gold-rush vigilantism and its aftermath. For the murder of Matthew Shepherd and the way the murder and trial fitted into community and wider politics, see Beth Loffreda, *Losing Matt Shepherd* (New York: Columbia University Press, 2000).

Page

161 *warning and whipping area residents for offenses:* Quotations drawn from contemporaneous newspaper sources by Noble, White Caps, Appendix, 177-190.

162 *at the mildest left wounds that took weeks or months to heal:* J. Edward Murr interview, *Corydon Democrat*, September 11, 1940, reported in Noble, White Caps, 74.

164 *the illiteracy rate of Kentucky highlanders tripled:* E. Merton Coulter, *The Civil War and Readjustment in Kentucky* (Chapel Hill, NC: University of North Carolina Press, 1926), is still a good, statistically based study of the region.

165 *"a dollar looked as big as a barn door":* New York Times, October 12, 1887.

165 *The seventy-six vigilante incidents in Harrison and Crawford counties:* All incidents described below are based on Noble, White Caps, Chapter 4.

168   *The reverend Mr. T. Dwight Hunt reflected on morals offenses:* The following quotation is from Hunt, *Sermon Suggested by the Execution of Jenkins, on the Plaza, by 'The People' of San Francisco during the Night of the 10th of June, 1851* (San Francisco, CA: Marvin and Hitchcock, 1851), 12-13.

168   *they were structured as a fraternal organization:* Henry Clay Duncan, White Caps in Southern Indiana, a paper presented to the Monroe County Historical Society, n.d., and quoted in Noble's thesis.

168   *signed their own threatening letters "K.K.K":* Hazen Hayes Pleasant, *A History of Crawford County, Indiana* (Glendale, CA: Arthur H. Clark, 1926), 339, reported in Noble, White Caps, 82.

14. "Serving Your Racial Needs"

The Southern Poverty Law Center, Montgomery, Alabama, prepared a concise, accessibly written report, A Hundred Years of Terror, on the history of the first and second Ku Klux Klan, 1865-1950. The undated text is posted on the website of Indiana-University-Purdue-University-Indianapolis, at http://www.iupui.edu/~aao/kkk.html. The facts are accurate to my knowledge, but no references are given. For more depth and local detail, and a look at the primary sources, see David M. Chalmers, *Hooded Americanism: The First Century of the Ku Klux Klan, 1865-1965* (Garden City, NY: Doubleday, 1965), Charles C. Alexander, *The Ku Klux Klan in the Southwest* (University of Kentucky Press, no place of publication, 1965), Kenneth T. Jackson, *The Ku Klux Klan in the City* (New York: Oxford University Press, 1967), and Arnold S. Rice, *The Ku Klux Klan in American Politics* (New York: Haskell House, 1972). Chalmers, though mainly documenting the second Klan, described the continuity of the group into present times through imitator organizations, involvement in labor politics as the South became industrialized, and a renewed focus on violence against African-Americans.

For the connection of Southern culture to Thomas Dixon's novel and the film, see Everett Carter, "Cultural History Written with Lightning: The Significance of The Birth of a Nation," *American Quarterly* 12 (Fall 1960):347-357. The work of Cesare Lombroso was probably equally important in shaping the public attitude. A bibliography of Lombroso's works in Italian, with those translated into English, French, and German, is online at the Stanford Humanities Laboratory website called Crowds, http://www .stanford.edu/group/shl/Crowds/theorists/theo.htm#lombroso. Also see Mary Gibson, *Born to Crime: Cesare Lombroso and the Origins of Biological Criminology* (Greenwood CT: Praeger, 2002).

Page

171   *the Alabama chapter's slogan:* Alabama White Knights' website at http://www.kukluxklan.net.

172   *"My only regret," Wilson is supposed to have said:* Eric Goldman, *Rendezvous with Destiny* (New York: Alfred A. Knopf, 1952), 228-229.

173   *Only in 2000 did an independent researcher disclose:* Stephen Goldfarb, posted in 2000 at http://www.leofranklynchers.com/leofrank lynchers.html.

174   *one researcher estimates over a thousand victims injured:* Alexander, *Ku Klux Klan in the Southwest*, 55-59.

175   *Arkansas, Oklahoma, and Texas urbanized far more quickly:* Alexander, *Ku Klux Klan in the Southwest*, 68, gives the following figures for increase of urban population 1910-1920: United States average, 28.8 per cent; Arkansas 43.3 percent; Oklahoma 68.5 percent; Texas 61.2 percent.

176   *the fraternal order and nonprofit mutual insurance society called Woodmen of the World:* A history of Woodmen of the World is online at http://www.woodmen.com.

178   *"Catholics, Jews, Negroes, immigrants, and radicals":* Stanley Frost, *The Challenge of the Klan* (Indianapolis, IN: Bobbs Merrill, 1924), cited in Alexander, *Ku Klux Klan in the Southwest*, 21.

178   *"efforts to preserve premarital chastity, marital fidelity, and respect for parental authority":* Alexander, *Ku Klux Klan in the Southwest*, 21.

181   *"I am, as a matter of principle, sorry to say that the lynching had a most healthy effect":* Theodore Roosevelt to George Otto Trevelyan, September 9, 1906, in Elting E. Morison, ed., *The Letters of Theodore Roosevelt*, vol. 5 (Cambridge MA: Harvard University Press, 1954), 401.

181   *factional strife like the New Orleans incident:* The only nationally com-
      piled table of dates I know of for racially motivated riots and lynchings
      together, using the best data that were widely available at the time, is in
      Richard Maxwell Brown, *Strain of Violence* (New York: Oxford
      University Press, 1975), Appendix 4.

182   *"Bombarded with antagonistic statements":* Eugene H. Berwanger, *The
      Frontier Against Slavery* (Urbana, IL: University of Illinois Press, 1967),
      59.

15. "Foreigners and Negroes"

Peter Rachleff summarily reported conflicting current views about racially
targeted lynching in "Lynching and Racial Violence: Report from a
Conference," *Z Magazine* 15:12 (December 2002); online at http://www
.zmag.org/ZMagSite/Dec2002/rachleff1202.htm. The scholarly conference
was held at Emory University in October, 2002, in conjunction with the
exhibit of lynching photographs, "Without Sanctuary." For some contexts of
American bigotry, see David H. Bennett, *The Party of Fear: From Nativist
Movements to the New Right in American History* (Chapel Hill, NC: University
of North Carolina Press, 1988), Eugene H. Berwanger, *The Frontier Against
Slavery* (Urbana, IL: University of Illinois Press, 1967), and Marcus Lee
Hansen, *The Immigrant in American History* (Cambridge, MA: Harvard
University Press, 1940). These sources provide some legal history of immi-
grant groups and some statistics that go beyond historical U. S. census data.
Josiah Royce, throughout his book *California* (Boston: Houghton Mifflin,
1888), brings to life the state's political struggles during the 1850s and the
impact they had on immigrants.

After "common sense," the next most slippery concept in human thought
is "the facts." What they are depends on how they're defined, how they're
counted, and where you get them from. I calculated present-day population
percentages by using the U. S. Census Bureau's online Table 2, Male
Population by Age, Race and Hispanic or Latino Origin for the United States
(2000), at http://www.census.gov/population/cen2000/phc-t9/tab02.xls.
Ethnicity of death row inmates and those executed 1976-2003 comes from
Death Row U.S.A., a project of the NAACP Legal Defense and Education
Project, online at http://www.deathpenaltyinfo.org/DeathRowUSA1.html.

As for the number of lynchings historically in the United States, I've learned since my colleague Liz Hines and I started Project HAL (Historic American Lynching) that the compiled total available is a serious undercount. The NAACP's *Thirty Years of Lynching in the United States* (New York: Arno Press, 1969 [1919]) covers only the years 1889-1918, but it also omits some local records—for instance, in Arizona, Texas, and Wyoming—that lynching researchers have found and made me aware of.

Page

185 *More people were lynched in just ten southern states:* Stewart E. Tolnay and E. M. Beck, *A Festival of Violence* (Urbana: University of Illinois Press, 1995), Appendix C.

185 *Roy Wilkins, former executive director of the NAACP:* From Wilkins's 1969 preface to *Thirty Years of Lynching.*

190 *"Ours is 'the land of the free',":* Mark Twain, *Roughing It* (Hartford, CN: American Publishing Co.), vol. 2, 128-129.

191 *The Chinese population of San Francisco County:* Elmer Clarence Sandmeyer, *The Anti-Chinese Movement in California* (Urbana: University of Illinois Press, 1991 [1939]), Table 4, quotes 1870 U. S. census figures for San Francisco County of 136,059 Europeans and 12,022 Chinese.

191 *Patrick Hamilton wrote of the Apache Nation in 1884:* In *The Resources of Arizona* (San Francisco: A. L. Bancroft), 293.

191 *he too recommended extermination:* Elie Reclus, *Primitive Folk* (London: Walter Scott, 1891), 123.

192 *nine Indian deaths for every European-American killed:* Henry F. Dobyns, "Inter-Ethnic Fighting in Arizona," *Journal of Arizona History* 35 (Summer 1994): 176. For indictment and conviction rates, see Clare V. McKanna, Jr., *Homicide, Race, and Justice in the American West, 1880-1920* (Tucson: University of Arizona Press, 1997), esp. 149-153.

192 *Samuel F. B. Morse wrote in 1835:* Morse, *Imminent Dangers to the Free Institutions of the United States through Foreign Immigration, by an American* (originally published anonymously 1835; reprinted as an unnumbered volume in the American Immigration Collection, ed. Oscar Handlin, New York: Arno Press and *The New York Times,* 1969), iv.

195 *the NAACP's reporting period 1889-1918:* NAACP, *Thirty Years of Lynching,* for all numbers in this paragraph.

195 *a state "composed so largely of foreigners and Negroes":* Quoted in Jacob Goldstein, "Shall Capital Punishment Be Abolished?" *The New Outlook* 116 (1917):19.

196 *Seven-eighths of all persons committed to the New York city prison:* Robert Ernst, *Immigrant Life in New York City, 1825-1863* (Columbia University, New York: King's Crown Press, 1949), esp. 57-58.

196 *studies of the Columbus, Ohio, jail and the Massachusetts State Penitentiary:* See Eric Monkkonen, *The Dangerous Class* (Cambridge MA: Harvard University Press, 1975), 85, and Robert Hindus, *Prison and Plantation* (Chapel Hill: University of North Carolina Press, 1980), 175ff.

196 *Italian-named persons were thirty to forty percent:* William J. Bowers, *Legal Homicide* (Boston: Northeastern University Press, 1984), Appendix A. Published records for New Jersey by name begin only in 1907.

197 *Lewis Lawes, who crusaded against capital punishment:* Lawes, *Life and Death in Sing Sing* (Garden City, NY: Garden City Publishing, 1928), 11.

197 *Italian immigration was 222,260 in 1921:* For immigration totals, see Edmund Traverso, *Immigration: A Study in American Values* (Boston, MA: D. C. Heath, 1964), 118.

198 *an African-American was lynched or legally executed every four days:* Tolnay and Beck, *Festival of Violence,* 100.

16. A Clean, Well-Lighted Place

My account of Progressive Era death-penalty abolition was grounded by the concise overview in Philip English Mackey, "Introduction," in Mackey, ed., *Voices Against Death: American Opposition to Capital Punishment, 1787-1975* (New York: Burt Franklin, 1976). But, in this instance, it's hard to beat the torrent of words from those who were alive at the time. Some are quoted from journals of the day, others from studies of individual states. My notes below contain a representative sampling of sources.

Page

203 *Warden J. A. Johnston of San Quentin wrote:* Reprinted in *La Gaceta, El Boletin del Corral de Santa Fe Westerners,* June 1964.

204 *Humanity dictated, said Gerry:* Elbridge T. Gerry, "Capital Punishment by Electricity," *The North American Review* 149 (1889), 322 for this and Gerry quotation in following paragraph. Also see L. Figueroa, "Making Death Easy," *Overland,* n.s. 77:4 (April 1921), 30-33.

207 *Turn of the Balance:* Written by Brand Whitlock, published in New York by Grosset and Dunlap, 1910 [1907]). Quotations: 596, 617.

207 *Cory Quirino, Filipina inspirational speaker:* See online interview by Anna Gamboa, Cory's Quintessence, at http://www.herword .com/aiadw/quirino06.24.02.html.

208 *Harold P. Brown explained this new humanitarianism:* Brown, "The New Instrument of Execution," *North American Review* 149 (November 1889): 592-593. Also: "Electrical Execution," *Scientific American* 62 (January 11, 1890), 26; *Public Opinion,* August 16, 1890:433-435.

208 *In the late 1870s, a patent had been applied for:* John Laurence, *A History of Capital Punishment* (New York: The Citadel Press, 1960); "Execution by Electricity," *Scientific American* 62 (March 1, 1890), 131.

209 *"The majesty of the law would be vindicated":* Brown, "New Instrument of Execution," 593, also see "Electrical Execution," *Scientific American* 62 (January 11, 1890), 26, and *Public Opinion,* August 16, 1890:433-435.

209 *"The great industry of the world for four long years was killing":* Clarence Darrow's debate with Judge Alfred J. Talley, at the New York League for Public Discussion, is excerpted in Mackey, *Voices Against Death,* 176.

210 *scenarios in a number of states ended with the same last act:* State-level abolition history is in Philip English Mackey, "Introduction," in *Voices Against Death.* Quotations from Oregon's governor and legislative committee in Robert H. Dann, "Capital Punishment in Oregon," *The Annals of the American Academy of Political and Social Science* 284 (1952), 111-112.

212 *Collier's and some other wide-circulation periodicals:* See quotations from the local press in *Public Opinion,* August 16, 1890, 433-435;

"Abolishing the Death Penalty," *Literary Digest* 86 (August 22, 1925), 29; "Attacking the Death Penalty," *Literary Digest* 88 (February 13, 1926), 7-8. Quoted newspaper opinion, not necessarily a random sample, ran two to one or better in favor of capital punishment throughout this period. Samuel P. Hays discusses the ambivalence of "the people" toward Progressive era reform in "The Politics of Reform in Municipal Government," *Pacific Northwest Quarterly* 55 (1964), 157-169.

213 *The first national polls during the 1930s*: See George H. Gallup, *The Gallup Poll: Public Opinion 1935-1971*, vol. 1 (New York: Random House, 1972), 45.

17. "Evolving Standards of Decency"

Robert M. Bohm, *Deathquest* (Cincinnati OH, 1999), 7-68, analytically reviews recent death-penalty history with an emphasis on the law. A good summary of Supreme Court decisions regarding the death penalty is in the class notes to CCJ 3934 Contemporary Issues (Death Penalty), a course offered by criminal justice professor Lisa Stolzenberg in the School of Policy and Management at Florida International University. Online at http://www.fiu.edu/~stolzenb/ccj3934/chapter2.htm. Franklin E. Zimring and Gordon Hawkins, *Capital Punishment and the American Agenda* (Cambridge: Cambridge University Press, 1986), 38-49, review and analyze the backlash against death-penalty abolition after 1972. Zimring's new book is *The Contradictions of Capital Punishment* (New York: Oxford University Press, 2003). For the Caryl Chessman case, see Theodore Hamm, *Rebel and a Cause: Caryl Chessman and the Politics of the Death Penalty in Postwar California, 1948-1974* (Berkeley: University of California Press, 2001), and Edmund G. Brown, *Public Justice, Private Mercy: A Governor's Education on Death Row* (New York: Weidenfeld & Nicholson, 1989).

Page

216 *the number of appeals filed in death-penalty cases grew tenfold*: For these data see William J. Bowers, *Legal Homicide* (Boston: Northeastern University Press, 1984), 16 and Appendix A.

217 *Policy analyses began to appear more frequently in law journals*: For example, L. E. Deets, "Changes in Capital Punishment Policy Since 1939," *Journal of Criminal Law* 38 (March-April 1948), 584-594; G. H. Dession, "The Gowers Report and Capital Punishment," *New York University Law Review* 29 (May 1954), 1061-1068.

217 *Twenty states' legislatures rushed to pass similar laws*: Bowers, *Legal Homicide*, Table 1-8.

222 *A poll that year showed 50 percent in favor, 41 percent opposed*: See George H. Gallup, *The Gallup Poll: Public Opinion 1935-1971*, vol. 2 (New York: Random House, 1972), 1518.

222 *the death penalty was about authority*: Zimring and Hawkins, *Capital Punishment and the American Agenda*, 38, for details of public and media reaction.

225 *One decision of the "anti-defendant" years has been revisited*: See Mental Retardation and the Death Penalty, at the abolitionist website of the Death Penalty Information Center, http://www.deathpenaltyinfo.org/dpicmr.html.

226 *Texas has carried out more than one-third of all executions in the United States*: "Death Row, USA," a project of the NAACP Legal Defense and Educational Fund, Inc., online at http://www.deathpenaltyinfo.org/DeathRowUSA1.html, as of January 2003.

226 *George Bush demolished the presidential campaign of Michael Dukakis*: Timothy Noah, "Did Gore Hatch Horton?" *Slate Online Magazine*, Monday, November 1, 1999, at http://slate.msn.com/id/1003919/.

227 *"racial and gender bias committee"*: See http://www.biascommittee.duq.edu/.

227 *"68 percent of all verdicts fully reviewed in that period were found to be so seriously flawed"*: James S. Liebman, Jeffrey Fagan, and Valerie West, "Death Matters: A Reply," *Judicature* 84:2 (2000), 72, or online at the site of the Columbia Law School, http://www.law.columbia.edu/news/liebman.pdf. The authors collected data on 5,760 capital verdicts imposed by American states between 1973 and 1995.

18. The Endless End of Capital Punishment

For theories of violence I drew on, among others, Charles Tilly, "Collective Violence in European Perspective," in Hugh Davis Graham and Ted Robert Gurr, *Violence in America*, vol. 1 (Newbury Park CA: Sage, 1989). The quote from Tilly is on page 62. Also see Peter C. Sederberg, "The Phenomenology of Vigilantism in Contemporary America: An Interpretation," *Terrorism* 1 (1978):287-305; Michel Foucault, *Discipline and Punish: The Birth of the Prison*, tr. Alan Sheridan (New York: Pantheon, 1977 [1975]).

Index